T0355699

Haunted by Chaos

HAUNTED BY CHAOS

China's Grand Strategy from Mao Zedong to Xi Jinping

With a New Afterword

SULMAAN WASIF KHAN

Harvard University Press

Cambridge, Massachusetts
London, England

First Harvard University Press paperback edition, 2022
First Harvard University Press hardcover edition, 2018
First printing

Library of Congress Cataloging-in-Publication Data
Names: Khan, Sulmaan Wasif, author.
Title: Haunted by chaos : China's grand strategy from Mao Zedong to
Xi Jinping / Sulmaan Wasif Khan.
Description: Cambridge, Massachusetts : Harvard University Press, 2018. |
Includes bibliographical references and index.
Identifiers: LCCN 2017052653 | ISBN 9780674977099 (cloth : alk. paper) |
ISBN 9780674271173 (pbk.)
Subjects: LCSH: China—History—1949- | China—Foreign relations—
1949- | China—Economic policy—1949- | Power (Social sciences)—
China—History. | Nationalism—China—History.
Classification: LCC DS777.56 K53 2018 | DDC 327.51—dc23
LC record available at https://lccn.loc.gov/2017052653

For the Gang of Three at Yale:

John Gaddis, Charles Hill, and Paul Kennedy

CONTENTS

CHINA 1949

RUSSIAN

U.S.S.R.

KAZAKH S.S.R.

Tacheng

Yili

KYRGYZ
S.S.R.

Urumqi

TAJIK S.S.R.

Tarim

PAKISTAN

XINJIANG

GANSU

CHINA

Xining

QINGHAI

TIBET AREA

H I M A L A Y A

Chamdo

Ganzi

XIKANG

Lhasa

Batang

Kangding

NEPAL

Ganges

BHUTAN

Xichang

INDIA

Brahmaputra

EAST
PAKISTAN

Kunming

YUNNAN

Bay of
Bengal

BURMA

Irrawaddy

Salween

LAOS

THAILAND

Disputed boundary

S.F.S.R.

HSINGAN

HEILONG-
JIANG

HEJIANG

Heilong Jiang

*Zhenbao
Island*

°Jiamusi

°Hulunbuir

Qiqihar°

NENJIANG

Songhua

°Harbin

SONGJIANG

JILIN

MONGOLIA

LIAOBEI

Jilin°

Liaoyuan °

Liao

REHE

LIAODONG

CHAHAR

LIAOXI

Chengde
°

Dandong°

SUIYUAN

Zhangjiakou

Hohhot°

⊚ Beijing

°Tianjin

NORTH
KOREA

Sea of
Japan

SOUTH
KOREA

JAPAN

INGXIA

Yinchuan

Baoding
°

HEBEI

Taiyuan
°

SHANXI

°Jinan

SHANDONG

*Yellow
Sea*

PINGYUAN

anzhou

Kaifeng
°

JIANGSU

ANSU

SHAANXI

°Xian

HENAN

Hefei°

NANJING

°Shanghai

Han Shui

HUBEI

ANHUI

Zhoushan

SICHUAN

Chang Jiang

Wuhan°

°Hangzhou

Dachen

East China
Sea

Chengdu

ZHEJIANG

Wenzhou°

*Senkaku/
Diaoyu*

hongqing°

Changsha°

JIANGXI

°Nanchang

Changsha°

HUNAN

Fuzhou°

Mazu

FUJIAN

°Taipei

GUIZHOU

Nanri

TAIWAN

°Guiyang

*Jinmen
Xiamen*

GUANGDONG

GUANGXI

Guangzhou
°

Xi Jiang

°Nanning

HONG KONG
MACAO

*Shangchuan
Xiachuan*

South China
Sea

PHILIPPINES

Red

NORTH
VIETNAM

°Haikou

HAINAN

Haunted by Chaos

INTRODUCTION

FOR ALL THE INTEREST China has excited in the last several years, its grand strategy—the way in which it marshals different forms of power to pursue national objectives—has yet to be explored properly. Those who invoke the term often miss its historical roots and scope; then too, their work tends to ascribe a menace to the country's goals that would surprise Chinese grand strategists themselves. Historians have done excellent work on Chinese foreign policy, but have yet to produce a comparative study of the basic ideas of national security underpinning the conduct of the People's Republic of China (PRC). Unremarked by much of the work on China, there has been, from Mao Zedong to Xi Jinping, a consistent definition of national goals and a harnessing of military, diplomatic, economic, and political means to pursue those goals.[1] Historical interest aside—and the history is fascinating—the subject demands attention for a practical reason. At a time when hopes and fears of China are fervent and ill-informed in equal measure, it is important to explore the calculus behind Chinese decision-making, to attempt to see the world the way China's leaders do. Understanding alone cannot make for sound policy, but it is a crucial first step.

This book seeks such understanding through a "structured, focused comparison" of the grand strategies pursued by the PRC's paramount leaders: Mao Zedong, Deng Xiaoping, Jiang Zemin, Hu Jintao, and Xi Jinping. What were the operational codes—the deep assumptions about life—that shaped their conduct?[2] How did they perceive the world around them? What were the goals they defined and pursued? How did they meld different categories of power in pursuit of their objectives? And how well did their grand strategies work in the real world? There are, of course, limitations to such an approach to the study of China's foreign relations and national security. China's grand strategists—like people in other walks of life—were capable of inconsistency, sometimes surprising themselves as much as the historian on their trail. Besides, there are only so many things that even the best grand strategist can account for. Much that has been important in China's life—the unemployed who take up the life of hired thugs, the cadres gambling in North Korea and Macau, the disappearance of mahi mahi from the near seas—has happened outside the realm of grand strategy, presenting problems that Beijing must then scramble to respond to. Nevertheless, the men in question did practice grand strategy, which, for all it left out, encompassed quite a bit too. A closer look at what those grand strategies involved is well worthwhile.

To use the term grand strategy is not to imply that there was a meticulously written master plan, threshed out to the finest detail and then followed as best as possible. These were not men of the staff colleges or Ivy League; theirs was a peasant wisdom, honed in combat and despair. What they had was a set of instincts, a sense of where they wanted to wind up and how. As with all national security plans, these instincts sometimes failed them and failed them badly. But they were no less powerful for that. And in gearing military power, diplomacy, economic planning, and domestic policy toward what were seen as long-term interests, these instincts did indeed constitute grand strategy.[3]

The dramatic changes modern China has endured have obscured the commonalty of purpose and power that binds this book's cast of characters. They all saw China as a brittle entity, in a world that was fundamentally dangerous. Their main task was to protect it. (This might sound platitudinous, but when one considers some of the other grand strategies the world has seen—containment, world revolution, global jihad—one realizes that the platitudinous is not always what grand strategists pursue. Nor was basic security as simple a goal as it might seem. All that China had experienced in its past showed that statehood was something fragile, easily lost; to the people studied here, it was never something that could be taken for granted, even in times of peace.) Doing so required seeking a balance of power during the Cold War and after, while maintaining control of one's own citizens. It meant modernizing one's military without disturbing the political economy. It meant constant caution—which, carried to an extreme, could look quite the opposite. Everything came together, in a bid to preserve the state. (That they themselves had to be paramount to preserve the state was an assumption our grand strategists took as a given.) The exact mix of power—the weight given to military over economic considerations, in particular—shifted from epoch to epoch, but the overarching goal remained the same. There were variations—massive ones, which this book explores at some length— in the way China's grand strategists implemented these precepts, but they were variations on a common theme. The ideas born in the Mao and Deng years were nurtured by Jiang Zemin and Hu Jintao, before being imbued with the purpose, the growing power, and the sudden fear that have marked Xi Jinping's tenure. Of all the great powers, China is perhaps the one that has seen the fewest changes in its basic philosophy of international relations between the Cold War and post–Cold War eras. For China, in a way, the Cold War never really ended.

This is in large part because of the enduring importance of geography in shaping the operational codes of Chinese leaders. Other factors—ideology, character, life experience—have mattered, but these factors were forged, inevitably, in a country that had a long, vulnerable coast and porous land frontiers.[4] Then too, the line between foreign and domestic has often blurred. The desert to the north, the high mountains of the west, and the jungle of the south made control difficult; groups that bridled at the state's rein were bound to emerge. For all its long history, China has been disunited often—and each of the grand strategists in this book carried a memory of that disunity with them. The state has had little experience of conducting foreign policy as a unified, secure entity. That inexperience has been the hallmark of PRC grand strategy. This is not to lapse into geographical determinism: as this book makes clear, our leaders were very different men. Personality was important, particularly in the case of Deng's incurable restlessness and Xi's insecure vigilance. But all these men came of age in a particular world. The threats that confronted them were a product of that world, as were the mental maps they bore with them. It was within the parameters of that world that grand strategy was crafted.[5]

In writing this book, I have drawn on the excellent work on China's foreign relations that has been published, but I have relied chiefly on primary sources. This has been far harder than it would have been a few years ago. Part of Xi Jinping's grand strategy has been a systematic assault on historical documents. Gone are the heady days when researchers could show up at Chinese archives in search of new stories. Documents that were once available have disappeared, and new ones are not forthcoming. "We, too, are unhappy about it. We would like to help you, but there is nothing we can do," one archivist informed me sadly. In happier times, however, quite a few documents were copied and borne away. This study, therefore, uses documents from Chinese archives. It also relies on the numerous edited volumes of documents the Chinese government has published on a range of topics: chronologies of the leaders' lives, memoranda of conversations, speeches, military directives and plans, official budgets and trade statistics that allow one to trace the sources and practical impact of high policy. The word "edited" is crucial. These publications have been redacted, pruned, glossed, and rearranged; they are often misleading and occasionally downright mendacious. Used with caution, however, they can be useful in tracing the broad contours of Chinese grand strategy.

I have also drawn on documents from other countries that had dealings with China. These documents, of course, are by no means explicit on Chinese national security planning, but by showing us policy in action, they provide some grounds for inferring what Chinese grand strategy was. The vast trove made available by the Cold War International History Project has been particularly useful.

The first grand strategy discussed in the book is Mao Zedong's grand strategy of reunification. The territory China held when Mao declared the PRC on October 1, 1949, did not include vast swathes that are part of China today: coastal stretches, the island of Hainan, those mountainous holdings of Xinjiang and Tibet, large tracts of forests and hills in the southwest. The story of how Mao decided to take these lands and weave their peoples into the social fabric of China, of the military adventures and misadventures this resulted in, of the diplomatic exchanges and economic rebuilding it involved, is crucial to understanding the PRC. From here the tale moves to Mao's reign, from the Korean War through to his death. The narrative encompasses much—the Sino-Soviet alliance and its collapse, the elusive quest for third world unity, the rapprochement with the United States, the Cultural Revolution—but for all the wild turns and plunges, Mao was driven by a consistent set of grand strategic instincts ("principles" might be too mechanical a word). It was only in their application that he was mercurial.[6]

Deng Xiaoping came to power in a China that had already undergone some reform and opening. (Of all the characters discussed here, Deng was the only one not to hold the position of chairman of the Chinese Communist Party or that of general secretary. Such obvious trappings of power were for other men: Deng would work from behind the scenes, moving his acolytes into office as his power grew, content to be, at most, a vice premier and chairman of the central military commissions for party and state.)[7] The very act of reaching out to the United States came with possibilities that Deng moved to exploit. But he did so with goals that Mao could have understood and approved—a consistency unrecognized in the pertinent scholarship. Focusing on economic development was a way of keeping safe. It was a means of preparing for defense in a world that remained unpredictable. So too were Deng's ideas of "one country, two systems" and "joint development." The Tiananmen Square massacre was part and parcel of the same grand strategy that made reform and opening so necessary.[8]

In the reigns of Jiang Zemin and Hu Jintao, one finds both a continuation of the Mao-Deng era concerns and a harbinger of the issues that would dog Xi Jinping. Jiang, for all his ideological rhetoric, was a practical man, capable of learning from the Southeast Asian financial crisis and from confrontation with the United States. Military modernization, diplomatic balancing, political economy—Jiang addressed all these with remarkable, if understated, effectiveness. So did Hu, who steered China through the 2007–2008 financial crisis and riots in Xinjiang and Tibet. Their sheer lack of personality was a strategic asset. But it was during their reigns that financial and environmental problems began to fester. These were natural problems in the system they had inherited, but they were ones that could prove lethal. And they would drag on through Hu Jintao's time to Xi Jinping's.

There is a curious paradox to Xi Jinping's PRC. The country is more powerful than it has been at any point since its founding, and yet it also feels more insecure than it has since 1968–1969, when a major war with the Soviet Union threatened. Those problems of strategic geography have become harder to deal with, principally because China's growing weight has led to greater resistance from its neighbors and competitors. Xi seeks to address China's problems by drawing on all the categories of power his predecessors did. There is the balance of power with Chinese characteristics: reaching out to Russia, envisioning a new Silk Road, developing a bank that can buy friends. There is military modernization, with the focus on the much-touted anti-access, area-denial capabilities; there is also an attempt to use older forms of warfare, such as militias. There is an attempt to bring order to a political economy wracked by uncertain debts, underemployment, and corruption—a combination that jeopardizes political stability. And there is the flair, the drama, greater than that of any

Chinese leader since Mao. Like Mao, Xi rules by force of personality; like Mao, he sees in his own person the best guarantee for party and national security. Whether or not that works remains to be seen. It is a grand strategy fraught with risks. Structural forces beyond Xi's control—rising seas and vanishing ice, an aging population—could rob him of success too. And success itself does not guarantee happiness; that so many Chinese are parking their assets abroad suggests something is absent, even if Xi's grand strategy is working.

But all that comes later. Before we delve into the grand strategies of modern Chinese leaders, it is important to examine the world they came from. For grand strategies are shaped by the world their makers know, and it was in a broken, violent, unpredictable world that these men came of age.

FORGING GREAT CHINA

FOUR-THOUSAND-YEAR-OLD GREAT CHINA, Mao Zedong observed in 1920, was mere form, not reality. It had no foundation. To construct a large country, one first needed to build up smaller regions. This, China had not done. The sole way forward, Mao said, was to "smash this baseless great China and build many small Chinas."[1] There was a note of sadness to his musings: the admission that a once mighty colossus had been dismembered completely. But there was hope too, a vision of the China that could be and of a way toward it. Unity was not something to be taken for granted. It had to be fought for, secured by heroes strong of arm and will, who, by shoring up small gains, could eventually bring stability to the land and make China whole.

He would set out, then, like some hero from his beloved *Romance of the Three Kingdoms*, and put great China together again. He would have to face down foes both within and without: the Chinese whose vision of great China differed from his, the foreigners who were at best uncertain of and at worst downright hostile to the China he sought to create. His success owed much to luck. But it also came from an instinctive understanding of grand strategy, of how to weave together different categories of power to win and keep a state. There would be no shying away from the use of force. Mao would become famous for the guerrilla tactics he practiced, but these were just part of his military strategy; when the state needed it, he was willing to use tanks, battleships, and massed troops. He understood, too, the importance of diplomacy, of playing competing entities off against one another, of how negotiation and compromise could contribute to the safety of his state. And he understood the need for policies that would keep the populace on his side; the greater the discontent in a country, the harder it is to govern. The relative importance of these tools could shift from one situation to the next, but all were directed toward achieving that overarching goal of great China.

The journey to that state would unfold, broadly speaking, over three phases: the war with Japan, the renewal of the Chinese civil war from 1945, and in the civil war's last stages from 1949 to 1951. And the definition of the state would change over time. At the outset, Mao too had been uncertain of how far great China would go, of the extent of its territory, the sum of its peoples. But one has to start somewhere, and he would start by aiming for something small: a state of his own amid the chaos of all these tiny, competing Chinas. His state was just a fragment of what it would later become, but that would change in time. Ambition alters with circumstance; as success followed success, Mao's China would sweep out to encompass ever more.[2] What did not change was the fierce pragmatism with which Mao pursued his goal. It did not matter how unpleasant the people with whom one had to negotiate were or how far one had to depart from the ideological doctrine one espoused. What mattered was dragging the colossus together again.

From Civil War to World War II

You would be hard put to glimpse great China beneath the wreckage in 1920, never mind plan its resurrection. The Qing dynasty, which had taken China to its greatest territorial extent since the Mongols, had fallen in 1911. Before falling, it had seen China invaded and broken, by land and sea. In the nineteenth century, maritime powers had ravaged the coast—the British, the French, and, perhaps most unforgivably, the Japanese—and forced treaties on the Qing at gunpoint. In the ports they prised open to trade, the foreigners set up enclaves where their own legal and police systems held sway. They took it on themselves to set tariffs on goods imported to the country; the Westerners insisted on their right to spread Christianity across China. Such territory as the invading powers did not control informally, they wrested away, the British taking Hong Kong, the Japanese seizing Taiwan. By land, the Russians jostled up against China's frontiers, seeking a zone of influence in Xinjiang and gaining territory in Manchuria; later, in the twentieth century, they would struggle with Japan for mastery of China's north and northeast. Foreign control survived the Qing. The republic that emerged in the dynasty's place was a myth; China was a mix of warring states and alien powers. It was not the revolving cast of premiers in Beijing who determined how things went but the warlords—men like Zhang Zuolin and Feng Yuxiang, seeking foreign money and arms, their forces dueling back and forth across a suffering country. Xinjiang and Tibet, those farther outposts of the empire, had long been going their own way (although Chinese governments would retain a nominal claim to them); with the fall of the Qing, a large part of Mongolia would be torn from Chinese sovereignty too. In the wake of World War I, the foreigners would preach self-determination, but this, it became clear at Versailles, was a hollow promise. Instead of returning the enclaves of defeated Germany to China, the Western victors awarded them to Japan instead. The world might talk of self-determination, but its purpose was plain: it was still bent on subjugating China and its people.[3] All was chaos and misery.

And yet, beneath it all, you could sense something moving: a broken civilization's stirrings to restore itself. The stirrings were, for the most part, disparate and uncoordinated, but they spoke of a longing to enter the modern world. There were the students protesting the Versailles decision, whose activities would become known as the May Fourth Movement. There was Sun Yat-sen, the politician who dreamed of a republic and founded the Nationalist (Guomindang; GMD) party, speaking of the Three Principles—Democracy, Nationalism, and People's Livelihood; these did not mean much perhaps, but they gave people something to rally around. There was Sun's successor as head of the Nationalists, Chiang Kai-shek, who added a forcefulness and fascism to Sun's slogans.[4] And there was the Chinese Communist Party, inspired by the revolution in Russia and founded in 1921. At the insistence of its patrons in Moscow, the CCP cooperated with the Nationalists at first, forming a united front with them on the northern march that unified much of China—only for Chiang to massacre them almost completely in 1927. Chiang was not a man who liked to share power, and he hated communism with all the fervor of a good fascist.

Mao Zedong had his own vision for China's future, and it was not one that tallied with that of the CCP he had joined. His elders talked of restoring China, of getting its workers to overthrow the existing system; they had, Mao believed, completely missed China's true path to revolution. It was all very well to focus on the workers, but it was in the countryside that China's beating heart was to be found. The peasants, Mao argued, were crucial to revolution; without an uprising among them, the revolution could not succeed.[5] They were the majority of the population, and their suffering was great. His fellow party members criticized him in 1929 for devoting too many resources to peasant mobilization and not enough to taking cities (the criticism would stay with him, as both grievance to be nurtured and tool to be used); Mao shot back that they were wrong. In this semi-colonial China, the peasants' struggle should outstrip that of the workers. One had to wage a particular kind of warfare to be successful against the Nationalists and here came Mao's famous formulae on guerrilla warfare: to split forces and rouse the masses, to concentrate forces and engage the enemy, to retreat when the enemy advanced, to strike when the enemy tired, to harass when the enemy was stationed, and to pursue when the enemy was in retreat.[6] Win the peasants of China, wage the war that that victory allowed you, and you could create and defend a state. Those basic insights lay at the heart of the state Mao founded in 1931 in the verdant hills that lie between Jiangxi and Fujian: the Jiangxi soviet.

Simply calling this patch of land a state was revolutionary. And what made it even more so was what the state stood for. The Jiangxi soviet was to be a haven for the oppressed workers and peasants.[7] Within Chinese territory, the soviet leaders declared, there were now two "absolutely different countries": the Republic of China, a state of warlords and landlords which oppressed the people, and the Chinese Soviet Republic, a state which belonged to the exploited and oppressed.[8] It was the creation of an order where once there had been none, a way of being that was different, more dignified, less chaotic than what had existed before.

Mao's overarching goal from this point on was simple: to keep his state alive. There would be no compromise on CCP sovereignty, no giving it away in the name of greater good. Later in Yanan, when the war against the Japanese became desperate and people were urging the Nationalists and Communists to come together, the main hurdle would be Chiang's insistence that the Communists be subsumed by his government. The CCP could not accept this: being a state means having the right not to be subsumed by another. True, they did not have much international recognition. But they had a political philosophy and land where they could practice that philosophy, even if they were on the move. And they had arms to defend the new country they represented.

The use of those arms, like the state itself, was rooted in the idea that the masses were a source of strength. Mao had argued early on that the peasants needed to organize their own weaponry, that they needed peasant self-defense units.[9] The troops were to be under the command of the party; their tasks were to fight the landlord class, fight the Guomindang, and help the peasants and workers and oppressed.[10] And they were to conduct propaganda among the masses, organize them, and help them establish a revolutionary regime.[11] To be strong militarily, an insurgent army must be strong on politics; it needs friendly terrain and friendly people to wage guerrilla war with any success. The Communists were beginning to learn too what did not work for them; after an unsuccessful campaign in Hunan, it became clear that, without mass support, occupying central cities and annihilating the enemy was hard indeed.[12] There were certain circumstances in which the Maoist way of warfare worked;

doctrine had to fit the circumstances. The corollary was that when the circumstances changed, the doctrine could too.

These lessons—and Mao's power—were cemented by the fall of the Jiangxi soviet in 1934. There was time for soul-searching on the Long March, as the Communists fled Chiang's forces, and Mao took full advantage of it. The reason the Communists lost, Mao argued, was not (as some suggested) that the enemy was strong and the Communists weak; it was that the Communists had made strategic and tactical errors. They had become bogged down in a contest of holding positions and fortresses; they had forgotten to wage the active, decisive warfare that had underpinned so many of their victories.[13] From here on out, warfare with Chinese Communist characteristics would be something nimble, active, perpetually on the move, instead of moored to territory. In this, it was like the state it sought to protect. One could relocate that state, from Jiangxi to Yanan, take it traveling if war demanded. It was the idea of the state, the commitment to it that mattered. If those were there, the physical space held or not could be compromised on. One could wait and fight to realize the vision of great China in the fullness of time.

The Sino-Japanese war that broke out in the 1930s did little to change this. It was a war that in the beginning was fought by Chiang's China, not Mao's. Mao would found a new base in the high mountains of Yanan, far removed from the action of the Sino-Japanese war. The Japanese seizure of Manchuria in 1931, the Marco Polo Bridge incident of 1937 that set off full-scale war between Japan and Chiang's China, the battle for Shanghai, the fall and rape of Nanjing— as far as practical effects on Communist power were concerned, these might as well have been happening in another country. Chiang, distrustful of the CCP, had been as intent on extinguishing them as on resisting the Japanese. It was good propaganda material of course—the Japanese were destroying the country, and Chiang was selling it to them. Mao made sure to point out that the Communists opposed Chiang's policy of not allowing them to fight the Japanese, that it was time for red and white (meaning communist and anti-communist) troops to come together in a bid to fight the Japanese.[14] But for all the talk of anti-imperialism, the Communists had not engaged—had not had the opportunity to engage—the Japanese forces in battle; they were too busy surviving in territory dominated by hostile Tibetans and Muslims as they sought, fruitlessly, to make their way to the border with the Soviet Union (where they hoped to find succor). One cannot help feeling that however vociferous Mao's protests, he found Chiang's policy rather convenient: it allowed the Communists room to fan out, form bases in the western mountains, and all the while it was Chiang's forces bearing the brunt of the Japanese assault.

Chiang's fellow Nationalists were far from agreed on the wisdom of exterminating the CCP while Japan muscled in on Chinese territory. Two of Chiang's generals kidnapped the dictator in December 1936. Chiang, they insisted, was to cooperate with the Communists against the Japanese. The generalissimo was unhappy about this (the generals would suffer later), but under the circumstances he had little choice. And so the second united front came about in 1937 (the first had been formed on that ill-fated northern march), a CCP-GMD front to defend China against Japan.[15]

As the CCP saw it, its contribution to the war effort would be much the same as it had been in the war against the Nationalists: creating bases, suppressing and killing the enemy, cooperating with friendly forces, expanding the Chinese Red Army, and working, above all, for the right to command the people's revolution. They would wage guerrilla war in the mountain bases and gradually send soldiers to foment revolution out in the plains. It was time now to awaken the people of this slumbering, broken country, summon them to battle for China whether in the highlands of Gansu or in the eastern plains. Where possible, one would concentrate forces to kill the enemy. All of this was to be done while maintaining independence of the Guomindang, and a detachment of troops was to protect the Communist base in the Shaanxi-Gansu-Ningxia (ShaanGanNing, as they took to calling it) highlands at all times.[16] For one never knew what the Nationalists might do. The United Front meant a suspension of hostilities, not of distrust. Meanwhile, plans were made to expand guerrilla war in Hebei and Shandong. An army had sprung up in the northeast, which had, as Mao pointed out, been fighting the Japanese the longest. With good leadership, they could harm the enemy; the main question now was how to connect the central Communist leadership with the armies in the northeast.[17] It was the creation of small Chinas, which would add up, over time, to a larger whole. And the way to do so remained through guerrilla war. Mao sought to fight the Japanese as he had fought the Nationalists: in a patient, elaborate dance across China, which would end with Japan exhausted.

As much as military doctrine, sensible diplomacy was crucial to Communist survival. Mao's struggles with the Guomindang and later with the Japanese were unfolding in a larger context; there were other players, both globally and within the as yet undefined borders of China to whom he could reach out. The Guomindang was but one piece on the chessboard. One's policy toward it and toward other pieces was best determined by how it affected the survival of the CCP's state. Thus, on the Long March, when first encountering the full force of ethnic tension, Mao was shrewd enough to draw the right lessons from it.[18] The Miao, he noted as the Communists went through their territory, were different from the Han, their ways of life distinct; everyone would have to observe discipline and the defense officials be told about the party's minority policy.[19] The CCP stood for self-determination; different minority groups, Mao promised, could either join an eventual Chinese federation or form their own countries.[20] One needed these people on one's side. It was a line that was self-serving—it aimed at alleviating fear among possible enemies—but Mao was probably sincere; he was young at this point, and young idealistic revolutionaries have a way of making promises that they later cannot keep. Minority policy was part of a larger diplomacy, which in turn was part of a larger grand strategy to keep his ever-moving state secure.

From his base too, Mao's diplomacy was welcoming. It was immaterial, the Communists declared, what political party or social group someone belonged too; if they were willing to oppose the Japanese and oppose Chiang (this was before the united front), the Communists were willing, not only to sign an agreement to wage joint war, but even to form joint forces and a joint defense government.[21] All the Communists asked was that people refrain from attacking the Red Army and their base in ShaanGanNing; if those conditions were met, it was immaterial which political party one came from, which troops one had fought for, what one's relations with the CCP had been in the past—there was room, now, to work together to fight Japan and save China.[22] All across broken China, Mao well knew, there were forces that were neither his nor Chiang's; he had to survive them and, if possible, win them over. This insight formed the basis of his diplomacy toward the ethnic groups in what would become China's west. The Mongols were told that the Communists saw the need for a joint struggle to overcome their mutual enemies, Japan and Chiang Kai-shek, that only through working with the Communists could the Mongols "maintain the glories of Genghis Khan's time, avoid national annihilation, and embark on the path to national rejuvenation." The Communists respected their rights, the equality of all nationalities.[23] A similar message went out to the Hui Muslims, both populous and powerful in the regions the CCP found itself in. The Hui's affairs, Mao said, were for the Hui themselves to decide; their mosques, their religious autonomy, would be protected. The reactionary forces of the warlord bureaucrats could be abolished. The Hui and the Han, two great peoples, could overcome Japan and the people selling out the country.[24]

Mao was careful too not to come across as overbearing at this time. With Ma Zhanshan, who had worked with the Japanese and Chiang Kai-shek before deciding to lead resistance to Japan in the northeast, Mao was cordial in 1939; his forces and Ma's were working toward a common goal. The Communists would court Yan Xishan, the warlord in charge of Shanxi, to see if he could be dealt with peacefully. One did not want him joining forces with the Nationalists, even though a united front had been declared; his neutrality would keep the Communists safer. Yan's eventual willingness to make an alliance of convenience (one that would come to an end much later, with Yan decamping to Taiwan) boded well for the war in the north and northwest.[25] Not all these attempts were immediately successful in bringing over large numbers of people to the CCP's side, although some would eventually come in handy. But they reflected one of the key precepts of Mao's grand strategy. With his China one among many, in a world vast and fragmented, one needed to pay attention to the smaller powers. Smaller powers mattered; they could help as one sought to cope with the larger ones.

In coping with those larger entities, Mao would seek a balance of power. There had been, in the days of intense conflict with Chiang, a tendency to lump the Japanese and the Guomindang together: the latter was portrayed as selling out the country to the former, standing in the way of revolution. But there was an understanding too that the Guomindang was far from monolithic, that there were people within it who thought Chiang's policies harmful, whom the Communists might reach. A letter was sent to Guomindang troops in the northeast in November 1935, urging them to stop fighting the CCP; it was better, instead, to cooperate to resist the Japanese and oppose Chiang.[26] One could peel away at Chiang's organization, depriving him, bit by bit, of the forces that sustained him.

Not that one would abandon Chiang altogether. As the war with Japan intensified, the emphasis on the Chiang-Japan relationship shifted too. The appropriate slogan, even before the united front, was no longer to "resist Japan and oppose Chiang" but rather to "compel Chiang to resist Japan."[27] There was room for accommodation with the Nationalists if they behaved reasonably—room that was explored well into the war and beyond. The CCP, Mao would assure Guomindang negotiators, had no intention of overthrowing the Guomindang government, of expanding beyond its current borders. All that was needed was for the Guomindang to recognize the CCP's right to develop behind enemy lines, recognize the current defense sector and the border district.[28] In short, although it was not phrased quite this way, the Guomindang was to treat the CCP as a sovereign state. The two sides could then refrain from mutual attack.[29] It was an intriguing offer—and one cannot help wondering if, had it been accepted, Mao might have been content with two Chinas. Given all that followed, it might at first glance appear unlikely. And yet there are so many instances of partition where it might once have been thought impossible—in the subcontinent, in Yugoslavia, in Eastern Europe. Mao might well have resigned himself to a situation like that which would later exist between India and Pakistan: two states always on the alert, bound by mutual suspicion and loathing, with sporadic clashes that could occasionally flare into war—but two states nonetheless. Mao did not like Chiang and would never trust him. This was insufficient reason to jeopardize his own state. In 1942, he would tell his comrade Liu Shaoqi that although renewed civil war was possible after the war with Japan was over, there was also the possibility of cooperation with the Guomindang, and this was a possibility that the CCP should strive to realize. Talks with the Guomindang about how to cooperate persisted into 1943.[30] There is wisdom to letting talks run as long as they need to; it buys time and avoids bloodshed. But if core interests are to be surrendered, talks become pointless. To acquiesce in Chiang's insistence at the talks that the CCP was subject to his government, not sovereign in its own right, was to surrender all that Mao had been fighting for. The CCP's line was pragmatic coexistence; that meant not compromising away its own existence as a sovereign power.

As a sovereign power, the CCP could reach out to Japan too. There being two main enemies, the Nationalists and the Japanese, the sensible thing to do was to use one against the other. As late as 1941, Mao could write to Zhou saying that the contradictions between Japan and Chiang could be used. If the Japanese attacked in force, it would be worth assisting the pro-Japanese forces; this would put pressure on Chiang and his allies.[31] These were balance of power politics that made perfect sense—if one assumed that the overarching goal was not the survival of all China but of Mao's. Subtle feelers went out to the Japanese; agents like Pan Hannian were sent to meet with Japanese officials to see if the CCP and Japan could find a modus vivendi.[32] There was nothing to be gained by shutting off the possibility of an understanding with Japan; if the CCP could reach such an understanding, it would strengthen its hand in the struggle against the Nationalists. One wanted to be closer to both Japan and the Guomindang than they were to one another. It did not matter that the Japanese were imperialists tearing China apart. It mattered only whether they were hindrance or help to the survival of Mao's China.

And beyond Japan and the Guomindang, beyond the ethnic armies and militias fighting across China's fractured expanse, there were the great powers being drawn into world war. The CCP's initial line on those powers and World War II had been fairly ideological: imperial powers, whether German or British, Italian or American (not yet formally in the war), Japanese or French, were intent on carving out colonies for themselves. It fell to the socialist countries to promote revolution, liberation. China's future was clear: a new, independent China would emerge.[33] But somehow, the Soviet Union was not helping as much as would be ideologically appropriate; the CCP had wanted to make it to the Soviet border, but that proved impossible—and Stalin never provided the aid that the CCP had been counting on. Nor did the Soviets enter the war against Japan, although there had been hopes that they would.[34] As the fighting wore on, the CCP's understanding of wartime alliances and the uses they could be put to deepened. Alliances could constrain Chiang Kai-shek, some more than others. "Chiang joining the Anglo-American group," Mao mused, "has benefits without harm; [his] joining the German-Italian-Japanese group has harm without benefits. We should no longer emphasize opposition to [Chiang] joining the Anglo-American group, though we should not advocate it (because they are an imperialist war group)." It was meet, under the circumstances, to forge diplomatic links with the Americans and British and move against the pro-Japanese and pro-German parties. And it was time to stop cursing Chiang and the Guomindang.[35] These inclinations could change, as the contemplated assistance to pro-Japanese parties suggests, but they showed the recognition that one had to be practical about ideology. It was all very well to be anti-imperial, but in this particular war, the interests of Communists and imperialists went hand in hand.

For Mao's core interest was the survival of his China. He was in no rush to oppose American and British assistance to Chiang via the Burma Road, because one might be able to use the contradictions among the imperialists against Japan. Besides, it might become more difficult for Chiang to fight the Communists as the struggle with Japan intensified.[36] (The allies would not, presumably, be happy to see resources that should be going to fight Japan being diverted to an anticommunist vendetta.) By much the same logic, he did not mourn the loss of the Burma Road in 1942. The closure of that southern supply route would make Chiang more reliant on the northwest, on the Soviet Union. And the increased economic difficulties and dissatisfaction Chiang would face would make it harder for him to conduct an anticommunist campaign.[37] The overall China war effort was immaterial to Mao. What mattered was how it affected the prospects of his China.

This was, in large part, what made the American entry into the war such a promising development. The outbreak of an American-Japanese war, he thought, might reduce Chiang's attacks on the border region.[38] The American and British desire to avoid a civil war in China had been, he told Liu Shaoqi, one of the reasons for Chiang Kai-shek's improved attitude. One could, circumstances permitting, even follow up with a gesture, such as offering to withdraw one's troops north of the Yellow River.[39] There was a touching faith in American rationality, in America's capacity to recognize and pursue its national interests. The Americans would see that Chiang was harming the war effort; they would compel him to behave decently. They would help the Communists in the war—not out of the goodness of their hearts, of course, but because they had an interest in winning World War II, and that meant keeping China free of civil war. They would have the good sense to rein Chiang in.

This was not bad reasoning; considering the Americans Mao had met—Jack Service, Edgar Snow—it was logical. There was tangible evidence of American willingness to cooperate with the CCP. When an American military delegation was due for a visit, the decision was made to speak with them frankly, telling them what the Communists could and could not do. The foreigners were impressed with what they saw in Yanan. The resulting cooperation included intelligence sharing.[40] Capitalist-imperialists the Americans might be, but they were useful partners in Mao's war.

The problem arose when the Americans sought to mediate between the Nationalists and Communists. Patrick Hurley, bluff, blustering, a little offensive perhaps, but still worth humoring, showed up with proposals to bring peace. Hurley started off with a suggestion that was seen as bringing the Communist forces under Nationalist command. This, Mao said politely, was not feasible. They were willing to work toward resolving problems, but the destruction of the liberated areas' capacity to make war and the hindrance of democracy (meaning CCP power) were unacceptable. Some form of joint effort against the Japanese would be worth exploring.[41] Chiang shot back that once the Communist soldiers had surrendered and the CCP had sent delegates to participate in a Nationalist government, their legal standing could be recognized—but not before. The proper thing for Hurley to do at this point—at least from the CCP's perspective—would have been to put pressure on Chiang to agree to the idea of joint government. Instead, Hurley sent Chiang's proposals back to the Communists. This was not the deal the Communists had contemplated.[42] There was no way they could have accepted it, despite Hurley's insistence; it would have entailed a complete loss of sovereignty. Hurley's conduct showed at best incompetence, at worst, bad faith.

Herein lay the source of the CCP's suspicion that it could not trust the Americans to be evenhanded. In a final talk with Jack Service, Mao would note that the CCP was searching for a friendly America, one willing to cooperate with China in realizing democracy and fighting the Japanese; the hope was that the Americans would not intervene in the event of a Chinese civil war.[43] One wanted American cooperation in opposing the Japanese; danger arose only when the Americans lapsed into helping Chiang fight the Communists.[44] Some of the later vitriol, one suspects, was all the more intense for the hope the CCP had had in American rationality. The Americans had seemed so reasonable—people like Service—empathetic, logical, understanding; and the CCP had invested so much time, so much face, in reaching out to them. For diplomacy to fail simply because the Americans were tied to Chiang was unforgivable.

To sustain war and diplomacy, a state needs a sound political and economic base. It was here that Mao was at his most flexible. Economic policy, as he laid it out in 1934, was far from doctrinaire. The land revolution was meant not only to turn land over to the peasants but to improve productivity. There was room for private enterprise—it would be subordinate to state-run enterprise and would have to follow the law, but within these constraints, it would be encouraged.[45] The economy had a purpose: to sustain the soviet state, its capacity to protect itself and its people. Governance meant supplying people's wants. Whatever worked for these larger goals, Mao would use. Private enterprise could be helpful and would, therefore, be permitted.

A similar flexibility marked land reform, for that too was part of the war effort. In 1937, he would tell his comrades Zhu De and Peng

Dehuai that land reform should be carried out in areas to the enemy's rear or where the enemy was being pursued, because seizing the great landlords' property was the key to rousing the masses, which was what was needed for a people's war. But the policy was to apply only to those great landlords who were traitors. And because the will of the people mattered, it followed that absent their agreement, there was no need to rush to seize property from middle-class traitors. In 1940, the CCP would mull the tricky, sometimes elusive balance to be struck: rent and debt needed to be cut but not so much as to create larger problems. Cut interest by too much, and the peasants might find themselves unable to get loans. It had to be made clear that the peasants had a duty to pay rent and interest; it would not do to disrupt the economy too much. Now was not the time to conduct serious land reform.[46] Ideology was philosophizing, but statecraft sometimes had to concern itself with prosaic questions. What does the state produce and what must it import? One had to monitor expenses, be aware the state could get too heavy for its own good and that state jobs might then have to be cut.[47]

Mao would, in fact, find himself in the position of having to rein in comrades more ideological than he (he was, ironically given what was to come later, even well disposed to intellectuals in 1944),[48] bent on a policy that he saw as needlessly swift and extreme. Many of the land reform policies pursued in the past, he would note in December 1940, were not appropriate for use now; some had not even been appropriate at the time.[49] There were truer believers in the CCP than Mao, and it was useful to have them around to criticize. Criticizing Zhang Guotao during the Long March had played a role in Mao's rise to power; this was a tactic that could be used again. Peng Dehuai, now—Peng was being too ideological; he was emphasizing the role of democracy in opposing feudalism, rather than the Japanese.[50] There was a war on, and Peng was targeting the wrong enemy. Wang Ming too would come in for criticism.[51] It was not that there were not genuine disagreements; there were, and Mao thought his policies crucial to the health of the CCP's state. It was just that prosecuting these disagreements ferociously would strengthen his control of the party, while minimizing errors in what was, after all, a dangerous situation. He himself, he would acknowledge in 1945, had made errors; it was only that, for the good of the party, they had not been registered.[52] Mao's good was the good of the party, which was the good of the state. It was, like most truly dangerous beliefs, at once self-serving and sincere.

Civil War Renewed

Then the bombs fell, and the Soviets declared war on Japan and came flooding into the northeast. The Japanese were defeated. The need for a united front was gone. How, now, were the Communists to secure their state against Chiang Kai-shek? On the state itself there was to be no compromise: the main conditions of talks, Mao made clear, were the recognition of the liberated areas and the troops.[53] Territory and the right to the use of force: these attributes the CCP was insistent on.

It is doubtful that Mao expected Chiang to be happy about this. They had killed far too many of each other's soldiers, fallen out too many times. Besides, as the CCP was well aware, the generalissimo was monopolizing the right to accept surrender on China's behalf. But the three great powers—the United States, the USSR, and Britain—did not want renewed civil war in China; some form of cooperation with the Guomindang might yet, therefore, be possible.[54] Not that the CCP would do anything so foolish as to rely purely on talks. They had long been aware of the geostrategic importance of the northeast and were quick to try to establish bases in the areas adjacent to the Soviet, Korean, and Mongolian borders.[55] There were skirmishes there; the Nationalists did not want the CCP to continue holding the cities of Shenyang and Changchun. But there was no harm in talking of the need for peace and exploring the possibility, however faint, of a modus vivendi with Chiang. If Chiang, under diplomatic pressure, succumbed to the need to accept the CCP's conditions, a deal could be struck. (Just how long it would have lasted is interesting to speculate on. Mao might have remained bent on the conquest of all of China, but he might also, especially if there were practical constraints, have been content to maintain the liberated areas and his forces as a separate or autonomous state. A Chiang who had set his lands in order, brought fiscal balance and social stability to the territory he controlled, would have been a formidable enemy—and therefore one not to provoke lightly. It would not have been an easy relationship between Mao's China and Chiang's, but it might have been a reasonably long-lasting one.) If, as seemed more likely, the talks failed, then the world would know it was Chiang's fault. A reasonable mediator, the CCP assumed, would see that it was the generalissimo who had scuppered the talks and renewed civil war, not they.

The CCP was always going to be suspicious of the American attempt at mediation. The Americans, honest brokers, had landed in China in 1945 and paved the way for the Guomindang to come in, allowing them a foothold in the northeast.[56] Their neutrality had already been compromised. But the CCP remained convinced that the Americans could be dealt with, that there were contradictions between the Nationalists and the Americans that could be exploited. Cordial relations between Zhou and American special envoy George Marshall—who was on one of the most thankless diplomatic missions of all time, trying to broker peace between the Nationalists and the Communists—should, Mao directed, be preserved insofar as possible. Zhou would try to convince Marshall of the need for an unconditional ceasefire in the northeast. The Americans were not bad friends to have; Marshall might even be touched for a loan.[57] Marshall seemed so reasonable, so understanding of the CCP's concerns. Mao did not fully grasp, as Chiang did, that America was larger than Marshall, that regardless of what the special envoy saw as practical policy, American domestic politics could and would override his preferences. It was a woeful misunderstanding of the nature of American politics—and one that hobbles the PRC to this day.

Because these negotiations were entered with little faith, the CCP would fight for mastery of the northeast. In Manchuria's eastern, western, and northern reaches—far from where the Americans could help the Guomindang—Mao directed that bases be set up in areas not too close to the Guomindang holdings. Preparations were under way for a guerrilla war, for rousing the masses and producing goods.[58] The CCP was already organizing for war to protect its state, to which Chiang was but one threat. Grand strategy from here on out would be about winning the war.

Thus began the transition—which would be completed in the final phases of the war, after October I, 1949—from a ragtag band of guerrillas to a modern military force. Guerrilla warfare remained the preferred military strategy during the early phases of the war. Mao was firm on the importance of holding the big northeastern cities: Harbin, Changchun, Qiqihar.[59] But places like Harbin and Changchun were not enough; smaller cities and rural areas were of prime importance.[60] For a guerrilla war to work, one needed to win the people, not the territory which was one of the reasons, despite the early loss of those big northeastern cities, the CCP was able to prevail. The role of the troops in the Central Plains, Mao explained, was to remain active and flexible in places like Sichuan, allowing the inner CCP line up in the north to hang on for victory. In the second stage of the war, the inner line—presumably once it was secure enough—would send its troops to join with those of the Central Plains to take the Xinyang, Dabieshan, and Anqing line.[61] The Communists would build from small pieces to a larger whole.

The way to do so, of course, harkened back to the older civil war. The warring state was to remain on the move: holding territory did not matter as much as doing damage to the enemy. Let the Nationalists disperse to occupy Communist-held territory, Mao thought; it would make it easier to destroy the enemy. He knew that although Chiang held territory, his grip on it was far from secure, that much of it was protected only by public security groups rather than proper soldiers, that people's livelihoods were suffering, leaving room for instigating a people's struggle.[62] If one waited Chiang out, staying on the run, the generalissimo would sink deeper into a mire of his own making and eventually drown. The results bore Mao out. But it was a strategy that entailed significant loss, including that of Yanan. Yanan hurt, reminding Mao perhaps of the loss of his beloved soviet; the story is told of how, even though his general, Peng Dehuai, urged him to leave, he insisted on staying until the last possible moment. He would maintain that the loss of Yanan reflected, not the enemy's strength, but the growing crisis of Guomindang rule. And yet it was on April 10, 1947, just after the fall of Yanan, that he declared the goal of annihilating Chiang's regime.[63]

Yanan was lost, but his armies fought and won elsewhere. In the summer of 1947, Peng Dehuai and Xi Zhongxun moved against the Muslim warlords in Ningxia and Gansu.[64] The loss of the major cities notwithstanding, Lin Biao and others had done well in the farther reaches of Manchuria; as Mao told them, "Under your leadership, the northeast has conducted land reform, mobilized the masses, and established a strong branch of troops."[65] That brief sentence crystallized many of the factors that allowed the CCP to move from the loss of Yanan to the massive campaigns in southern China and the occupation of cities. First, there was a sense of geography, of China's vastness. There was more to the country than just its cities; there were mountains and forests, farther worlds where Communist forces could recuperate. Second, there was a willingness to praise subordinates who had done well. Lin Biao was a superb general, and Mao would recognize this and commend him for his leadership. Third, there was the awareness that categories of power other than the military mattered. Mobilizing the people and getting the economic system on a suitable footing mattered for victory. Political and economic power could overcome a military deficit. Those strengths might not tell immediately, but they could over the long run prove decisive. Mao was confident that Lin and his forces would move to establish bases in southern Manchuria soon.[66]

By 1948, those strengths began to make themselves felt—most obviously through a changed military strategy. Directives went out to avoid the needless destruction in the north and northeast.[67] The enemy's strength was diminishing in these regions and the CCP would, presumably, need intact rail lines to administer its new territories. By September 1948, the CCP was preparing for the withdrawal of Guomindang forces from Shenyang and Changchun.[68] Suddenly, cities like Beijing and Tianjin were being occupied. There was no more retreating when the enemy advanced; warfare was no longer being waged predominantly on the run. The CCP was drawing up plans for an army that was five million strong.[69] And at Zhu De's suggestion, the CCP would explore how to get troops trained in aerial combat in the

Soviet Union; one would need an air force to take Taiwan.[70] This was no longer guerrilla war. It was modern warfare, waged by a state grown strong.

There was little reason, back when the CCP lost Yanan or even Changchun, to contemplate events such as this. At the time, they were losing and losing heavily; the best that they might have hoped for would have been a dying resistance in the countryside. Luck helped, as did some superb tactical planning and execution. But so did careful attention to the political economy. Mao was no economic genius. He did not have to be; he merely had to do better than Chiang Kai-shek. Ideology, he had observed back in January 1945, should "accord with the circumstances we are currently in." It was this practical streak that had led to his endorsement of capitalism. China too needed to develop capitalism, he declared in May 1945. But whereas Chiang had developed a capitalism that was half fascist and half feudal, what the Communists would develop would be the capitalism of new democracy. The capitalism of new democracy was revolutionary, useful, conducive to socialism.[71] Ideology was flexible; words could mean whatever one wanted them to. The important thing was to get the economy to function.

This meant striking a tricky balance. Independent capitalists were to be isolated politically, but, properly supervised, they had a role to play in economic recovery. On one hand, one wanted to be wary of making further concessions to rich peasants, particularly on the principle that they needed to till the land; on the other, in areas where the populace seemed content, there was no need to rush through with further changes.[72] Even a revolutionary state needs a certain amount of stability and predictability, for these minimize resistance. When giving directives on the implementation of land reform, Mao was careful to specify that there was room for compromise, although it was to be left unwritten, informal; if the middle-class peasants were amenable, there was no reason wealthy middle-class peasants could not get a little land. The troops might find it best to stick with existing ways and customs in newly liberated areas. Creating chaos would only help the enemy and isolate the CCP. "To the extent possible," as Mao put it, killing should be avoided.[73] It was not that he was averse to killing; rather, killing unnecessarily would alienate the populace and undermine the larger goal of winning the civil war and securing the new state. When people carped that the economy had become capitalist, Mao fired back that it was not; it was a "new democratic economy." Agriculture would be socialized in good time, but this was not the moment; to socialize it now would only hurt production.[74] He was trying to have it both ways: to be ideologically proper while doing what reality demanded. It was not that ideology was irrelevant; it was just that there were other considerations that could trump ideology. Mao's pragmatic streak was alive and well, and he knew that to win China and keep it, he needed to keep his more reckless subordinates in check.

The other component to sound economic planning was making sure that the military did not grow too heavy or alienate the social base. On January 9, 1948, Mao made clear that once a place had become a base, the government, not the troops, would be in charge of managing the economy. The troops must neither confiscate nor destroy property; their provisions were to come from enemy warehouses, landlords, land taxes, and appropriate taxes levied by the government.[75] This would keep things predictable for the populace and confine the military to its proper sphere in the new Chinese order. By the summer of 1948, he was worried that the war and economy were not in synchrony; it was no longer possible to add more troops without creating serious difficulties of provision. The solution was to fill the ranks with

Guomindang prisoners and locals.[76] Cutting down on expenses was the key to sustaining a long war.

One of the things that kept costs low was skillful diplomacy. The Guomindang was not a monolith. The CCP could be intent on annihilating Chiang's administration, but if his soldiers and representatives could be co-opted, it would save much blood and money. Chiang's was a government that relied heavily on powerful warlords; this made a policy of peeling them off much easier than it might otherwise have been. There were long, patient negotiations with Fu Zuoyi, the Guomindang commander guarding Beijing; it was possible, the CCP believed, to divide him from Chiang. If Fu would just allow the CCP's forces to take Beijing and Tianjin, he could be absolved of war crimes, keep his private fortune, and live in Beijing or anywhere else he wished. But there were to be no further concessions.[77] Mao knew how to negotiate. One had to specify what one wanted, what not to cave on, carry on until there was a reasonable chance of getting it, but be prepared to walk away if the other side asked for too much. He would be generous to Fu where he could afford to be, for generosity made conquest easier. It helped too that Fu's inner circle and family had been penetrated by CCP spies. So Fu, who was a sensible man, accepted the CCP's terms on January 22, 1949. Under those terms, Guomindang troops stationed in Beijing would be transferred to locations outside the city, pending reassignment.[78] By January 31, Fu's troops had all vacated Beijing and the People's Liberation Army (PLA) began streaming in.[79] Fu had had enough of warfare; when he met Mao, he wanted nothing more than to work in hydraulics. But the chairman, menacing in his benevolence, explained that he was releasing Fu's forces who had been taken prisoner and sending them to Suiyuan, where they would come in handy (many of them had been stationed there during the war with Japan). Fu himself, Mao pronounced, could still do military work. "I see you still have great ability," said Mao.[80] Negotiation meant getting Beijing much more cheaply and easily than by fighting Fu to the finish. And the man himself could then come in handy. Why punish a resource when he could be used?

The CCP would reach out to other Guomindang leaders too. It would not work on Bai Chongxi or Li Zongren—stubborn men, as wary of Mao as they were of Chiang—but there was no harm in trying. There were now two governments holding capitals in China—the CCP in Beijing, the Guomindang in Nanjing—and secret talks between the two were as much an opportunity for recruitment as for negotiation. The negotiations would fail: Chiang could not stomach the idea of making terms with the CCP. But they gave Mao the chance to meet Zhang Zhizhong, the Guomindang's erstwhile governor in Xinjiang. Zhang was a shrewd, practical man; he had had some success in winning over the Muslims of China's far northwest, only to be undercut by Chiang's hardline policies. Mao met Zhang on April 8, 1949, to discuss how to end the war. The chairman understood the difficulties of the Nanjing representatives' position. He was willing, he said, to drop the idea of naming war criminals in the peace clauses, in order to make the representatives' task easier.[81] Zhang was unable to bring the Guomindang as a whole to make the agreement, but he was willing and able to join the CCP himself. Mao was aware that out west, the CCP needed expertise like Zhang's, needed people with firsthand experience of the turf where the CCP was encountering difficulties. Zhang, with his deep knowledge of Xinjiang, could be tasked with establishing a military and political committee there. Deng Baoshan could be handy in Qinghai. And Qinghai was where the Panchen Lama, one of the most powerful figures in the Tibetan laity, was now based; he was to be protected and respected, as were the

Tibetans living in Gansu and Qinghai, for this would be the key to resolving the question of Tibet.[82] The people to his west mattered to Mao too; he was willing to do what it took to win them over.

The Nanjing government's refusal to come to terms meant that the CCP would use force to move south, which raised the question of diplomacy toward foreigners. What was remarkable was the restraint the fervently anti-imperial Communists aimed for. The PLA was to avoid engaging foreign troops.[83] Mao ordered that the troops be educated to protect American and British expatriates (all foreigners, but those two groups in particular) and officials. There was good reason for this: Mao believed that those countries had an interest in dealing with his China. There were hints that diplomatic relations with Washington might be possible; the British were interested in doing business. If the Americans and British would sever relations with Chiang—and it seemed as though the "old American policy" of helping the Guomindang and opposing the Communists was dying—it was possible to contemplate establishing diplomatic relations with them.[84] Huang Hua, then working in the foreign affairs office in Nanjing, was asked to meet American ambassador John Leighton Stuart to see if it was possible to get clear on American intentions. While doing so, he could communicate China's intentions too. It was not that China—Mao had genuine pride—needed America to do something for the Chinese people. It was simply that America had to stop helping Chiang, stop participating in China's civil war. That was the key requisite for establishing diplomatic relations.[85]

This was not quite as outlandish as it might have sounded to the Americans. If one wishes to establish a working relationship with a state, it seems reasonable to stop supporting its enemies—especially those bent implacably on its destruction. Had the Americans accepted these terms, some sort of working relationship might well have been established. It might not have been intimate, but it would almost certainly have been an improvement on what was to come.[86] At the time, the CCP still hoped that relations with America and Britain could be restored, and this was the hope that inclined it to be solicitous of the foreigners on their land—partly because foreign intervention could yet tip the balance, partly because these countries remained crucial to the Chinese economy. Trade dependence on the United States had shot up. In 1936, 19.7 percent of China's imports came from the United States; by 1947, that figure was at 51.7 percent.[87] If the emerging new China were to survive, it would need solid relations with the capitalists. Therefore, Mao made clear that although he did not recognize the existing diplomatic apparatus of foreign powers or any agreements they might have concluded with the Guomindang, he was fine with business continuing—even with capitalist powers.[88] He would protect foreign residents, so long as they respected the law of the land.[89] Revolutionaries needed to eat too, and trade would help with this. The CCP was anti-imperial, but its anti-imperialism was rooted in the understanding that imperialists were aiding the Guomindang, thereby keeping China from achieving greatness. Should the imperial powers stop assisting the Guomindang, the CCP could work with them.

Because he was a believer in both the balance of power and in communism, reaching out to the Americans and British did not mean abandoning relations with the Soviets. Josef Stalin had been more receptive of late. The Soviets had turned over weaponry and territory in Manchuria to the CCP after the Japanese surrender; the emerging Cold War had inclined them more favorably to the CCP.[90] Mao wooed the visiting Soviet minister of foreign trade, Anastas Mikoyan, assiduously, explaining to him that the CCP was not too eager for recognition by Britain and the United States, that there was reason to be careful in dealing with foreign enterprises in China, that the party was now free of Trotskyist influence—in sum, that the CCP was really and truly a communist power.[91] This did not necessarily mean that Mao was willing to become utterly subordinate to the Soviet Union (as Soviet archival records might suggest); it meant simply that he was willing to tell the Soviets what he thought they wanted to hear. In classic Cold War fashion, he was trying to get what he could from both Washington and Moscow.[92] An agreement with the Soviets seemed to be on the table, and a visit to Moscow was in order. On July 25, 1949, he cabled his delegates in Moscow, agreeing to the establishment of a Chinese university there.[93] Closer relations with the Soviets would be useful. Not that these were to preclude decent relations with the capitalist world; "leaning to one side," to use Mao's phrase, did not require falling over. Mao would deal, the track record suggests, with whoever was willing and able to help him.[94] For much of 1949, the CCP, like Otto von Bismarck, sought to be closer to other players in the balance of power than they were to one another; the prospects for their relationships with both Moscow and Washington seemed brighter than those for the relationship between the two superpowers. In diplomacy, as in all else, Mao would do whatever worked.

Defining China

"We the four hundred and seventy five million Chinese people have now stood up," announced Mao, founding the People's Republic of China.[95] After the fall of the soviet and that wild, desperate march through the mountains, after being savaged by Chiang and betrayed by the United States, the colossus was finally whole again and could rise as one. But who were the Chinese people who had stood up? How far did their lands go? Where did they give way to the claims of another people, another state? Mao Zedong, even as he founded the PRC, had no memory of a China that was one, no template for what China really was.[96] And much of what would become the PRC was still outside Mao's control on October 1, 1949. The southern hills and forests where the Guomindang forces were still holding on; long stretches of the east coast and the islands of Taiwan and Hainan; those far western territories of Tibet and Xinjiang—it still remained for these places to be conquered, still remained, indeed, for the PRC to decide that they should be conquered at all. Some form of action against the Guomindang in the south was probably necessary. There had been too much blood spilled for the PRC to tolerate a second China now. But the CCP, so it had said, believed in the right of self-determination for ethnic minorities; they could, if they wished, have autonomy, even independence. At the time, the CCP probably genuinely meant this. But circumstances had changed and a new state would have to be governed. And governing might mean that faraway places had to be woven into the new state.

For, on the frontier, the state would need protection. Ideology and anti-imperialism contributed to the decision, but the principal motive for Chinese expansion was geopolitical. The clearest explanation of the policy had been given by Zhou Enlai on September 7, 1949:

China's minority nationalities should also be included in the People's Republic of China; [we] recognize their right to autonomy. Therefore we think the People's Republic of China, as the country's name, is really appropriate.

... We advocate nationalities' autonomy, but we must prevent imperialists using the nationalities problem to foment discord against China's unity. For example, the British imperialists' conspiracy in Tibet and southern Xinjiang, the American imperialists' conspiracy

in Taiwan and Hainan island. It is correct that these places have national minorities, but they have all along been within the territory of
China. . . .

All nationalities have the right to self-determination. . . . But today,
imperialists seek to divide our Tibet, Taiwan, even Xinjiang. Under
these circumstances, we hope that each nationality will not listen to
the imperialists' provocation. For this reason, our country's name
is the People's Republic of China, and not federation.[97]

The borders and nature of the new state, in Zhou's formulation,
were based on an understanding of threats, not on ideological principle.
This was not a Marxist way of establishing a state (although the
notion that being "the people's" is a provision for autonomy was). It
was the old-fashioned geopolitical thinking of an empire. Enemies
menaced China from different directions; China would therefore have
to assert a strong claim to territory that lay in those directions. Like
the Qing empire and others before it, the PRC was claiming land so
as to secure itself.[98] The objectives had expanded dramatically since
the days of the Jiangxi soviet. With growing strength came a broader
definition of what it took to stay safe. Success fuels insecurity and
ambition.

To get all the territory still outside his control, Mao would employ a grand strategy similar to the one he had used throughout the
civil war: the judicious use of force, diplomatic outreach, and appropriate management of the political economy. The war was far from
finished; the battles that unfolded after October 1, 1949, were no
mere skirmishes, dying blows in a contest that was over. The Guangxi
campaign alone, according to Chinese sources, meant crushing some
172,900 enemy soldiers.[99] These were battles that marked the PLA's
coming of age, the completion of its growth from guerrilla force to a

modern military capable of waging war by air and sea, as well as by land. For simplicity's sake, the battles following the establishment of the PRC can be divided into three categories: battles for southern land, battles for the coast and islands, and battles for what would become China's far west.

Bai Chongxi's forces had been driven back to his Guangxi stronghold. In neighboring Guangdong, the Guomindang general Yu Hanmou was still fighting. Mao's sense of geography was useful here: he agreed that the plan was to sever links between the two provinces. This meant isolating Guangzhou, the main city of Guangdong, rather than attacking it immediately. Thus cut off, so the PRC hoped, the enemy soldiers stationed in Guangzhou would simply surrender, thereby allowing an easy liberation.[100] (Even if they did not surrender, the soldiers in Guangzhou would be less dangerous for being unable to join forces with Bai's troops in Guangxi.) Force was something to be used judiciously; the troops were resources that needed to be husbanded with care. There was no point in unleashing destruction if the same object could be accomplished without it. As it was, a demoralized Guomindang fled the city. The PLA had conquered Guangdong by November 4, 1949.[101]

Guangxi was more challenging. The south had been good to the Guomindang, and Bai, personally, had a base here, local support; he was operating in terrain he knew well. Nor was the risk confined to the man and place. Left undefeated, he could connect with fleeing fighters in Yunnan, Guizhou, and Sichuan to form a southwestern defense line that would keep the Guomindang intact in the region. That line could eventually get American support.[102] (The fear of American involvement was not utterly without foundation. The United States had been in contact with Bai and Li Zongren, although the intelligence community eventually concluded that there was little possibility of their providing effective resistance to the Communists, even with American support.)[103] There could be no tolerating an enemy like this at one's backdoor.

The first step in dealing with the problem was to seal off Bai's escape routes. PLA forces took Guiyang in Guizhou, thus making it difficult for Bai to flee west or even north. They also took the route that would have allowed Bai to move seaward and thence to Hainan.[104] These were no guerrilla sorties; it was overwhelming, purposeful force. By December 14, 1949, the PRC had taken Guangxi.[105] Farther west too, the PRC had been making progress. Mao had long held that Sichuan was the key point of the southwest.[106] By November 30, 1949, the Communists had taken Chongqing; by December, they had Chiang Kai-shek surrounded in Chengdu. The generalissimo fled to Taiwan by plane on December 10, 1949.[107] Chiang had directed his general Hu Zongnan to hold firm in Xichang, but there was only so much holding firm Hu could do. By the end of March 1950, Hu's resistance was at an end. The PLA had taken Xichang, and with some local help, conquered the small towns at the edge of the Tibetan plateau—places like Luding, Kangding.[108] What was remarkable about these encounters was the role reversal. It was Guomindang forces that sought to employ guerrilla warfare now—folly in the Sichuan-Xikang-Yunnan theater given how hard it would be to get minority support, how unfamiliar they were with the terrain—and the PLA that conducted regular warfare, using large, standing armies to surround and cut down a dwindling foe. The success of the CCP had led to expanded goals, a larger definition of the Chinese state; this, in turn, cemented the shift from the small, nimble guerrilla war doctrine to the massed forces that defeated Bai, Chiang, and Hu.

But standing armies were only one part of what it meant to be a modern fighting force. To truly compete militarily in the new world, the PRC would need an air force and a navy. That naval warfare was a different game became clear with the one great exception to the PLA's string of victories: defeat to the Nationalists at the island of Jinmen. The island lies off the coast of Fujian, and here, at the battlefield of Guningtou, the Nationalists vanquished the PLA's forces. The PLA was not well-informed on the enemy's strength. More importantly, it knew nothing—had not had the opportunity to learn anything—of the elements of naval warfare. How could its soldiers have known what it took to move troops across the sea, of the importance of currents and beachheads? Their great victories had come by land. Now suddenly they were scrambling to find sufficient sailors; most of the new recruits were from the recently liberated areas of Fuzhou and Quanzhou, familiar with neither the PLA's way of warfare nor the local sealanes. The three units involved lacked an integrated command.[109] The prudent thing to do would have been to wait, but enthusiasm and impatience impelled them to battle and defeat. Mao was incensed. He had warned them, so he grumbled, not to rush to Jinmen, to occupy Xiamen before turning their attention across the waters, to attack as a coordinated force, but they had paid no heed.[110] In grand strategy, the gap between theory and practice can sometimes yawn frustratingly wide.

There would be many consequences to Jinmen's fate, but one of the more significant was the military modernization it triggered. To be secure (and to take Taiwan), the new Chinese state would have to become adept at naval warfare. There were lessons to be learned from what had gone wrong at Jinmen, and these would be applied in the conquest of Hainan. Hainan, Mao noted approvingly, was different from Jinmen in two ways. One was the enemy's comparatively poor combat effectiveness. The other was the presence of Feng Baiju, who had led Communist resistance against both Japanese and

Nationalists on the island.[111] Feng's band of warriors had emerged in 1927, a group of peasants in uprising.[112] Having them there gave the Communists local allies, local knowledge. But there would be no rush to glory this time. War at sea, as Mao had cautioned, was entirely different from what the Communists had experienced. It required paying attention to the tides and the winds; it meant having to transport an entire army in one fell swoop. It meant fighting with what one had, without counting on reinforcements.[113] The PRC had a way of learning from its mistakes. The conquest of Hainan, completed by May 1, 1950, marked the arrival of a major power on the South China Sea. By May 1950, the PRC had also completed its conquest of the Zhoushan islands, giving it access to the East China Sea.[114] It had gone from being a land power to a land and sea one. That change would bring both danger and ambition.

In the northwest, the PRC fought its way to the edges of Soviet Central Asia. PLA forces took Lanzhou; from here they moved westward to Xining, pushing toward Xinjiang. Here Mao's troops would face a different challenge. It was not the Guomindang they had to combat here, so much as distance and local discontent. In Yili, Tacheng, and Altai, locals had taken up arms against the Guomindang, battling Chinese forces in an arc that went all the way south to Aksu.[115] Most of the resistance could be co-opted, but some could not, which meant that the PLA had to use force. Even where it did not, it needed to put soldiers, to keep an eye on things, to make sure that the Guomindang and the British and the Americans were not scheming to destabilize the western front. But Xinjiang was massive, impenetrable; the places that Chinese forces needed to reach were separated by miles of desert and mountains. To fully control it, Chinese forces needed to take to the skies, and the Soviets were immensely helpful here. The Soviets, far more familiar with the region than the Chinese were, educated the Chinese in the ways of the air and transported Chinese soldiers and equipment across Xinjiang's vastness.[116] Later, when the PLA was moving onto the Tibetan plateau, airpower would be used again. Here aviation was harder, partly because the Soviets were unable to offer the same degree of local knowledge and assistance, partly because Chinese soldiers found the flying conditions immensely difficult. Uncharted mountains loomed suddenly out of the mists, catching unprepared pilots in downdraft or blasts of icy wind. Nevertheless, planes were used to supply the troops in Batang and Ganzi, on the eastern rim of the Tibetan plateau; their use would contribute to the success of the Chamdo campaign and the eventual conquest of Tibet.[117] The new state was adding airpower to its military capacities. Mao followed Soviet advice and established two air force academies in China. He set his officials to securing and repairing airports in eastern China; these, he realized, would be important.[118] China's military revolution was moving along, trying to meet the tougher security demands that its growing state placed on it.

But military power alone would not be enough. Diplomacy, too, would be needed. Mao wanted to minimize resistance. Getting along with people, instead of fighting them, would make it easier to hold China together. While many of the civil war's last battles were unfolding, Mao was traveling to Moscow. He did not necessarily like Stalin at this point; there had been too many slights, too many disappointed hopes to forgive easily. But Stalin, driven by the exigencies of the Cold War, had released captured territory and weapons to the Communists in the early days of the civil war; the Soviets could yet be useful. So on December 16, 1949, Mao Zedong and Josef Stalin sat down for a talk.

Mao's first concern was the preservation of peace. There had been too much warfare; China needed breathing space in which to pull itself together. Stalin felt that peace was possible; it could last, he suggested, not just for five to ten years, but twenty to twenty-five, perhaps more.[119] The Sino-Soviet relationship would move to a more equitable footing. Port Arthur, in China's northeast, would be governed by the existing Sino-Soviet agreement until peace was made with Japan, after which the Soviets would withdraw their troops. Dalian would no longer be an international port, but, in Mao's phrase, "a base for Sino-Soviet economic collaboration." There would be credit agreements and trade agreements; Mao made clear that trade agreements with Manchuria and Xinjiang were to go through the central government, not the provincial ones.[120] There were no more little Chinas, only one big one. That China was sovereign again, and it had won back some of the trappings of sovereignty through patient talks with Stalin. The CCP diplomats had had a receptive interlocutor of course—it was Stalin, not Mao, who was eager to make trouble for the west at this point, Stalin who, when Mao mentioned that changing the agreement on Port Arthur violated the Yalta agreements, responded, "True, it does—and to hell with it!"[121] But they had had to talk to him; they had done so because they realized that diplomacy was necessary in order to survive. A treaty of friendship and alliance was signed on February 14, 1950.

The Soviets would be especially useful and especially problematic in Xinjiang. As Deng Liqun, posted to the Foreign Ministry's Xinjiang office, would note, Xinjiang's Uighurs and Kazakhs paid little attention to Chinese news, making propaganda work difficult; students were much more familiar with the Soviet Union than with China. This meant that the Soviets might have useful advice on what to do. An informal trade existed, which was of use to the local economy. But the boundary between the two countries was unclear, as was the citizenship status of the residents. There were minorities who had had

Chinese citizenship, but had acquired Soviet citizenship too. Some had been trying to escape the consequences of the Yili rebellion; others were former Guomindang soldiers or members who were trying to protect themselves now that the Guomindang had lost. Some were nomads, to whom national boundaries were irrelevant. The Soviets had suggested forming a boundary commission; this, if pursued, would need cadres.[122] It was a harbinger of problems to come; in Deng Liqun's plaintive tones, in his mention of Soviet "prestige" in the region, one could discern the disquiet of a man who felt that foreigners were too influential in the realm, a disquiet that he would later give full vent to in Deng Xiaoping's reign. But the Soviets were necessary. It was the perennial problem of a vulnerable state: having to tolerate serious inconvenience for overall gain. As Peng Dehuai had pointed out in December 1949, the region's economy was under severe strain. If things were to work out, Peng argued, China would need help from the Soviets. The Soviets could assist with transport, restore the normal flow of goods by engaging in formal trade, and develop energy resources in conjunction with the Chinese.[123] These were powerful considerations, inclining Mao to cooperate with the Soviets. Trade and finance were important and would help. But Deng Liqun's concerns were powerful too; they cut to the heart of what it meant to stand up and be sovereign, of whether or not China was master in its own territory. The Sino-Soviet relationship was one of mutual convenience and some ideological affinity. But it was rarely comfortable. Mao was working with Stalin principally because it was in his interests at the time.

It would be imprudent in China, then, to become entirely dependent on the Soviets. There were other countries China needed to get along with; when Stalin floated the idea of spreading rumors that the Chinese would cross the borders to Southeast Asia to "frighten the imperialists a bit," Mao demurred.[124] There was chaos enough in

China itself, and this was no time to go looking for unnecessary trouble, whatever Stalin might have to say about the matter. And trouble aside, those other countries could be helpful. The recognition of new China by India, Pakistan, and Britain, Mao realized, was conducive to entering Tibet.[125] Diplomatic successes could make military ventures safer. Economic diplomacy, too, was not to be confined to the Soviet Union. While still in Moscow, Mao was telegraphing his subordinates to let them know that although the Soviets were obviously of prime importance, they were to prepare for trade with Poland, Czechoslovakia, Germany, Japan, Britain, and America.[126] Imperialists and capitalists the latter three might be, but there was no harm in reaching out to them. The possibility of peaceful coexistence was being pursued well before either Mao or Nikita Khrushchev would give it a name. China needed all the friends and economic boosts it could get. Ideological preference would not constrain it. And it would not neglect smaller countries; they too had a role to play in China's success.

The line between diplomacy and state-building is blurry in an empire, and Mao knew that dealing with the appropriate power brokers was important. He had plumbed the depths of ethnic resentment on the Long March; he knew how important it was to assuage such feelings. Local collaborators, therefore, were sought everywhere. Disgruntled Tibetans and Uighurs, defecting Guomindang soldiers, and stranded Japanese—if all these people felt that they had a stake in the success of new China, new China might do well. True, the leaders of the short-lived Eastern Turkestan Republic, which Ahmed Jan Kasimi had helped found in Yili, were on their way to Beijing for negotiations when they died, in one of those mysterious plane crashes that appeared to afflict those for whom Beijing had mixed feelings.[127] But Burhan Shahidi, the Uighur governor of the region, was a sound ally, and Mao wanted the locals on his side. The key to resolving the

Xinjiang problem, the chairman lectured Peng Dehuai, was intimate cooperation between the party and the Uighurs. Burhan's current provincial government had ten Han and fifteen Uighur or ethnic minority members; this ratio was best left unchanged for now.[128] Xinjiang's forces had suffered under the Guomindang and done sterling work on their own revolution; there was room to work with them, as an elder brother might with a younger, to establish people's democracy in Xinjiang.[129] Of course, their existence as separate armies was not to be countenanced; as Mao had already directed, they were to be renamed the PLA.[130] But they were to be integrated into the existing military system, not alienated from the state.

Similar policies were followed in Tibet. The CCP worked hard to get the laity, including the Dalai Lama, on its side. The agreement between Tibet and China reached in May 1951 allowed for substantial autonomy; China would retain control over military and foreign affairs, but religion and culture were to be left untouched.[131] Religion was to be respected in Xinjiang too; although communists were atheists, the argument went, they were also supposed to be respectful of the religious freedom of those within the country.[132] Mao was in no rush to foist societal reform on China's minorities; the impetus for reform would have to come from them.[133] And it would be important to get cadres from the minority ranks; this would make governance easier and give people a reason to feel part of the new state.[134] Mongol or Tibetan, Kazakh or Han—all were equal in new China. It never worked out in practice; changing social attitudes is harder by far than cutting a trade deal or seizing territory. But the ideal was held out, and for practical reasons as much as moral ones: it was conducive to getting and retaining territory that the state needed.

The focus on economic diplomacy showed how vested the PRC was in stabilizing the economy. At this time, its economic policy remained practical. Mao was in no rush to divide land belonging to rich peasants at this point, despite murmurs from more ideological comrades; the defeat of Chiang, he explained on April 6, 1950, made it unnecessary. It was one thing to use land reform to mobilize the masses in time of war; it was another to conduct it in peacetime. The CCP had gone too far with land reform earlier, he recalled, isolating itself. It was better to go slow than to go fast; there would be less chaos, less damage to production. There might even be ways of compensating for unequal land distribution—some sort of taxation and subsidy policy perhaps.[135] Not that he was ruling out an assault on rich peasants for all time to come; they could be useful enemies tomorrow. But he was arguing—and arguing forcefully—against embarking on a campaign against them for the moment. To truly exploit peacetime, one needed to be prudent.

The troops were to be part of economic consolidation. When not fighting, they were to be put to work, boosting agricultural and industrial production. China's economy, after all, had suffered under the long wars, and the troops could make useful contributions, to fisheries, to irrigation work, to the things without which no country can function, never mind be prosperous. They could, Mao declared, be a "production army."[136] Not that they would be allowed to go into business for themselves. Private enterprise in the hands of men with guns could be dangerous; it could carve out a space where they would profit at the expense of the people, becoming unjust, a source of resentment. There would have to be order to the PLA's dealings; they would have to fit within the planning of the local government.[137] There was good reason for such caution. China was emerging from the warlord era, a time when troops had struck fear into the hearts of the people. To succeed, the PRC would have to exercise control over its soldiers, lest they lapse into old ways. Mao Zedong had a sound understanding of the dark side of human nature. He just believed in his capacity to succeed despite it—and by using it.

By mid-1950, then, Mao Zedong had put great China together again. The scale of the goal had adjusted to circumstance over time: it had gone from soviet to liberated area to all of the PRC as we know it today. It was possible that territorial ambitions had been set back in 1920, when he first mused on the need to build up from smaller pieces. But this seems unlikely. At various points, he seemed satisfied with the territory he had. It is possible that had Chiang compromised during the civil war and taken the opportunity to focus on economic rebuilding, China would have come together in a joint government that provided for some regional autonomy, with warlord Mao and warlord Chiang masters of their own spheres of influence. Mao was a man capable of resigning himself to constraints. Had Chiang been too strong, he might have been content with the territory he had. But each success allowed him to redefine his goals (it also, of course, deepened Chiang's anger and thus the insecurity of Mao's regime). Grand strategic objectives can alter over time. Getting the state was always a goal; what that state would be—its borders, its peoples—was open to adjustment.

The forces crafting that state had changed too. The guerrilla band had become a modern military, evolving with the changing goals the state set. The key organizing principle of Mao's diplomacy was simple: he would deal with whomever he could to get the state he wanted. Diplomacy required carefully probing for schisms in the enemy's loose-built coalition of warlords and seeking closer relations with other players than they had with one another. Patient talks with Nationalist leaders as well as minority groups had saved the CCP expenses in money and blood. The prospect for China's relations with both the United States and the USSR was brighter, in 1949, perhaps, than the prospects for relations between those two superpowers. Sustaining this grand endeavor meant departures from communist orthodoxy in diplomacy and in economic planning. Ideology could take the CCP only so far. Mao would use whatever tools he had to in order to get that grand China he had talked about so long ago.

Just how far Mao could have extended his China remains unknown. He had seen the check at Guningtou as merely temporary and was eager for a renewed assault on Jinmen. In a note to Stalin asking for the various goods the air force would need, he mentioned 1951 as the time when work on taking Taiwan would be launched.[138] Had he got the three to five years of peace he and Stalin had been counting on, the nascent navy might well have taken Taiwan, or at least its offshore islands. The United States might even have come around and recognized the PRC; there seemed to be little eagerness to help Chiang in Washington in those dying months of 1949. The relationship between Beijing and Washington might not have been cordial, but with the United States no longer moored to a rival regime, the main obstacle to a modus vivendi would have been gone. This would have left the PRC almost perfectly poised, leaning toward the Soviet Union but not estranged completely from the other Cold War superpower. Thus happily situated, it could have focused on nothing more than economic recovery.

That, at least, was the plan. But those three to five years of peace it had assumed were about to be shattered—by Korea.

2

MAO ZEDONG and the BALANCE of POWER

M AO ZEDONG had dragged great China to its feet again, but there were still forces determined to tear it back down. It was so fragile, this colossus he had created, so easily broken apart. In Mao's world, there were foreigners, imperialists who would carve China up again if given the chance, and they might find support within. He could not be too vigilant in working to keep the state whole. Throughout his long reign and all its vicissitudes—from the glorious rhetoric of anti-imperialism to the rapprochement with the United States, from the abyss of the Great Leap Forward to the beginnings of reform and opening—this remained Mao's guiding star. There was one great aberration from 1966 to 1969, but barring that, he pursued a grand strategy aimed at securing the state that had been so hard to win.

To be safe, China needed a balance of power in the world surrounding it: support or at least neutrality from the superpowers, friends where it could get them, and, ideally, buffer zones between its far-flung outposts and the rest of the world. Diplomacy would be geared toward this balance of power. Beijing would give voice to specific disagreements, but those disagreements did not have to destroy the relationship, provided it was friendly enough to serve core Chinese interests. There would be a quest for economic growth too. People revolt if not well fed, and besides, a sound economy is the foundation of military power. Military power would be necessary, for in a hostile world, it was the only real guarantee of safety. And China would find itself fighting on several fronts—beginning with Korea.

The Strategic Environment

Mao Zedong had not committed to participating in a Korean war—such participation, he had made clear to the Soviets in 1949, would depend on "coordinating with Moscow"[1]—but he was keeping a careful eye both on the divided Korean peninsula and on American policy toward Asia as a whole. He was willing to do all in his power to help his North Korean comrades: they had fought side by side with the Chinese against the Guomindang in Manchuria. Conditions permitting, Mao was in favor of a North Korean attack on the South in the beginning of 1950. China would provide training, food, supplies, and even troops to help their brothers in arms.[2]

But the Americans showed no signs of leaving. The North Koreans, after much dreaming and much pleading with Stalin for support, finally got to attack South Korea on June 25, 1950. It seemed perfectly safe: Dean Acheson, the American secretary of state, had given a speech in which he sketched out a perimeter of defense America needed to protect in Asia, a perimeter that left South Korea out. But then, on June 27, once the North Koreans had moved to unify their country, President Harry Truman leaped to the defense of South Korea—a place that Washington had thought it had no interest in protecting. And Truman did more: he sent the U.S. Seventh Fleet to neutralize the Taiwan Strait. Truman, Mao grumbled, on June 28, 1950, had said the Americans would not interfere in Taiwan; here was proof that that statement was false. There were signs, too, that they wanted to interfere "in the internal politics of Korea, the Philippines, and Vietnam." None of this meant that a military clash between the PRC and the United States was certain, but it would be foolish in Mao, unrecognized and communist, to be unprepared. China would have to reduce its land troops and focus on building up its navy and air force.[3] The Americans were utterly unpredictable; all that lay between them and China's northeast were stretches of North Korean volcanoes and lakes. It was best to be prepared. The PRC therefore mobilized troops to defend its northeastern border; Stalin would provide air cover.[4] Ethnic Koreans had been serving in China's northern armies; these started trickling back across the frontier, to fight in their war.[5] The PRC began to contemplate quiet measures to provide support to the North Koreans: ammunition, vehicles.[6] It was discreet movement in shadows, thus far, very different from what the Korean War would become. Not that Mao was unprepared for a worst-case scenario; if the Americans won, he believed, success might spur them to threaten the PRC. The Koreans, therefore, had to be helped, using armed forces in the form of volunteers. But it would have to be at the right moment.[7] That moment was not now. The Americans were unpredictable, but it was worth trying to reason with them. Which was why Beijing's diplomats had such extensive talks with K. M. Panikkar.

Panikkar, then ambassador to the PRC, was the quintessential Indian diplomat of his time. He was interested in world peace, urging everyone to work for it; he saw his role as educating east about west and west about east. He was, in sum, a willing channel between the estranged Chinese and Americans, and Beijing used him as such. It was, Zhou Enlai explained to Panikkar, the American Seventh Fleet, along with its aircraft, that had occupied Taiwan; it was American planes that were bombing China's people and destroying its property along the Yalu River. To eliminate Chinese opposition to the Americans, Zhou said, "the Americans should change their policy of invasion." "The American government," he continued, "has forgotten its own history. Did not Washington oppose the British invasion? . . . Did not Lincoln fight a war to liberate the slaves? Was this not a civil war? Now they don't let others be Lincoln."[8] There was a reason Zhou was invoking those hallowed presidents of American yore; he was hoping that Panikkar would communicate what he had said to the Americans and that respect for America's past would induce an understanding of China's present. China too wanted to throw off the yoke of the Guomindang, unite its country. Surely, the Americans, with their own heritage of liberation, could understand as much. This was no ideological tirade, no implacable denunciation of American imperialism. It was a listing of specific grievances—the bombing and Taiwan—with the corollary that if those grievances were addressed, China was more than willing to improve relations with the United States. Washington would find this incredibly hard to understand, but to Beijing, these issues were fundamental to national security. The PRC would protect that security by military means if it must, but it would try too to reach an understanding with its foe.

Such understanding could be achieved only if the other side understood what China would and would not stand for. On October 3, 1950, Zhou warned Panikkar that if American forces crossed the thirty-eighth parallel to broaden the war, China would have to be concerned with the matter. It was not clear at this point, Zhou said, if such troops as had crossed the line were South Korean or American. But any American troops that had done so would have to withdraw. "It might be too late for any peaceful formula," sighed Panikkar. "That," said Zhou, "is the Americans' problem."[9] There were some things that the PRC would not compromise on, and it was important that the Americans know what those were.

The curious thing was that there were at least some Chinese leaders who felt differently. Mao Zedong, torn, as he often was, between strategic prudence and revolutionary fervor, was dreaming of war regardless of who crossed the thirty-eighth parallel. The day before Zhou's talk with Panikkar, he had composed a cable to Stalin saying he was ready to send volunteers to Korea in force; to let all of Korea fall to the Americans would sap Korea's revolutionary strength and harm the entire East. One would have to be prepared, of course, for the American air force to bomb Chinese industrial bases and for its navy to ravage the coast. In the first phase, China would send forth the divisions in southern Manchuria to suitable places in North Korea. This phase would be a defensive war, fighting the enemy north of the thirty-eighth parallel. Once Soviet equipment had arrived, the Chinese would join their Korean comrades in a counteroffensive, eliminating the American troops. It was a grand plan—and Mao left the cable unsent.[10] War, as envisioned in this telegram, was to be launched before the Americans crossed the thirty-eighth parallel. But he still had his doubts, both about the wisdom of the enterprise and about whether he could get the consent of his comrades. He did, however, do one more thing to ease the road to war. He asked Zhou Enlai to send a plane to Xian so that Peng Dehuai could return to Beijing.[11]

On October 4, the day after Zhou's talk with Panikkar, Mao chaired an enlarged meeting of the politburo to discuss Korea. And here too, the thirty-eighth parallel was far from being the key point of the discussion. Korea might be geostrategically significant, but there were Chinese leaders who were deeply opposed to going to war for it, hostile forces north of the thirty-eighth parallel or not. China had been fighting for so long. There were still Guomindang agents scattered across the land who had to be dealt with; the economy was a wreck; the PLA was ill equipped, and China did not have control of the skies. It was, in sum, both too hard and unnecessary to go to war with the Americans. Such were the arguments of many among the gathering. Mao listened. He admitted that they had a point, and yet, he said, when another country was faced with a crisis, "to sit watching from the sidelines is hard on the heart." "Hard on the heart"—this was not grand strategy; it was emotion: the tug of loyalty to the North Koreans who had helped the CCP in the days when the revolution was young, the desire to prove to Stalin, to the world, to his own people that China was no coward, that it would stand and fight no matter how powerful the forces ranged against it. He closed the meeting by saying that they could continue the discussion the next day.[12]

Peng Dehuai had sat silent through the meeting. He had fought in the warlord armies, defended the soviet, held the Nationalists at bay when they attacked Yanan, and worked in the far west. When Peng spoke, people listened, and Mao, not as inured to outside views as he would later become, wanted to hear from him. It would help, of course, if Peng thought as Mao did, if he could help the chairman overcome some of the resistance to intervention. And it was Peng who made the case for war the next day, not as some gallant adventure, but as a matter of survival. "If American troops are stationed on the banks of the Yalu River and on Taiwan," Peng argued, "if they want to launch a war of invasion, they can find a pretext any time."[13] There was a geopolitical dimension to the marshal's thinking: where most would think of Taiwan and Korea in isolation, he saw a single arc that menaced China, the capacity of a power that held both to threaten the Chinese state by land and sea. How could one possibly allow an enemy to come sweeping down through the northeast—that same northeast that the CCP had held on to during the civil war, thereby making its eventual victory possible—while simultaneously sending ships to bombard and seize that long coast? Geography made China vulnerable, and Peng was acutely alive to that vulnerability. In retrospect, it would seem obvious, axiomatic even, a truth buried deep in China's history of invasion. At the time, it took Peng to disinter it and give it voice, Peng's words to carry the day.

So the troops on the northeastern frontier became the Chinese People's Volunteers Army, which would be deployed to Korea.[14] Whatever Mao's feelings about this adventure, he knew that this was a fight China could not win alone. He had already sent a message to Stalin saying that he was glad that the Soviets saw it as a "joint struggle" and that air cover would be crucial; without it, American attacks against Chinese industry could stir discontent, jeopardizing PRC security.[15] Zhou Enlai and Lin Biao were sent to Moscow to ask Stalin what kind of support he could provide if the Chinese entered Korea.[16] The Soviets had proved so unreliable in the civil war; how could one be sure that they would actually help with this war that they were urging the Chinese to undertake? There were grounds for wariness. The Soviets were willing, Zhou reported on October 12, 1950, to provide planes, bombs, and tanks, but the Soviet air force needed time to prepare; it would be two to two and a half months before it could be deployed to help the Chinese volunteers.[17] Air cover had been crucial to Chinese war plans. But even though air cover was not immediately forthcoming, the politburo decided on October 13 that the plan to send the troops to Korea should remain unchanged—for by now the Americans had crossed the thirty-eighth parallel. Nevertheless, the

PRC would be cautious. For the first phase of the fighting at least, Chinese activity was to be confined to the north, helping the North Koreans expand their bases (there was a memory here, of how China had been unified; one strengthened little bits of turf to gain the larger whole) and rousing the Korean masses to organize people's armies. Only six months down the line, once fully trained and equipped with Soviet artillery and tanks, were they to take offensive action against the Americans.[18]

The decisions about the Korean War highlight several key points about China's grand strategic thinking. First, there was a national security calculus behind the war. China's safety, as much as Korea's, was at stake.[19] The PRC needed a buffer zone to the northeast—ideally, an ideologically sympathetic one—and it was willing to protect it. There might have been some confusion over the precise nature of that zone—whether it was endangered only once the thirty-eighth parallel had been crossed or whether the mere threat to North Korea was sufficient to merit action—but to the official mind of the PRC, it was of existential importance. Second, in addressing that threat, the PRC used both diplomacy and military power. One could try to reach out to the Americans—all the more comfortably because if negotiations failed, military preparations were underway and troops would be there to defend the northeastern frontier. The Indians were far from being the perfect diplomatic channel, but given Stalin's eagerness for war and the American reluctance to recognize the PRC, it was probably the best Beijing could do. Third, ambition could not outstrip perceived capabilities. Until such time as they had the necessary air cover and support, the Chinese were not supposed to take the offensive. Ideally, of course, they would drive the Americans off the Korean peninsula altogether, but given the limited means at their disposal, this might prove unrealistic. They would settle, therefore, for second best in the short term: not allowing North Korea to fall. On this, there would be no quarter; there was a sense of what China could and could not live with. The corollary, of course, was that if China's estimate of its strength changed, objectives might too. Thus, once Chinese forces had managed to beat the Americans back past the thirty-eighth parallel, the goals expanded. The evidence of the battlefield suggested that the Chinese could take the entire peninsula. By December, Mao was convinced that the Americans could not organize a long-term defense of South Korea. The reason the Americans and British were calling for China's troops to halt north of the thirty-eighth parallel, he wrote to Peng Dehuai and Gao Gang (political commissar of the Northeast military region), was because it would allow their troops to make war again. Given respite, they would regroup and renew the attack. "Therefore," the chairman argued, "we must cross the thirty-eighth parallel. To just stop north of the thirty-eighth parallel would be a great political disadvantage."[20] Where the Americans had made war once, they might do so again. It was best to drive them away from Korea entirely. The starting point for peace negotiations became a withdrawal of all foreign troops from Korea, the withdrawal of American forces from Taiwan, and the PRC's assumption of China's seat at the United Nations.[21] It troubled the Indians, who had worked hard to rally countries around the idea of a ceasefire that would be followed by negotiations. An exasperated Panikkar kept trying to get Chinese diplomat, Zhang Hanfu, to see how this was the best that could be done, only for Zhang to reiterate Zhou's statement of Chinese terms.[22] Beijing's demands on Korea, Taiwan, and the United Nations were the first steps to a peaceful settlement, not goals to achieve in talks after a ceasefire had been reached. Strength made ambition possible.

One could, of course, overestimate capabilities, and with the benefit of hindsight, this was exactly what Mao did. And yet, at the time, the decision made sense. The Americans could not be trusted; several long decades of fighting had taught Mao that it was a mistake to trust anyone. Besides, China's forces were winning; they had beaten the Americans in battle. They were far from the only participants in the Korean War to let victory on the battlefield tempt them to further ambition. And as ambitions go, Mao's was a sensible one. If the PRC rid the peninsula of the Americans now, it would not have to worry about fighting them later. So the war raged on—and when its fortunes turned, with American forces beating the Chinese back across the thirty-eighth parallel, Mao was prepared to negotiate. While negotiations with the U.S. forces were under way, in the summer of 1951, he would ask Peng to make sure that the talks went smoothly; it would be bad form if chaos were to break out. Not that this meant trusting the enemy; troops were to be ready for an enemy assault during the talks.[23] But there was the idea that force could be dialed up or down. (Practice did not always match theory. Armed Chinese soldiers would wander into the negotiation site in August.)[24] These negotiations would be fraught—American insistence that Chinese POWs be returned only voluntarily was a particularly heated issue—but the Chinese were willing to compromise in a way they had not been in the winter of 1950. Goals were flexible. If one could come away with national security more or less intact, one might compromise on an earlier, grander vision of how assured that security could be. The eventual armistice left the line between the two Koreas exactly where it had been before the war began.

But perhaps the most crucial point about the Korean War, from Beijing's perspective, was that it was not occurring in isolation—a fact that forced some hard choices on the PRC.[25] There was another war unfolding along the coast, a contest with the Guomindang for the tiny islands that lay in unquiet seas. The Nationalists had not abandoned their dream of retaking the mainland, and although Mao would postpone the invasion of Jinmen, he would not reduce the three armies stationed in Fujian.[26] One had to remain alert on the coast, at points like Xiamen, where the enemy might attack. The air force was busy with the Korean theater and unable to help on the coast. All defense here, Mao directed, would have to be undertaken by the east coast alone, without hope of outside aid.[27] He was still wary of naval warfare: his preferred method for fighting these prospective coastal invaders was to let them enter deep inland and then annihilate them.[28] But on the countless islands ringing the coast from which an enemy could harass PRC vessels, this was not possible. Dachen Island remained untaken and would have to be left thus until the Korean War was over.[29] Nanri Island was lost to the Nationalists in 1952, when they sent in some nine thousand soldiers. The defense of the islands had to be sharpened, grumbled Mao (even as he made clear that those charged with that defense could not expect reinforcement); defeats like that at Nanri had to be avoided. The enemy on Taiwan and Jinmen, he was convinced, was coordinating its threats to the Fujian coast with that of the American war in Korea.[30] Once again, there was that sense of two regions being connected. But how many fronts could China fight on? It was all very well for Mao to ask that Nanri-like defeats be avoided, but he himself had, just earlier that year, told his naval officers how he hoped that the foreign exchange used for ships could be redirected to the air force; the Korean War made it necessary. He consoled them by saying that by using domestic funds to purchase materials for shipbuilding they could move faster, spend less money, and that they would develop China's own shipbuilding capacity. (Notable too was Mao's tone here: it was, unusually, cajoling rather than imperious; he was trying, perhaps, to minimize the risk of a revolt by armed sailors along the coast at a time when China could ill afford it.)[31] But the consolation was an attempt to mask an unpleasant truth: fighting multiple wars, the PRC would simply have to compromise and make do as best it could. "The Pacific now," as Mao would become fond of saying, "is still not pacific."[32] So China would have to fight a war along that troubled sea, all the while still locked in combat with the Americans in Korea. The experience would spur the quest to develop a proper navy.[33] But that would take time, and the war was happening now.

Southward too, in Guangdong and Guangxi, the Nationalist threat remained intact. As early as November 1950, PRC officials were pondering an enemy attack on Guangdong. The troops still mopping up GMD forces in Guangxi would, it was decided, have to spare some soldiers to reinforce Guangdong's defenses.[34] To the west, there was Tibet: that massive plateau, where intelligence reported GMD and American interference, still to be brought under control of the new state.[35] This was a very different type of warfare from the island battles. It was waged in high mountains, where the altitude alone made soldiers ill, and transport was the key problem. The conquest of Tibet would require a cavalry from Qinghai to accompany the PLA with food.[36] The decision to take Tibet had been made well before the Korean War broke out, but the battle of Chamdo—the most serious military engagement of the campaign—began on October 6, 1950, and dragged on till October 24.[37] Tibet could have been far harder to take than it proved. Barring the battle at Chamdo, there was little organized, cohesive resistance on the plateau. Its communities were united by little but religion, and the laity was amenable to a negotiated peace with the PRC: the famous seventeen-point agreement that would, in essence, allow for religious autonomy in exchange for Chinese control of defense and foreign affairs.[38] But even with Tibet won, the troops could not leave and head for another of the many theaters where they were needed. They had to be sent farther into the plateau's wilds, building roads, providing food, guarding the new territory and the approaches to it, doing what was necessary to protect the Panchen Lama—once in exile in Qinghai, now a friend of the new regime's to be escorted back home.[39] For Mao too had his client warlords and beneficiaries, men who had to be protected that they may protect his empire. All the while, the American special forces menaced the northeastern borderlands with a view to establishing bases for guerrilla war; they were doing the same in Xinjiang, in the Xinjiang-Mongolia borderlands, and along the eastern edges of the Tibetan plateau.[40] Korea was just part of a larger problem for the China Mao had put together. There was war on every front. And meanwhile there was still the basic work of governance to do. There were people to feed, far-flung regions to consolidate, an economy to heal, weapons to be modernized, trade links to be forged. As it fended off danger across its vast perimeter, Mao's China would have to find a way of completing those tasks too.

Finding a Balance of Power

The first step was to forge friendships abroad. It was easier to be safe if outside neutrality or even support was assured. The key relationship would be the one with the Soviet Union, but there were also the smaller countries surrounding China: the perpetually feuding India and Pakistan, a divided, turbulent Indochina, Japan, defeated and locked in the American embrace. These were countries vulnerable to American pressure; they could become part of a great web designed to constrain and ultimately garrote the Chinese state. It would be best if China could persuade them to keep the Americans distant. It would be prudent too to reach beyond the immediate neighborhood; friendship farther afield, in places like Africa, could be useful. As to the

Americans themselves, there was no harm in trying to reason with them. Mao's China was not bent on quarrelling with the United States; it asked only that its integrity not be compromised. The basic precepts of Chinese diplomacy were deceptively straightforward. Beijing would try to maintain as close a relationship with every country as it could get; this would keep the balance of power in order. There could be no caving on core interests, but there was no reason to sever relations altogether either. If you could agree on the need to keep the conversation going, Beijing was, for the most part, more than willing to reciprocate. Specific disagreements, no matter how vehement, did not have to devolve into complete alienation.

The Soviet Union was to China a model and a benefactor.[41] This did not mean the relationship was easy. There is, in all client-patron relationships, a mixture of dependence and resentment at having to be dependent, and this one was no different. Stalin had channeled massive amounts of money into the PRC, although he had insisted that they pay for the arms used in the Korean War. He had come through with that much-needed air support, albeit far later than Mao had hoped.[42] He could provide the means for China to build its own aircraft, and experts to work in China's factories.[43] It was to Stalin that the PRC turned when it wanted help keeping American aircraft out of China's northeast, or with boosting naval growth stunted by a focus on the needs of the Korean War.[44] But there was something galling about such dependence. Peng and Zhou had had to listen respectfully while Stalin grumbled about Chinese pilots. "What are they doing?" Stalin asked. "Are they afraid?" When Peng explained that they could not yet fly in formation, Stalin lectured that they needed to spend more time in the air, railed against their "anarchical disdain for orders and medals."[45] This while China's young men, who had upped and gone to Korea from far away, were fighting the Americans, dying in a foreign land, while Stalin only sent aircraft to battle and loftily directed Mao on how to fight. Soviet support being crucial to national security, China would stomach the insult. But it rankled.

With Nikita Khrushchev, Stalin's successor, relations proceeded, at first, on a more even keel. Khrushchev was bumptious, overenergetic, but he was also eager to prove that he was better than Stalin, a gentler ruler of the communist world. He continued to provide the aid, agricultural implements, and advisors that China needed, and for this he deserved thanks.[46] He needed to be educated on how impossible the idea of "two Chinas" was and how important the offshore islands of Jinmen and Mazu were to the PRC—but he could be worked with.[47] With Stalin dead, Moscow was interested in peace initiatives from Korea to Indochina.[48] It was an interest that dovetailed well with Beijing's; it fit with that old idea of reaching a modus vivendi where possible. Soviet foreign minister Vyacheslav Molotov suggested that the Geneva Conference could be an opportunity for exploring how to ease "tensions in Asia" beyond Korea and Indochina. For Beijing, fearful of the American presence in the region, this was welcome counsel, although as things turned out, it did not bear fruit.[49] Zhou, after discussions with the Soviets at Geneva, wanted to adjust Chinese negotiation policy "to persistently take the initiative to pursue peace."[50] This would help China in its overall goal of achieving a stable neighborhood. That Soviet and Chinese diplomats would come to such a conclusion together showed how much things had changed since Stalin's day.

Of course, the alliance had its problems. In his infamous secret speech of February 25, 1956, Khrushchev criticized Stalin; the speech leaked and the criticism spread across the globe. Mao was incensed. It was not that there was any great love lost between him and Stalin; rather, it was that Khrushchev had, without warning, attacked one of communism's holy saints, a saint who had been used to sanctify communism in China. If Stalin could be criticized today, Mao could be criticized tomorrow. The speech threatened the new order he had worked so hard to create. He could attempt to limit the damage. Hence the attempts to point out that to err was human, that "Khrushchev will similarly make mistakes... and we too will make mistakes," that Stalin's mistakes were severe, but he "also had great achievements."[51] But that damage had been done was obvious. Khrushchev had opened a dangerous door, and there was no knowing where it could lead.

The first effects were felt in Eastern Europe. There had been a simmering discontent in Poland after collectivization; Khrushchev's speech and the Polish leadership's interest in genuine reform only fueled discontent, as hope for a more liberal regime took hold. News spread to Hungary, where protests also broke out. The Soviets would eventually threaten (and in Hungary launch) military intervention if the communist parties in each country could not quell the disturbances.

The PRC's response was twofold. The first, of course, was that it was Khrushchev's fault, for criticizing Stalin: this was what had paved the way for attacks on the communist system.[52] But second, and more importantly, Mao sought to shift the basis on which communist countries related to the Soviet Union from one of subservience to equality. The mere act of counseling Moscow on how to handle the crisis was a signal; China might be economically reliant on the Soviet Union, but there was no reason to avoid criticizing and guiding the Soviets when they went astray. Liu Shaoqi was dispatched to convey a message from Mao to Moscow: that the five principles of peaceful coexistence could be realized among socialist countries. The principles were simple: mutual respect for territorial integrity and sovereignty, mutual noninterference, mutual equality and benefit, nonaggression, and peaceful coexistence. Moscow would, after some heated discussion, adopt the Chinese idea of issuing a statement incorporating those five principles into dealings with socialist countries.[53]

This was a radically different model of dealing with fellow socialists than the communist bloc had known. In Stalin's time, Moscow's orders were meant to be obeyed; defiance, everyone understood, came with costs. Tito might defy Stalin, but Tito was Tito, mad, bad, "our son of a bitch," as Dean Acheson had proudly called him; most importantly, he was not dependent on Moscow for arms. Mao himself had been willing to go against the Soviet leader's wishes when necessary, declining, for example, to make too much trouble for the British in Hong Kong, but he had understood that if he wanted the aid and weaponry the Soviets could provide, some show of deference would be necessary. The five principles, by contrast, which first emerged in 1954 as part of the Sino-Indian agreement on trade in Tibet, were designed to be anti-imperial. In their harping on mutual equality, in their call for noninterference (regardless of ideological differences), they defined a relationship that was the complete opposite of that which Stalin had enjoyed with his satellites. And it was this equal, noninterfering relationship that Mao had cajoled Khrushchev into accepting, at least nominally, with Eastern Europe. Mao approved of the statement that held that one Warsaw Pact country's forces could be stationed in another with due agreement; as he told the Polish ambassador to China, it implied that in the absence of agreement, the host country could send those forces back home. Stalin had done many great things, but he was, it could not be denied, a big country chauvinist.[54] It was a theme Mao returned to in Moscow when visiting in 1957 to commemorate the October Revolution. He was happy that contradictions between socialist countries could be discussed; in Stalin's time, nobody would have dared speak of this. "'Fraternal parties'—this was a sweet-sounding phrase," he mused, "[but] in reality it [the relationship between the Soviets and other socialist countries] was unequal. I now feel a sort of equal atmosphere."[55] In that insistence on equality, one can hear the undertones of China's feelings toward the Soviet Union. It was an intimate relationship—and like so many intimate relationships, it came with the need to assert independence every now and then.

Asia was, given China's location, the most important theater in the balance of power. Ideally, it would be free of American influence, and this was why Zhou invested so much energy in the Geneva Conference of 1954. The whole, often unrecognized, point of Zhou's efforts at Geneva had been to bring an end to the first Indochina war and, in doing so, to eliminate any excuse for a foreign military presence in China's near abroad. Geneva was about so much more than getting recognition as a diplomatic player; it was China's attempt to secure its backdoor.[56] This did require prodding old friends, who, left to their own devices, might undermine that goal of an Asia free of America. Ho Chi Minh, the communist leader of North Vietnam, was an old comrade; he had supported the CCP since the 1920s, visited Mao's base in Yanan, and given succor to Communist troops during the Chinese Civil War.[57] But now Mao had to urge him to engage in peace talks, arguing that it would give the Communists the moral high ground and would deepen the contradictions between the French and the Americans.[58] At those peace talks, Zhou, realizing that the boundaries in Indochina were far more complex than the Chinese had at first thought, that Laos and Cambodia were real countries, pressed the Vietnamese to make concessions so that the conference could reach some sort of agreement about Indochina. (Notably, he would mention working with the Soviets on this.)[59] Vietnamese forces were to withdraw from Cambodia and Laos.[60] Ho Chi Minh did not like this, but he, like Mao, understood patronage and its impositions. He had received money and weapons from China throughout the first Indochina war, and he could accept, if reluctantly, a temporary setback in the name of survival.[61] Mao, for his part, was seeing a bigger picture: Ho might be a brother in arms, but his struggle was just one piece on a larger chessboard. The PRC needed hostile forces to keep their distance from Chinese borders, and it could use the moral standing that a successful peace agreement would confer. Compromises on Ho's part would help to achieve those goals. The Vietnamese, therefore, would be pressed to make them.

This set the pattern for Chinese policy toward Indochina. North Vietnam was by far the most important partner, and it would remain so. Trade flourished between China and its southern neighbor, and as of 1959, the Vietnamese struggle was held to have achieved much.[62] Between 1950 and February 1959, the PRC sent 5,443 advisors to Vietnam, to help with economic restoration, development, and the establishment of a socialist base.[63] (Later, when the Chinese and Soviets started squabbling, the success of the relationship with Vietnam would be measured in part by how strongly the Vietnamese supported China's position.) But the need to develop solid relationships with the other Indochinese countries was taken seriously too. Cambodian visitors would become frequent guests in Beijing; Laos would be repeatedly reassured that China meant it no harm. China needed a balance of power in Indochina that maintained a suitable buffer zone. Sacrificing Indochina's overall security to the relationship with Vietnam would be foolish, and China was not going to do it.

Indian prime minister Jawaharlal Nehru could be also enlisted in the quest for an Asia free of foreign military bases. Nehru, proud, patrician anti-imperialist, was a man of vision if not wisdom, and he and Zhou found common ground. If the five principles of the agreement they had just reached could be applied to Southeast Asia and

Asia as a whole, the region would become a zone of peace, free of military bases, outside interference, and occupation. Nehru suggested that Burma and Indonesia might be interested in signing such agreements; a prudent first step might be for China to issue a statement of respect for the five principles.[64] Zhou wanted a demilitarized zone on Chinese borders; Nehru had one eye on Pakistan and another on world peace. The five principles might give them both what they wanted. There were, they held, forces in Asia that favored a freedom from Western presence; it was their task to help these forces along. Later, the matter would be formalized at Bandung, Indonesia, when one of the ten principles promulgated there would demand abstention from collective defense arrangements that served the interests of the great powers.[65] In an Asia where no one hosted foreign bases, China could be safe.

Zhou's visit to India marked the beginning of a beautiful, if short-lived, friendship. Nehru made his own visit to Beijing that year, and through the mid-fifties, India would interpret American behavior to Beijing and try to get Beijing to be reasonable. Indian talks with Portugal over Goa's status were followed closely; if Portugal returned Goa, it might make the return of Macao to China easier. India could sympathize with how unjustly the Americans had acted in Taiwan, interfering in China's internal affairs.[66] And sympathy meant standing up for China at the United Nations. They had their differences, of course—there was a disputed border, which Zhou promised to "research"—but they had much in common too. Desire for world peace aside, both were large countries, with large populations, and both had been invaded by empires in the past. Chinese diplomacy, in keeping with the five principles, would focus on what the two countries had in common. "We don't need a great wall between us," said a visiting Indian vice president. "We have the Himalayas." Mao could not accept this. "We need neither a great wall nor a short wall," the chairman said. "What we have between us is friendship."[67] Friendship there might have been, but it was friendship with a purpose: economically and politically, India could be of use to an isolated PRC. And in showcasing how friendly the PRC could be, it could ease concerns about the PRC among other neighboring countries.

It was one thing to revel in a vision of Asia free of military pacts; it was another to convince countries like Pakistan and Thailand to share in that vision. Pakistan and India still disputed Kashmir, and Pakistan, as Nehru reminded Zhou, was a recipient of American aid; East Pakistan was also of key strategic importance if a war broke out in Indochina again.[68] Pakistan's willingness to participate in the Southeast Asia Treaty Organization (SEATO), a military pact headed by the United States, did little to alleviate those concerns. Meeting with a Pakistani women's delegation to China in the fall of 1954, Zhou brought the matter up. It was an odd forum; decades later, Sultan Khan, the Pakistani diplomat charged with arranging the delegation's travel, would complain, that to the women it was a "social junket. . . . First of all they were crazy in Hong Kong, shopping . . . they started buying like crazy. And the shopkeeper thought they were all my wives. . . . He said, you are a very good husband; you are spending money so lavishly."[69] But the women were connected to the scions of Pakistani officialdom, especially Begum Shah Nawaz, who was heading the delegation. So Zhou was earnest in his representations; he talked of his hopes for unity between China, Pakistan, and India, and of how "nothing good comes of foreign interference." Which was why, he went on, China could not understand why Pakistan had joined SEATO. SEATO was directed against China: how could the Pakistanis, toward whom China had been friendly, be part of it?[70]

The explanation was simple. Small country that it was, the begum explained, Pakistan felt that the growing intimacy between China and India might leave it friendless on the Kashmir issue; it was only natural, therefore, to seek outside protection. The pact, she reassured Zhou, would never become a vehicle for attacking China. Pakistan had signed it only to protect itself.[71] Beijing's problem was that what Pakistan did for defense had the capacity to threaten China. It was all very well for the begum to vow no harm was intended; the pact allowed American military power to function on China's borders. Trusting to goodwill in such a situation was folly. The United States, Zhou warned, would drag Pakistan into the war, whatever the claims about defensiveness; Pakistan would have no choice but to participate. He suggested a joint statement supporting the five principles instead. This the Pakistanis eluded.[72] It would have meant, as the begum was shrewd enough to realize, getting rid of American support: an anticommunist pact like SEATO was a pact that would be aggressive to a communist neighbor. Thus emerged the pattern for Sino-Pakistani relations throughout the fifties. The Pakistanis would complain about the Indians and Kashmir; Zhou would maintain that Asian participation in an American-sponsored military pact was unacceptable to China; he would cajole and threaten; the Pakistanis would make their excuses about needing security against the Indians; and so the recriminations began again. Not that Zhou would alienate them altogether. It did not do to sever relations; differences could be managed, if not overcome, and one never knew where a friend might come in handy in the future. As long as the Chinese maintained a relationship with Pakistan, they might eventually be able to talk it out of the American embrace. Chinese diplomats emphasized that the relationship between the two countries was a friendly one (which was what made it all the more hurtful that

Pakistan would bind itself to an American military pact). But for the relationship to remain friendly, it would be best if Pakistan knew where the Chinese stood.

There were attempts to reach out to Thailand too. The Thais were also part of SEATO, but there was no reason not to attempt to find common ground with them. "We just received a report that the SEATO countries are conducting exercises in the South China Sea," Zhou told two visiting Thai naval officers, "but at the same time you were visiting our naval forces in Shanghai." This was proof of friendship: "You participate in SEATO, but we do not see you as we do the Americans; we see you as friends." Of course, Zhou added, participating in SEATO was not in Thailand's interests; he hoped officials there would come to recognize this in due time.[73] But they would recognize it more quickly if China were friendly rather than hostile. "The Chinese people need peace, need to develop their own country," Mao told a Thai delegation in 1956. "We need many friends, the help of many foreign friends. It does not matter which country these friends are from, including Americans and Japanese."[74] China was willing, Zhou said, to sign an agreement on the status of overseas Chinese in Thailand as it had in Indonesia, mandating single citizenship so as to quell fears of insurgent activity. It was willing to reach agreements with Thailand based on the five principles, just as it had with India and Burma. Nothing prevented countries like Thailand, the Philippines, or Pakistan from reaping the benefits of such agreements—except, perhaps, that the Americans would be unhappy. Meanwhile, there was always trade.[75] The tone was carefully crafted, designed to play on all the feelings of insecurity and resentment that come with accepting military protection, holding out promises of commerce and goodwill. The Thais might be in the American orbit, but there was no saying they had to stay there forever. If reassured that China was not a threat, they might, at the very least, moderate their support of Washington's goals.

This attempt to woo American allies stretched beyond SEATO. Japan might not have formal diplomatic relations with the PRC, but there was a multitude of channels through which Beijing could reach Tokyo. Tatsunosuke Takasaki had spent time in China supervising the development of heavy industry in Manchuria; he had been interned for two years after the war in the Soviet Union, the PRC, and the Republic of China (ROC). The experience had somehow left him without much ill will toward China. He had represented the Japanese at Bandung, where the anti-imperial of the world had pledged unity; he was invited back to China in 1959 and arrived in 1960. He and Zhou discussed normalization; although both wanted it, the continuation of the U.S.-Japan alliance made it difficult. Zhou maintained that the security treaty, "which the Japanese people courageously fought against," would sooner or later drag Japan into a war of aggression against the PRC. (Zhou also said that aggressive though Japan had been during World War II, its aggression had led to the fall of the Qing and the Nationalists, leaving China more grateful than anything; it was a telling remark, for it showed just where the CCP's priorities had lain at the time.) It was not that China objected to a close U.S.-Japan relationship; it objected, rather, to the aggression symbolized by the security alliance, as well as Japan's role in perpetuating "two Chinas."

The peace treaty, Takasaki responded, was rather "like a scab which has formed over a deep wound. Once the UN begins to function effectively or once Japan's strength is fully restored, this treaty will automatically vanish. If this scab is taken off, bleeding will resume and infection will set in." The Japanese had, he maintained, no position on Taiwan. His key interest was trade: it was important, he argued, not merely as an economic proposition but as a prelude to normalizing relations. It was an exchange in which the differences were stated without softening, but not allowed to destroy the relationship. Japanese public opinion could be swayed; hence Zhou's emphasis on the opposition of the Japanese people to the alliance. One needed, therefore, to reassure Japan; China, the premier said, had no intention of liberating Taiwan at present and would certainly not seek to impose its ideology elsewhere. Such diplomacy could be effective. Takasaki reported that he had "come to respect" Mao's policy and "firm leadership."[76] Ideological flexibility and a courteous tone went a long way.

Further American allies could be reached too. The British, practical people for all their faults, were open to recognizing the PRC, as eventually were the French. The PRC let it be known that anti-imperialist though it was, it recognized that the British had a stake in the region. The British, as Zhou pointed out to the Indians, had legitimate interests in Asia, investments that they needed to attend to in Singapore and Malaya, not to mention India, Pakistan, and Ceylon. He had, he continued, told people from both Singapore and Malaya that remaining within the Commonwealth was a good thing—it would protect them from being sucked into the American orbit. Relations between China and Britain should be better; there were mutual interests.[77] For a card-carrying communist and anti-imperialist, the notion that capitalist investments by an aging empire were something that should be welcomed was quite a leap. Pragmatism, at base, was what drove grand strategy. It was wiser to court and win American partners, instead of just letting relations with them deteriorate because they were friendly to the Americans.

There was one alliance that was intolerable, and that was the one between Chiang's ROC, securely ensconced on Taiwan, and the United

States. Chiang's was not China, not a state; for it to be allied with the Americans was unacceptable. And the alliance began, ironically, with a PRC attempt to prevent its emergence. Mao continued to believe that force could be used in a controlled fashion to signal intent, and it was this signaling that drove the Americans to a treaty with Chiang. The intent itself was benign. The story of the first Taiwan Strait crisis is usually confined to the shelling of Jinmen and Mazu, which began in the fall of 1954.[78] But the shelling was just the crest of a wave of low-intensity warfare that had been waged more or less constantly since the Korean War broke out. The Americans remained just off the coast, cruisers hovering near the Zhoushan islands, planes flying overhead. At high sea, Mao directed, his soldiers were to make sure that they not attack foreign forces.[79] He wanted the Americans to realize that China did not want to fight them. One of the key problems with the idea of an American security treaty with the GMD, for Mao, was that it would cause intense long-term harm to "our relations with America." He was aware too that the struggle to liberate Taiwan would promote domestic unity.[80] But he was not planning on seizing Taiwan immediately. He knew, with painful certainty, that China did not have the naval capabilities to launch an attack on the "Chiang Kai-shek who is in the water." China would have to concentrate on building up its air force and navy; only then could it recover the lost archipelago.[81] The shelling, carefully calibrated, was meant to convince the Americans not to sign the defense pact. Its effect was quite the opposite. President Dwight Eisenhower had had no intention of signing the treaty, but found himself forced to do so to maintain credibility as a defender of the ROC and, by extension, of the noncommunist world.[82]

It had been a massive miscalculation on Mao's part, but there was a logical goal to it: to show the Americans that the PRC meant business on Taiwan, without taking away all hope of finding a modus vivendi. This caution informed the decision to postpone the liberation of Yijiangshan Islands till 1955. With the American Seventh Fleet conducting major exercises in the neighborhood, 1954 was simply not the time. The Yijiangshan Islands were won in 1955. And when the Nationalists were defeated at Dachen, Mao said that they were to be allowed to withdraw safely.[83] That conquest caused American activity to intensify—and not just in the coastal theater. On May 10, 1955, news arrived of an American plane crossing into China's airspace out in the northeast; the directive went out that if enemy planes invaded PRC airspace, local forces were to strike.[84] But even here, there was no suggestion that combat be initiated. The idea was to keep China's defenses strong, not to provoke a war that could prove lethal. And the PRC had altered, ever so slightly, the balance of power along the coast: little islands, ringing PRC fishermen and vessels, were now in CCP hands. One builds up to larger territories by cobbling smaller bits together. If one could do so without alienating a superpower completely, so much the better.

For there remained the hope that some sort of rapprochement could be achieved. The PRC was willing, despite all the recriminations and betrayals of the past few years, to try to reach a modus vivendi with the United States; it would signal that willingness through back channels and try to communicate it directly. Thus the emphasis in talking to the Thais that China needed friends from all over, including the United States. Having denounced anticommunist military pacts to the Pakistanis yet again. Zhou would suddenly ask if Pakistan could reshape the pacts to be peaceful and broaden them to all Asian-African countries, all the way to the Pacific.[85] It was a bizarre suggestion—akin, really, to Soviet foreign minister Vyacheslav Molotov's proposal that the Soviets join NATO—but the idea was that China might be able to join SEATO. In a pact based on equal relations that included China instead of attacking it, there would be no need for Beijing and Washington to be antagonists. The Pakistanis did not feel up to the task, so the idea died. But Beijing would continue to reach out to Washington. Field marshal Bernard Law Montgomery, visiting Beijing and working past Mao's initial dislike, was given a subtle hint. Mao, having taken a break from discussions for a swim in the river, sighed that he would like to swim in the Mississippi.[86] It was too subtle, perhaps, but it was meant to signal Beijing's willingness to reach out to America. Given changes in American policy, PRC policy could change too.

The problem was that there was only so far American policy would change. Direct talks between the two countries, which took place in Warsaw, came to nothing because the gap on Taiwan was too great. Taiwan being a part of China, the PRC saw simply an invading power that had interfered in a domestic Chinese matter. If the Americans withdrew their forces from Taiwan and the offshore islands, there was no reason China and America could not get along. In September 1958, Chinese negotiators would produce a draft of what peace terms could look like. Beijing and Washington would agree to resolve their differences peacefully, without recourse to arms. China would insist it was sovereign over Taiwan, Penghu, and the coastal islands (notably, there was no insistence that the United States accept or respond to that claim). The United States would undertake "to withdraw all its armed forces from Taiwan, the Penghu Islands, and the Taiwan Straits." China would seek immediate recovery of Jinmen, Mazu, and any islands that could be used to menace the mainland; if the Guomindang officers there withdrew, the PLA would not pursue them. And China would agree, for an undefined period of time, to try to liberate Taiwan and the Penghu Islands peacefully instead of taking them by force.[87]

Given that Mao would later insist on the right to use force, this was quite a remarkable offer. It was a gesture of goodwill, meant to reassure the Americans, give them a little face. It was certainly not giving Taiwan away—but it expressed a willingness to wait.

It was spurned. The American ambassador explained that there was no way the United States could abandon an allied state—it was that word "state" that would have stung; Chiang Kai-shek did not represent any Chinese state—although if the mainland would cease its attacks and reach an agreement not to use force, the United States could reduce the number of troops stationed in the region. To China, this was a blurring of the distinction between international tensions (those between the PRC and the United States) and the domestic matter of liberating Taiwan; the two were utterly distinct. Taiwan had had no right to sign a treaty; it represented no government and was part of China. And as such, American concerns about Taiwan need not stand in the way of a Sino-American rapprochement. "Between China and America," Wang Bingnan, the Chinese diplomat conducting the talks, would say, "there is no war."[88] There being no war between the two countries, tension could be reduced if only the Americans would stop interfering in China's internal affairs. But to Washington, the ROC had global recognition and was not occupied by America.[89] There was nothing wrong with a defense pact between the United States and the ROC: the PRC—"your side," as the American ambassador was careful to put it—had a security pact with the Soviet Union. That equation of the two pacts spoke volumes; to the Chinese official mind, it meant that Washington was creating two Chinas, rendering rapprochement impossible. Chiang making a pact with the Americans was no different from Wang Jingwei making one with the Japanese in World War II. But to the Americans, Chiang headed an allied government, which had fought the Japanese in World War II.

The alliance was a defensive one, between America and a sovereign state.[90] A Chinese listener, with that bitterly torn China so recent, was bound to hear in this an attempt to create two Chinas; those furious if unsung battles along the coast made it hard to perceive the U.S.-ROC alliance as anything other than provocative. But these were considerations lost on Washington. There was no geostrategic reason, at this time, that the United States could not have made the deal National Security Advisor Henry Kissinger later would, which reversed the American position on Taiwan completely. It chose not to do so. The PRC wanted a rapprochement, but it knew its red lines; there was to be no negotiating away core interests. Diplomacy was meant to serve the larger goal of keeping great China safe. It was not meant to be an instrument of that state's continued dismemberment.

In a world like this, China needed the means to protect itself. Because it was now a state, not just a movement, it had to complement people's war with a modern military. In addition to a proper navy and air force, this meant nuclear weapons. On January 15, 1955, a small conference was convened to discuss developing the bomb. It was now known that there were uranium deposits in China; from here on, Mao said encouragingly, one would certainly find more. Trained scientists were available to supervise the project. The Soviets were being helpful right now, but with or without the Soviets, this was something that China would do well.[91] The bomb would be seen as a defensive weapon. It was one more move toward a modern military, one that stood in the same ranks as that of the United States or the Soviet Union. But such a military was not an alternative to diplomacy; it was meant to back it up. Military and diplomatic power enhance one another's effectiveness.

China's plan, then, was to limit threats to national security by maintaining as many friendly relationships as possible. But the relationships were meant to keep China secure. If they ceased to serve that purpose, China would rethink them—although it might try to walk back to a friendlier time.

The Balance Shifts

In the late fifties and early sixties, a series of overlapping conflicts would cause Beijing to reorient its approach to the balance of power. Not that that earlier approach would be abandoned; realpolitik and a willingness to compromise remained as important as ever. But there would be a need to change strategic partners—beginning with the Soviet Union.

The term "split" does not quite do justice to the Sino-Soviet relationship.[92] Beijing followed each bout of conflict, each insult traded, with an attempt to find common ground with Moscow. This had always been the case; whether suppressing annoyance at Stalin's arrogance or at Khrushchev's de-Stalinization, the PRC had found a way of getting along with the Soviets. It approached the differences of the late fifties and sixties in the same spirit. The chief cause of those differences was the idea that Moscow was willing to barter away PRC national security. As Beijing saw it, there was mounting evidence to support that idea. Moscow did not give the PRC the weaponry it wanted. It refused to stand up for the PRC in the Taiwan Strait crisis of 1958; it castigated Beijing for its role in the Sino-Indian dispute; it withdrew its workers from Chinese factories in 1960 and refused to stanch the flow of nomads from Xinjiang to Soviet Central Asia in 1962. Soviet leaders spoke mockingly of Mao (Mao, not given to empathy, perhaps found it difficult to understand that his own behavior toward Soviet officials had been less than polite); under Leonid Brezhnev, the Soviet Union would fight China along that unresolved border in 1969. Such was Soviet policy. But policy could be changed. Beijing continued, throughout all this, to believe that it could reach an understanding with Moscow, provided it was made clear what the PRC would and would not compromise on. For the relationship to work, it would have to serve Beijing's interests, not sacrifice them.

On June 7, 1958, Peng Dehuai reported a Soviet proposal to build a joint wireless system. Mao suggested that the Soviets provide the expertise, the Chinese the investment; the final product could be used by both sides, governed by a formal agreement.[93] He had, given the troubles on his coastline, asked the Soviets for nuclear submarines, and Pavel Yudin, the Soviet ambassador to China, offered a suggestion. Since the common enemy was America, why not establish a joint submarine fleet on the Chinese coast, which Vietnam could participate in too? Mao Zedong said he would do his research. It sounded to him a little like the peasant cooperatives that had been established across China—and the meaning of the term cooperative would therefore have to be contemplated.[94]

"After you left yesterday," he told Yudin the next day, "I could not sleep and I did not eat." It was proof, the chairman said, of the Soviet refusal to trust the Chinese, of the Russian inability to stand the Chinese people—the same attitude that lay behind their refusal to share nuclear weapons. It was as though Stalin had returned, ranted Mao; he would not have done this even in Stalin's time. Khrushchev could come discuss it with Mao himself. Mao had already been to Moscow.[95]

The tone was a massive overreaction. But beneath the hurt national pride, there was an understandable precept: Mao did not want to be dependent on the Soviet Union for prosecuting his grand strategy. Dependence carried constraints. Having the submarines and using them as he saw fit was one thing; having them on his territory with the Soviets directing if, when, and how they were to be used was another. So Khrushchev—this was the trip where he was infamously humiliated in Mao's swimming pool—had to fly to Beijing. There must have been some misunderstanding, clucked Khrushchev; the Soviets had their own submarines so how could they possibly have proposed a joint project? Mao had the transcript ready to show Khrushchev. There had been another proposal too for a radar station in China's south, which Soviet naval units in the Pacific might use. "Well, isn't that a cooperative then?" said Mao. Khrushchev offered investment. "We don't want you to pay," shouted Mao. "If we want to do it, we will do it ourselves. If you pay, we will not build it." "Fine," said Khrushchev.[96]

This done, however, Mao moved to find common ground. There was room for agreement on Soviet experts—over 90 percent of whom, the chairman admitted, were good.[97] Over the succeeding days, he spoke with Khrushchev of the march of the imperial powers, of the danger posed by America's aggressive military pacts. The Soviets had sought to limit nuclear testing, but how would that position be affected by other countries going ahead with such testing? We are independent, replied Khrushchev. Mao had a final cunning hint to throw out: were not American bases the world over in the communists' interest? It split American strength. (An attempt, perhaps, to see how Khrushchev would react.) Khrushchev did not commit to an opinion.[98] But his opinion did not matter. What mattered was that they parted with the relationship intact. There would still be Soviet advisors, Soviet aid, and the perception of a common enemy. Mao had no intention of giving the Soviets more levers with which to control China's military adventures. Because he had the prickly pride of a wounded nationalist, the memory of having to plead with Stalin, the bitterness of fighting a war in Korea without Soviet comrades fighting by him, and because there was an uncontrollable part of him that delighted in being cruel, he had expressed himself more intemperately than necessary. But he had highlighted the differences in the relationship without letting the relationship be destroyed; he had stayed close enough to the Soviet Union without becoming too close. It was the same policy that marked relations with Pakistan or Japan, and it was the same policy that would subsequently mark relations with the United States. The tone differed, not the substance.

Then the shells flew across the Taiwan Strait again and widened the gulf between Moscow and Beijing. On August 18, 1958, Mao directed Peng to prepare to shell Jinmen. Here too, the sense of a connection between theaters informed planning. Since they would be attacking the Nationalists and, indirectly, the Americans, it was best not to conduct exercises in Guangdong as these would disturb the British. One had to avoid engaging too many foes at once. Pursuit was not to extend beyond Jinmen and Mazu.[99] Mao, once again, wanted to avoid bombing Americans, although he was informed that this was impractical.[100] The shelling started on August 23, 1958.[101] It was just shelling: the PRC would not attempt to land on the island or send ships and planes to the open seas. It would not attack the American forces, although if the Americans invaded the PRC's sovereign seas and airspace, it would respond.[102] The use of force was limited, because the objectives, though numerous, were limited too. China wanted to show the Soviets that dependence did not mean subservience; there was the idea that the American involvement in Lebanon made this a good time to shell the islands, that shelling might get the Americans to resume some form of dialogue. There was the idea, too, that it would promote internal unity, particularly needed now that the Great Leap Forward was to be launched.[103] And China was tired of being hemmed in: Xiamen, as Mao would observe, had basically been turned into a dead port.[104] All this justified some form of military adventure. It did not justify a full-scale war.

The perception of American intent, however, shifted. Even as he grumbled about the death of Xiamen, Mao was wracked by the suspicion that the Americans would seek a compromise: withdrawing from Jinmen and Mazu, and focus on maintaining an independent Taiwan. This was unacceptable.[105] The question now became how to keep the Americans in Jinmen and Mazu, for to gain the offshore islands was to lose Taiwan. Mao declared—was he perhaps trying to save face?—that Jinmen and Mazu could be left in Chiang's control; they created an easy pressure point, where one could bomb or not, as required.[106] The military commission explained that since the Americans were conspiring to get Chiang to release Jinmen and Mazu in order to create two Chinas, it made sense to lighten the shelling for a while.[107] So the shelling came to a temporary halt on October 5, 1958.

The episode reflected an ability to keep an eye on overarching goals, despite self-created chaos. The PRC had started this round of shelling, but once it became clear that the shelling might cost it sovereignty over Taiwan, it stopped. There was a larger cause: sovereignty, and it was not to be jeopardized by the desire to send a signal to the Soviets, the Americans, or Chiang. The PRC could regulate the use of force, engage Chiang without engaging the Americans. Part of what gave Mao confidence was the hunch that it was unlikely, although not impossible, that the Americans would go to war over Jinmen or Mazu; he retained, oddly, a faith in American rationality.[108] For all the risk taken, he was behaving logically himself. By suggesting that they might abandon the offshore islands and hold on to Taiwan, America had put two Chinese goals in competition: having a coastline free of the American presence and maintaining China's claims to sovereignty over Taiwan.

Having decided that Taiwan was and always would be part of China, a little tension on the coastline was just something that had to be tolerated.

To the Soviets, China's use of force in the strait was a terrible idea. Moscow had, after all, committed to the defense of the PRC—but defending it against the United States for a tussle over Jinmen and Mazu was pointless. Zhou would tell the Soviets that China was doing all this to avoid the creation of "two Chinas." If chaos broke out, the Chinese would handle it themselves; they would not drag the Soviets down with them.[109] (A hint, here, that one would not care for allies so lily-livered in a real battle.) But the episode showed the limits of the alliance—and the wisdom of rejecting a jointly controlled naval force. Were the Chinese to rely on Soviet officers for coastal defense, taking the initiative on things like a shelling campaign might become much harder. Alliances can be constraining.

Khrushchev returned to Beijing in 1959, fresh from America. He told Mao that he had spoken with the Americans about the China problem (how that must have rankled; this bumpkin discussing his China with a country that did not recognize it). The Americans, Khrushchev thought, were unwilling to go to war for Taiwan. But to Mao, it seemed as if Khrushchev, who should have been on China's side in all this, was pleading for Washington, taking the same position the Americans had at Warsaw and asking China to refrain from the use of force. "The Taiwan question," Mao reminded him, "is an internal matter; China must definitely liberate Taiwan. There are two ways of liberation: one is to use peace; the other is to use war." Since Zhou had declared China willing to negotiate, Mao continued, China had done so for four years. "In the negotiations, we just raised one point with them, which was that they should withdraw their troops from Taiwan; if they withdraw their troops there would be no problem. . . ." In a Taiwan without American troops protecting it, the CCP could talk to Chiang openly, Mao held—and this was what the Americans were afraid of. Khrushchev pushed: Eisenhower, he said, understood. "Yes, America understands," said Mao. "They want to talk, but they want to talk by their line. They have hinted that they can persuade Chiang Kai-shek to evacuate Jinmen and Mazu, and want us to guarantee that we won't use force towards Taiwan, though we can make demands regarding it. This way their domination of Taiwan can become legal. . . ." Khrushchev was upset. The Communists had not said that they would not go to war over Taiwan, which allowed the Americans to portray the Communists as warmongers to the world. This, as Mao pointed out, was no different from the American line on the matter. To renounce the right to use force in Taiwan would be to recognize "two Chinas." Khrushchev was frustrated. "We talk tactical problems," he said, "and you come back at us in full strength with a question of principle." "This too is tactical," said Zhou.[110]

Khrushchev shifted ground. He did not understand why the Chinese had fallen out with the Indians; he could not understand how they had let the Dalai Lama escape. (Unrest across the Tibetan plateau had wound up with the Dalai Lama fleeing China and repudiating the seventeen-point agreement; the Soviets would not be above hinting that Beijing's Tibet policy was flawed.) The Indians opened fire first, the Chinese countered; as to the Dalai Lama, the border was a few hundred kilometers long, and he could have slipped out anywhere. Here too there was no agreement.[111]

But despite all the hectoring and the heat, they ended on an amicable note. "Our basic line is the same," Mao said, "we only have divisions over specific problems." This, he continued, should not affect unity. It was how Beijing saw relationships: people can agree to disagree about specifics, as long as there is a reservoir of goodwill underneath. Khrushchev agreed (although perhaps he did not quite know what he was agreeing to. It was difficult to separate specific disagreements from the larger relationship—Kissinger could do it, as could Mao—but it was a tricky balance, demanding fortitude, a willingness to stomach harsh tones, an impatient drive to larger concerns. Khrushchev could nod agreement to a kind sentiment; whether or not he grasped the philosophy of relationships behind it was less clear). "When we were in difficulty," he said, "China supported us. We have supported you too. . . . If you have an opinion about us, bring it up; if we have any opinion about you, we will speak frankly." "Good, good," said Mao, and the meeting closed.[112]

It had not been pleasant. But it had not shattered the relationship either. China preserved an independence of action. It had reason to do so. What Khrushchev took as a responsible effort to make world peace, the Chinese saw as his trying to pressure them to accept the American line. The Soviets, it appeared, were vulnerable to American temptation. Eisenhower was no fool; he wanted, the Chinese suspected, to improve relations with the Soviets, the better to oppose the PRC.[113] Mao had been reading John Foster Dulles. Dulles aimed to change the Soviet world (which Mao interpreted as not just the Soviet Union, but the entire socialist world) from within.[114] One could see in Khrushchev's diplomacy not just the fumbling of an inexperienced leader, but the success of a malevolent American grand strategy designed to bring the communist world and great China down.

Seeing Khrushchev in this light, the PRC needed to make a decision: to abandon the Soviets altogether or attempt to win them back. Abandonment was difficult; it would upset the balance of power, and China still depended on the Soviets for food. It could yet, of course, come to that. But even now there might be room to reason with

Moscow firmly while leaving the prospect of friendly relations open. Properly dealt with, Moscow might not succumb to American temptation. The basic interests of the two countries were such, China suspected, that they should incline to unity. He believed in the rationality of other countries, in their ability to perceive their interests clearly and act accordingly.

Chinese diplomacy, therefore, sought a balance between letting a revisionist Moscow advance the imperialist line and alienating the Soviets altogether. In 1960, Moscow withdrew its advisors from Chinese factories. This was a serious blow to the Chinese economy. The response was measured: the withdrawal, the Chinese Foreign Ministry wrote to the Soviet embassy, violated the Sino-Soviet pact and the norms governing friendly relations between socialist countries. The Chinese hoped that the Soviets would reconsider; it would be greatly regretted if they did not.[115] But it was one more bit of evidence of Soviet ill intent, one more move that undermined Chinese strength.

Then the nomads began to move across the Sino-Soviet frontier (the border was still undemarcated). To its far west, the Chinese state blended into the fourth world: a zone where the ways of life were defined by statelessness. Nomads and traders of mixed blood roamed back and forth across uncharted borders, shifting easily between languages. The distinction between China and the Soviet Union was, at best, a semantic one to them; theirs were paths of movement rather than states; they neither knew nor cared where the boundary might lie. In the spring of 1962, as the hunger caused by the Great Leap Forward ravaged China, Kazakh nomads poured into Soviet Central Asia.

The PRC could have simply wished them good riddance and been done with the matter. But this would be to admit that the state had somehow failed them. The exodus could harm Xinjiang's productivity, which depended on the presence of people. And there were rumors that Soviet officials had been behind the movement, promising the nomads a better life on their side of the border. One did not know what kind of malcontents were taking advantage of the offer, what evil they might plot against the PRC from the safety of the Soviet Union. It was one thing to have such movements when one trusted the country on the other side of the border; to have them happen at a time when the Soviets seemed to be falling further and further into revisionism was another matter altogether. The relationship was no longer secure enough to stand such movements. So a note was sent to the Soviets demanding that they take appropriate measures to deal with the matter. By the Chinese count, some twenty thousand nomads had already made the crossing. Not only had the Soviets not prevented these people from crossing the border, they had also provided them with assistance on the other side: transport, money, food, the promise that in three months they could go wherever they wanted. If allowed to continue, the PRC warned, this situation could harm Sino-Soviet relations.[116]

The Soviet ambassador could not believe that the Soviets would encourage the migrants. Of course, if they had crossed over bringing nothing, one might make some arrangements, but encouraging them to leave China was something the Soviets would simply not do. Zhang Hanfu, the Chinese diplomat who was taking the matter up with the ambassador, was unyielding. The Chinese knew what they knew; they hoped the Soviets would take all appropriate steps to deal with the matter.[117] On April 25, a memo from the Soviets explained that the Soviet border officials tried to tell the border crossers to return to their own territory, but these measures had been fruitless; the people kept coming. Many of them, the border officials reported, had been coming empty-handed, in desperate need of help.[118] This was precisely the sort of response that would have stung the Chinese to the core; it implied that they had failed to provide their people with what was needed. On April 29, Zhang made clear to the Soviet ambassador that China expected the Soviets to return the people who had crossed the border illegally. It was, Zhang argued, their responsibility.[119]

This, the Soviets responded, could not be done. It was one thing to send people back when there were just one or two of them; this was unprecedented, a flood. How could the Soviets round up tens of thousands of people and send them back? They had welcomed the Chinese to take appropriate measures themselves, whether preventing border crossings or sending a team to try to persuade the border crossers to return, which the Chinese refused to do. Among the border crossers, there were children and people who were ill. The two countries were fraternal, the Soviet diplomat continued; everyone involved was a communist, including the border crossers, who were mass educated under a communist system. Why neglect to work for them?[120] The Chinese maintained that the Soviets could have stopped it if they wanted; in the past, when nomads approached the border, Soviet guards would ward them off, taking up weapons if necessary. This the Soviets denied: there was no way they would raise their weapons against the working classes of a friendly country. In any event, they argued, the trouble began in China. These people had prepared to cross the border in China, had traversed Chinese territory to reach said border, and had had to go through the Chinese side of the border before they could reach the Soviet side.[121] The problem, this argument hinted, had originated in the PRC.

They had reached an impasse: the Chinese insisting that the Soviets do their duty and return the border crossers, the Soviets insisting that they had done nothing more than help the needy and could do no more than let the Chinese come work with the refugees. Only once that impasse had been reached did the Chinese decide to shut the border trade down. The border markets in Xinjiang were to be removed; trade would henceforth go through the center. Such Soviet citizens as chose to remain in Xinjiang were to obey Chinese law; if they created chaos, they would be deported or punished in other ways.[122] The cosmopolitanism of the borderlands, the easy back and forth that had once defined life there, was being erased.

This was a significant step: it terminated the commerce that had sustained Xinjiang for so long and had thereby facilitated Chinese rule of the region. Beijing was calculating that the risk of Soviet-sponsored subversion in Xinjiang outweighed the economic benefits that the PRC had, back in 1950, been so keen to get. Then, the PRC had needed the Soviets. It still needed them in 1962, but need was now tempered by the fear that the Soviets were working to undermine Chinese security. A balance had to be found between economic prudence and protecting the integrity of the state. That security threat did not diminish with time. Xinjiang's officials were on the frontlines of a war as yet undeclared: they wrote of increased patrols and heightened troop presence, suggesting preparations for war. They feared that the Soviet revisionists were plotting to provoke a border incident; the Soviets might even do so in conjunction with the Indians and Chiang Kai-shek.[123] In retrospect, the fears might seem overblown, and yet, if you were stationed in the Yili valley at the time, the gathering Soviet troops and the muttering Kazakh herdsmen could only inspire fear. The PRC could no longer count on Soviet protection. The main threat to its national security might come from the Soviets themselves.

Even now, dealing with the threat did not mean alienating the Soviets altogether. When the Soviets suggested talks between the two countries to find a way out of the present situation, Mao approved the sentiment—although he reminded the Soviet ambassador of how

Khrushchev, despite calling for an end to public criticism, had criticized the Chinese party in Germany. If Khrushchev wanted to stop at Beijing while traveling in Cambodia, he was more than welcome to. If that was inconvenient, Mao would send a delegation to Moscow. He himself would not go, because officials in Moscow cursed him. But he would explore a way forward.[124] The problem was that it was hard to read Khrushchev; he changed his mind and tone so easily, and Beijing struggled to devise an answer to these changes. It would boycott his call for a conference of all communist parties, answering all letters from him in the sparest of terms.[125] He was basically a revisionist, bent on following the American path. Although it was unlikely that he would attack China, it was best to be prepared. But revisionists had to be dealt with too. The PRC would continue to talk with the Soviets in the hope of getting a reasonable settlement on the disputed border between them.[126] When Khrushchev fell in 1964, there was a mix of caution and hope. The Soviets were revisionists, but they now had some misgivings about the Americans, which meant they would need Chinese friendship.[127] Mao was still thinking in terms of balance of power politics, and it was this thinking that led him to send a representative to the commemoration of the October Revolution.

In Moscow, Rodion Malinovsky, the Soviet defense minister, told Zhou that the Soviets did not want "any Mao, any Khrushchev impeding our relations."[128] This could have destroyed Zhou's career; Mao might well have construed it as Malinovsky urging Zhou to topple Mao. The Soviets had attacked the Chinese leader directly in the presence of a Chinese premier. But instead of escalating the matter to the furthest conceivable point, the PRC lodged a complaint and demanded an apology, which the Soviets duly made.[129] There was an interest, even now, in containing the damage to the Sino-Soviet relationship—much as there had been in containing the damage to the Sino-American one. China needed friends, and the Soviets were useful friends to have. One wanted to retain the option of rapprochement, no matter how difficult it might seem.

These nuances of Chinese policy were little comfort to those who relied on both Soviet and Chinese support.[130] For Ho Chi Minh and North Korea's Kim Il Sung, the tensions between Moscow and Beijing raised serious questions. Would they have to take sides? Would the fallout affect the aid given to them? How far would their two sparring patrons go? For Beijing, the problems raised were just as difficult. The PRC had key geostrategic interests in Indochina and on the Korean peninsula; to lose influence there would tilt the balance of power even further from its favor. Kim and Ho would have to be persuaded that in the matter of Sino-Soviet relations, China was not to blame.

In Kim's case, this was fairly straightforward at first. Zhou welcomed Kim to discuss the continuation of aid—China was providing motors, technical support, food exports—and a border agreement.[131] In 1963, the North Koreans would inform Beijing that China was completely right and the Soviet Union utterly wrong; proof lay in the weakness of Soviet support for North Korea at the UN and Moscow's desire to establish diplomatic relations with South Korea.[132] Pyongyang's prospects too were shaped by Soviet policy toward the West; if the Soviets were not serious about fighting imperialism, they might not be serious about defending North Korea. In Moscow, Pan Zili, the Chinese ambassador to the Soviet Union, would meet with his counterpart from North Korea, telling him how even though the Chinese asked for more aid for the North Vietnamese struggle, the Soviets simply suggested an international conference to bring about peace. Khrushchev, Pan suggested, wanted to improve relations with the United States. He hoped, of course, that the Soviets would change their position, but good revolutionaries would have to keep a close eye on what they did.[133] It was shrewdly done. If the Soviets were wavering on North Vietnam, they might well waver on North Korea. Why not put the idea in the North Korean official mind?

With Khrushchev's fall, however, Soviet policy changed. Aid to Pyongyang resumed; the Chinese embassy there reported that the Koreans had said that they no longer needed Chinese planes, which probably meant that the Soviets had agreed to provide MiG-21s or some other aircraft. Whatever the Koreans asked for, it seemed, the Soviets would provide.[134] Pyongyang had options. China could lose North Korea if it did not get what it wanted—that fear would haunt Chinese grand strategists long after Mao.

The impact of Sino-Soviet relations on Chinese policy toward Indochina would be far-reaching. Ho Chi Minh, who had long relied on both Moscow and Beijing for support, wanted his two patrons to get along again and said so. He visited Beijing to discuss the matter. On the morning of August 10, 1960, Mao and Ho went swimming in the sea before settling down to talk. Mao found Ho's proposal basically, though not completely, good. It was good to promote unity, encourage peace. But revisionism had to always be fought. Ho asked what he should say to the Soviets. He wanted to be able to spell out the differences between the two sides to Moscow, to then be able to say that the Chinese comrades were willing to talk to the Soviets. And Mao was willing to let Ho do so.[135]

Ho returned to Beijing with the Soviet response. The Soviets, he said, were wary of the PRC, of its communes and its Hundred Flowers movement, its Great Leap Forward and its talk of the east wind—which they took to mean China—overcoming the west. China's military strength was growing. And why was it repairing Genghis Khan's mausoleum: had not Genghis's armies invaded Europe? Such was Ho's report of Soviet concerns. The military was defensive, Mao explained. This of Genghis was new to him. As far as he was concerned, Genghis might as well be cast into the ocean—but the Mongols worshipped their ancestors, so what would the Soviets have him do? He, Mao, did not worship Genghis. "The ones we worship are Marx, Engels, Lenin—and we have tremendous respect for Stalin." He added, "We also worship Ho Chi Minh and Hoxha."[136] That last bit sounded playful, but it was a reminder too: China was on Vietnam's side in a way the Soviets might not be.

Ho closed with the hope that talks between the two parties—which he had suggested and which both Khrushchev and Mao seemed interested in—would have a good result. Mao said that China shared that hope.[137] But it was not quite the same. Ho wanted the rift to heal. So did Mao, but not at the cost of the Soviets going revisionist and harming China. With the Soviets on his border, he was suspicious of them in a way that Ho was not. Ho's fight was with the Americans; besides, he was separated from the Soviet Union by all of China; he did not need to be wary of Moscow. Such differences of opinion would have to be managed carefully. Vietnam was too important a buffer zone and revolutionary partner to lose completely. One would have to make it clear that China valued Vietnamese friendship and that the Vietnamese, for their part, had much to gain from a friendly Beijing. Mao would thank them, in 1961, for serving on the frontlines to China's south—the phrasing showed just how important the Vietnam War was—and acknowledge how great their duties were: establishing socialism in the north, waging revolution in the south, all the while helping the Cambodians, the Thais, the Malaysians with revolution too. It was with the Vietnamese premier that Mao discussed the state of revolution in Laos and the possibility that Sihanouk, the Cambodian prince, might become another Nehru.[138] The Chinese embassy in Vietnam could report that although the Vietnamese were trying to promote Sino-Soviet unity and were hesitant to criticize the Soviets in public, they were, privately, dissatisfied with revisionism.[139] One could, of course, turn the interpretation around, and speculate that whatever the Vietnamese might say in private, their reluctance to denounce Moscow openly suggested that they might yet abandon China. Mao was not a man to extend trust lightly, and such trust as he extended was easily withdrawn. One could not count on Vietnam forever—which was probably why the Chinese began courting Cambodia. Beijing needed a favorable balance of power in Southeast Asia, and having good relations with both Phnom Penh and Hanoi was the surest way of attaining that balance.

So Sihanouk was befriended. Zhou was eager to extend the hand of friendship: he would discuss trade with him and offer to assist Cambodia in developing its industry. Cambodia's diplomatic connections could be useful for Beijing too. The country's neutrality meant that it had decent relationships with most countries in the neighborhood; only with Thailand and South Vietnam, Sihanouk explained, was his country on bad terms. There were still threats to Cambodia's national security. Song Ngoc Thanh, an opposition figure, although defeated, remained in Thailand. From there, Zhou said, he had been to Taiwan. There was an array of enemies under the American umbrella—the special forces of Chiang, Thailand, South Vietnam—that would cooperate to support Song Ngoc Thanh and make trouble for Cambodia. Zhou shared Chinese intelligence on this: a gesture of support, which would deepen the intimacy.[140] (The notion that such coordination to undermine Cambodia existed might seem far-fetched, but this was a time when extraordinary things were happening; it is perfectly plausible that someone in Langley or

Taipei dreamed up such a policy.) Sihanouk was far from being communist in his inclinations—but here were the Chinese, committed, so they said, to the fight against revisionism, sharing intelligence with a man who was wary of socialists coming to power in his country. Mao approved of such ideological openness. Afghanistan, Nepal, and Cambodia were all kingdoms, not communist countries, but the PRC was friendly with them: had not Stalin said that the Afghan king was better than the British Labour Party?[141] Ideology went only so far; one could compromise on it to retain friendship in an important neighborhood. Cambodia was a decent candidate for friendship. It had recognized the Algerian government before the French withdrew, thereby helping the Algerian struggle; it would support the People's Liberation Armed Forces in South Vietnam (the military arm of the National Liberation Front or Vietcong, as it was better known, in that region), Sihanouk told Zhou in 1964, in the hope that the Vietnamese would achieve peace, neutrality, and independence.[142] A country like this deserved support. Liu Shaoqi promised Sihanouk military aid.[143] As to American aid, Sihanouk refused it, saying it was like opium. And having said this he was careful to point out that if the Americans escalated the war and invaded his country, there was nothing he could do—but the Americans feared China, because China would not tolerate an invasion of Cambodia.[144] It was deliberately flattering, exactly the sort of thing Mao liked to hear (there was a reason the relationship with Sihanouk was warm enough to survive the later coup in Cambodia and earn him refuge in Beijing). But that specter of an American invasion showed why Cambodia mattered to the PRC. The regional balance of power was important. Beijing would try to remain closer to both Phnom Penh and Hanoi than they were to one another—and it would do so to keep the Americans at bay, in order to protect its own national security.

The same cool-headed approach to the balance of power marked China's dealings with South Asia. The Sino-Indian relationship, based on the five principles, had been the touchstone of third world unity. In some ways, its unraveling was remarkably similar to that of the Sino-Soviet relationship. In each case, a border had long been left blissfully unresolved; in each case, fourth world movements across that border became problematic once there was cause for mutual suspicion. The Chinese believed that the Indians were using the Tibetan uprisings—a result of flawed, cruel policies that created a refugee crisis and subsequent rebellion in Tibet—to push for territorial gains, thereby jeopardizing national security. Such acts reflected a lack of goodwill, and the Chinese would have to do something about it. The first step, as with the Soviets, was to try to reach an understanding with India while making clear that core interests could not be compromised on.[145] Zhou offered Nehru a territorial swap: Chinese sovereignty over the disputed western sector (Aksai Chin) and Indian sovereignty over the eastern sector. Nehru's refusal of the offer did not close the path to a peaceful solution altogether; in 1961, hosting Indian foreign secretary R. K. Nehru, Zhou would point out that the Indians had failed to agree to any of his suggestions in New Delhi and were sympathizing with the Dalai Lama, but he would also point out that friendship and cooperation were still possible.[146] Beijing was reluctant to give up on India. Reasonable people could compromise on boundary issues, as recent experience with Burma and Nepal had shown.[147] There were, however, two additional measures to be taken: negotiating a boundary with Pakistan and going to war.

The negotiations with Pakistan had begun before the Sino-Indian war started, but they would conclude in a boundary agreement only after the war was over. The negotiations were meant to show Nehru that the PRC was not entirely dependent on New Delhi. To China, the war was a defensive one, and it came at a time when the PRC was facing a threat on two fronts: India's encroachment in the west and a possible American-ROC assault on the coast. (The concern would have been all the more pressing given reports of ROC cooperation with Tibetans in India and Indian permissiveness toward supporters of Chiang Kai-shek in its territory.)[148] China was in danger again, hostile forces gathering at its edges, trying to drag it back into pieces. One could try to reason with those forces. On October 8, 1962, Zhou told the Soviets that if the Indians attacked, the Chinese would defend themselves.[149] The hope was that the Soviets would pass the message along; there was still time for the Indians to desist. But if reason did not work, the PRC would not shy away from using force. On October 17, Indian troops engaged their Chinese counterparts north of the McMahon Line. The Chinese did not recognize the McMahon Line but there had been a certain respect for it; it served, in the absence of an agreed border, as a line that would allow both sides to live amicably (though there were clashes throughout the 1950s, these appear to have been minor affairs, easily contained and with little detriment to the overall cordiality of the relationship). With that line crossed, Mao gave the order for a counteroffensive. The troops in Tibet and Xinjiang would repel the Indian forces that had crossed over.[150]

Victory was swift and decisive—but it meant that China needed to find new partners in South Asia. (Concerned Afro-Asian countries would try to bring about a Sino-Indian rapprochement, but these efforts did not bear fruit.) Pakistan was a natural country to turn to. The Pakistanis had long denounced the Indians to the Chinese, and were only too pleased to arrive at a border settlement. The negotiation of the Sino-Pakistani boundary exemplified all that was missing from Sino-Indian negotiations: a willingness to compromise on territorial claims, to sacrifice stretches of rock and ice for overall good-will. When the Pakistanis found that they needed to adjust the pre-liminary agreement reached to allow movement around a mountain spur, the Chinese were willing to oblige; the Pakistanis would do the same in 1965, when it was discovered that K2 was not quite where the negotiators had thought.[151] That Pakistan had reached the agree-ment despite pressure from the Americans and the British went some way in winning China's trust; Pakistan, said Zhou, could be an advo-cate for China within pacts such as SEATO.[152]

Not that leaders on either side, for all the rhetoric, saw it as any-thing other than a practical relationship. Beijing was highlighting its credentials as a responsible Asian power and buying support in the region. Friendship with Pakistan was expensive; Mohammad Ayub Khan liked the Chinese aid he received because it came without in-terest, and he would freely ask for more.[153] The Chinese were not very happy with this, but it was the cost of finding friends in South Asia. They drew the line at intervening militarily to protect Pakistan against India in 1965 and 1971, but Ayub Khan, at least, would probably not have expected intervention. Had Indian action actually threatened Chinese national security, the response might have been different, but Pakistan's losses did not materially alter China's geopolitical situation. (If anything, the division of Pakistan that followed from the 1971 war improved China's security. The more countries there were to ne-gotiate with in a neighborhood, the easier it was to achieve a suitable balance of power.) China reached out to Ceylon and encouraged it to be friendly with Pakistan.[154] Plans were made to fete the Afghan king in Beijing; he could be offered more trade and economic assistance.[155] These countries mattered, and China would not neglect them: as with Southeast Asia, it would remain closer to all of them than they were to one another. Perhaps because of its own relationship with the

Soviets, China could understand, better than India could, how sensitive they were to the power of their larger neighbors, how desperately they needed reassurance, and how their resentments could best be used.

Beyond the continent too, Beijing sought friends, to burnish its revolutionary credentials and get diplomatic support. Algerian independence was one of the great causes to fight for, the point anti-imperialists could rally around. Mao would promise the Algerians that Chinese help for their cause would not be sacrificed to improving relations with France.[156] This was a long-term investment: Algeria, after it had gained independence, was willing to support China's position on Vietnam at the UN.[157] Absent a seat of one's own at the UN, such support was essential—and it explains in part why China was so willing to court the third world. Newly emerging countries were flocking into the ranks of the UN at the time, where they could criticize U.S. conduct or make sure that China's position was understood; building a railway for Tanzania, for example, was one way of finding diplomatic support.[158] Zhou visited Africa in 1964: he promised aid, spoke of the need for peaceful coexistence, affirmed China's support for an Africa free of nuclear weapons, and pointed out that regaining China's rightful place meant not just the accession of the PRC to the UN, but also the expulsion of Chiang Kai-shek.[159] Nor was the quest confined to the UN: it was important that Beijing have friends in the communist world, to establish that being communist did not mean kowtowing to Moscow. The split between the Soviets and Albania provided one such opportunity. When Ho Chi Minh made the mistake of supporting Moscow's position in the dispute, it was Beijing that soothed Albanian feelings. Ho, as Vice Premier Chen Yi explained to the Albanians, was a good man, an old comrade, but he had, on this occasion, fallen under Khrushchev's influence. The rest of the Vietnamese Communists did not necessarily share Ho's position. Beijing stood by Tirana.[160] Ideological credibility among fellow travelers was important. The principle of equality needed reinforcement in the communist world; it meant that there would still be support for Beijing's position and that there would be just a little bit more pressure on Moscow to be reasonable. And so Beijing sought to pick off Soviet allies, much as it had sought to pick off American ones.

The geopolitical landscape, then, had shifted—and with it, so had Beijing's strategic orientation. The PRC would diversify its friendships, court favor in places where it had not had to in the early fifties. It would do this by spending money and manpower—often to its detriment.[161] The underlying strategic precept, however, was the same: careful diplomacy to foster a balance of power that kept China safe. There was room for compromise, even disagreement. Such room was not infinite; the PRC would not yield to threats to its territorial integrity. But that such room existed went a long way in ensuring that China was not utterly friendless. One might not always be able to reach an understanding with another country, but there was no point in giving up on the prospect. There was no harm in continuing a conversation.

This did not, of course, mean neglecting the use of force. The PRC had been prepared to use it in the case of both Taiwan and India. As those cases would suggest, military doctrine remained essentially defensive. And it would marry guerrilla principles with military modernization. Having tested a nuclear bomb successfully on October 16, 1964, the PRC announced a principle of no first use that very same day: "At no time, under no circumstances, will China first use nuclear weapons."[162] That sense of being threatened and unable to count on anyone else for defense (Khrushchev, who should have been providing the nuclear umbrella, was basically parroting the

American line) was still alive. The third line strategy, which Mao came up with in 1964, demonstrated both defensiveness and that oddly malleable concept of Chinese geography. Think of China as a stretch of lines, or fronts. The first was the coast; the second stretched to Lanzhou; the third was southwest. In the nuclear age, one needed a place to fall back to, and there had been, Mao felt, insufficient attention to this.[163] Such thinking was perhaps a legacy of his guerrilla days, when the Communists had had to move from one base to the next, retreating, advancing, then retreating again; it was always best to have something in reserve. So the PRC would move forces and goods to the southwest, where they would remain safe from American attack. By 1965, there was growing fear that America would expand the Vietnam War to North Vietnam. This would threaten China's national security—so clear was the threat that the Chinese were careful to signal as much to the Americans. Support to Vietnam went up too; Chinese experts were sent to help the Vietnamese with defense, construction, and work on railways and airports.[164] The southwest thus became, for a brief while, a hub of economic and military activity. Once again, Mao believed that not all of China's territory had to be held if war came; the PRC could abandon certain parts of it in order to lure enemy forces in deep, the better to annihilate them.[165] That concept of China as something movable still informed defense policy. Geography meant that there were many potential fronts to fight on; it also meant that there was space for the PRC to withdraw into. Force modernization would continue: there would be research on missiles and missile defense; the navy would grow strong enough to conduct patrols of Yongxing Island in the Paracels, and to start construction there.[166] But guerrilla instincts never left Mao's defense planning. People's warfare and modern weaponry went hand in hand. It was all very well to try to reason with people, but one never knew when or where one would have to fight.

There was one other realm important to grand strategy: political economy. Chiang had been defeated not least because of economic mismanagement and the social unrest that had triggered, causing his generals and the people to abandon the generalissimo. Besides, the economy was the foundation of military power, which was the state's key safeguard. Mao grasped that basic problem—and it was the desperation that problem engendered, coupled with ignorance, that led China, step by step, to the Great Leap Forward.

By 1953, the government knew it was short of food. Chen Yun, a high-ranking CCP member, called for strict control of private traders and the elimination of food traffickers. The state would proceed with collectivization.[167] Eliminating food shortages, so it was believed, required a bigger state. The curious thing was that Mao, as in the days before the PRC was formed, was ambivalent on economic policy. In early 1955, sensing dissatisfaction among the peasants, he suggested slowing down on collectivization, calling it to a temporary halt. But even then, the official diagnosis of the problem was telling in its assumption that expertise resided in the central government. As Beijing saw it, sales in the districts were exceeding the amounts the center had specified, which was dangerous. The masses needed to be mobilized and the cadres told that central directives were not to be violated.[168] Reports of success from Anhui and Guangdong encouraged Mao to resume collectivization in July 1955: if those two provinces could do it, why not others?[169] It was never the policy that was at fault, just the implementation; tweaks here and there—motivating the masses properly—would fix any problems. And there were provincial reports to support these conclusions. The tragedies of Mao's China were not solely his fault; he did immense damage, in which he was ably assisted by a whole system of people.[170] When it came to economic policy-making, the PRC was deeply confused and deeply cruel.

What Mao did understand was just how high the stakes were. The announcement of the Great Leap Forward and that insane call to surpass Britain's steel production in fifteen years did not come in a vacuum. How, he asked, could you modernize defense without modernizing industry?[171] China would have to build nuclear weapons and missiles, strengthen its navy and air force; to do all this, it needed modern industry, agriculture, science. War, if it came, would require not merely fighting defensively, but launching a counteroffensive to drive the invaders out.[172] Leaping forward was not a luxury; it was a matter of survival. (A matter too, if one probes deeper, of standing up: China would not be behind Britain and the United States any longer.) In the summer of 1958, with the Korean War still fresh in his mind, the Americans still refusing to recognize the PRC, and Chiang bent on reclaiming the mainland, this was true. The goal was wise; it was in the means that China erred.

The means involved going big. The cooperatives were to be transformed into massive communes, served by ever-larger waterworks; in the factories, the quest to raise output consumed workers and resources alike.[173] News came in of how wonderfully the Great Leap was going. In eastern China, it was reported, food production was going to go up; within the year, the food problem would be essentially solved.[174] "My health," Mao declared, "has improved since the Great Leap Forward."[175]

Then the reports came in from Anhui. People were starving. Mao sent a team to investigate. The reports turned out to be true.[176]

Mao had expressed doubts as early as November 1958 (though, as was typical with his grander plans, the doubts were abstract, philosophical, at best only tenuously connected to practical policy). Perhaps the pace had been too fast; perhaps it was best to let the Soviets enter socialism before China did. If one tried to develop too quickly, there might be great chaos under heaven.[177] His comrades had their doubts too: on December 8, 1958, it was announced that Mao no longer wished to be chairman of the country. He would remain a chairman of the party; he would focus on ideology. If the people and the country needed it, he could be reappointed to his former duties.[178] He had, it seemed, been effectively sidelined. And yet, for someone supposedly out of power, Mao remained astonishingly active. He met foreign leaders and issued directives. His basic foreign and domestic policies would remain in place (although Liu Shaoqi, notably, was a little cooler on the economic policies, admitting to foreign leaders that there had been mistakes). He would admit to error— "We have issued inappropriate directives, myself included"[179]—but he had not fallen as far as some of his comrades might have hoped. China persisted in the Great Leap Forward.

It was given a reason to persist by countless cadres who reported on the Leap's great successes. If those cadres were succeeding, as Mao wanted to believe, then the failures were obviously somehow the fault of the cadres reporting them. Zhao Ziyang, who would later gain fame as the architect of Deng Xiaoping's economic reform and the man who stood up for the students at Tiananmen Square, provided the explanation Mao longed for. Zhao was serving in Leinan, Guangdong, at the time, where, he reported, the Leap was doing well. Problems had arisen only because food was being embezzled and privateered. If policy were executed properly, the problems could be fixed in ten to fifteen days.[180] It was not the system that was at fault, merely the personnel charged with executing it. Adjustments to the Great Leap's implementation would deliver on the promise. There was always a way of interpreting unfavorable evidence away, and always someone willing to provide such interpretation. On January 27, 1962, when Liu Shaoqi warned that one could no longer deny the policy's failures, it was Mao who interrupted him repeatedly, and Lin Biao, two days later, who would say that the Great Leap Forward was correct, that one needed to rely on the leadership of the party and the leadership of Mao.[181] It was thinking and pandering of precisely this sort that made policies so hard to reverse. And while China's leadership squabbled about the matter, between thirty million and fifty million people died of hunger.[182]

The strangest part of the tragedy is that there was an alternative policy before them: one that Mao himself championed. Little plots of land had been left to the peasants. These were proving astonishingly productive, and Mao suggested raising such land from 5 percent of the commune to 7 percent. If the household plots were working, why not increase their size?[183] It was, in many ways, a similar observation to the one that would later guide Deng Xiaoping: what was happening outside the state's realm was proving worthwhile, and was, therefore, worth permitting, even encouraging. Household plots were not as spectacular as massive communes, but they provided the growth Mao was seeking; China's subsequent economic miracle would begin with them. But tinkering by two percentage points was too little, too late. The desire to have it both ways on economic policy meant that the little shoots of productivity that survived were never allowed to bloom. If the tragedy of the Great Leap Forward lay in the death and suffering of so many, the irony was that the path to economic growth Mao sought was there, waiting to be taken, all the while.

There was, then, a grand strategic vision that informed Mao's thinking in the late fifties and early sixties. To keep China safe as the world changed around it, one needed to find a new balance of power and modernize one's forces. The latter required massive economic growth—and it was in a deeply ignorant attempt to achieve this that Mao made his greatest mistake to date. Sifting through the debris of the Great Leap Forward, one could see the forces that would lead to economic reform. But one could also see the tendencies—an unwillingness to believe bad news, the notion that grand plans were being undermined by corrupt personnel, the idea that mass mobilization solved everything—that fueled the Cultural Revolution. And it was in the early years of the Cultural Revolution that China would depart from the grand strategy that had sustained it all this while.

From Chaos to New Balance

The Cultural Revolution has become so convenient a catchphrase that it obscures how many different things the years 1966 to 1976 involved. The first was the chaos: the attacks on foreign missions and Chinese government offices, Maoist upheaval in foreign lands, the complete abandonment of the balance of power politics that had hitherto marked Chinese conduct. It is difficult, if not impossible, to explain this period: why would people perpetuate collective madness? It might have been Mao's lust for power, his eagerness to differentiate himself from the Soviet Union, his belief that what had gone wrong with the Great Leap Forward was down to human beings and that the human beings needed to be fixed. Why the Chinese people, traumatized and hungry, agreed to perpetrate Mao's program is much harder to fathom. Whatever the reason, China plunged itself into insanity. The next phase was a return to grand strategy: the attainment of a new balance of power with the Sino-American rapprochement and an opening to commerce with the outside world. Then, with the PRC more secure than at any point since its founding, the party's political feuds would almost undo all its successes.[184] Delineating these phases does not lessen Mao's guilt or excuse the tragedy; it serves only to demonstrate that evil and folly can coexist with cunning. The latter was missing in the first phase; it came to China's rescue in the second, and would almost be snuffed out again in the third.

The phrase "cultural revolution" had cropped up as early as the Chengdu conference in March 1958. There had been some, Mao noted, calling for a "cultural revolution," and this could be researched.[185] The moral of the Great Leap Forward, for Mao, was that people mattered for policy. Absent proper spirit among those charged with carrying the revolution out, little could be achieved. On March 20, 1966, Mao declared that there were many things the government had not understood and that it was time for the young to rise. It was time now to break through, time to create.[186]

So the young rose in righteous rebellion. Dubbed the Red Guards, they dueled among themselves on campuses; they hauled out intellectuals and forced them to make self-criticism. They tortured and crippled Deng Xiaoping's son; they laid siege to foreign embassies and legations. Maoists sprang up across the globe. In Burma, this sparked anti-Chinese riots; in Pakistan, it was tolerated.[187] In China, no one was immune; the young could do as they wished. This pleased Mao. Even some of the cadres, he told a visiting Australian Communist proudly, were afraid of them.[188] The breakdown of state authority was something to be celebrated.

Swiftly, however, the need to limit the chaos made itself felt. Several officials, including Zhu De, Mao's partner in arms from the days of the Jiangxi soviet, emphasized the need to protect the stability of the troops.[189] The government swiftly issued a directive: no individual or organization was to attack the PLA; to attack a military organization would amount to destroying the Cultural Revolution.[190] Mao insisted that the troops could not stand entirely apart from the fray.[191]

But they themselves were supposed to be above attack. There was the unspoken realization here that China needed a fighting force capable of defending the country—and it also needed to keep the military on its side: armed men had overthrown civilian governments in China before. Besides, one did not want the Red Guards getting their hands on PLA weaponry: there would be swift penalties for doing so.[192] These directives did not always work: in Guangxi, some revolutionaries did seize PLA weaponry.[193] But when a mob created havoc on the rails of Xuzhou, Zhou could ask for a military response; there were, still, troops capable of coming in and maintaining some form of order.[194] That Mao felt the need for and approved such measures showed how murky his thinking on the Cultural Revolution was. Having encouraged destruction and creativity, he approved Zhou's suggestion that the destruction of state property was best not tolerated; having encouraged attacks on officialdom, he would sound caught between pride and annoyance that anarchism had developed and that some of the attacks extended to foreign ministry officials— pride because he could say he would protect them, annoyance that he would have to do so.[195] He was trying, bizarrely, to set up regulations for the very chaos that he himself had called for. In those tempestuous years, Mao Zedong had no idea of what he wanted: he was an old, confused man, who in his arrogance and confusion had unleashed forces that could not easily be stoppered again.

Then in 1968, Soviet leader Leonid Brezhnev sent tanks into Czechoslovakia. There would be many consequences to this particular display of Soviet power, but one was to draw Mao's attention back to geopolitics. The Soviets could not help their revisionism, he said, and there was nothing to be done to help Czechoslovakia; it was completely occupied by now and had been utterly dependent on the Soviets for food and petrol. Romania was a different story: it had its own resources—and this difference demanded Chinese attention. If China's oil fields in Daqing were occupied, Mao pointed out, the country would be left without petrol. There were rumors of oil in Sichuan and western Hubei; it would be wise to exploit these swiftly.[196] There were indeed hydrocarbons in Sichuan, but the key point was Mao's preparation for a foreign seizure of Daqing, that dark, sprawling oil town in China's far northeast. There was only one country that could realistically do this: the neighboring Soviet Union.

Mao, then, was concerned about the possibility of a Soviet invasion. It had been on his mind in 1964, and Brezhnev's conduct would only have heightened his worry. The Soviets, meanwhile, had no way of knowing what a country bent on the Cultural Revolution might do next. It remains unclear which side initiated the Sino-Soviet border clashes of 1969, but out in that spirit-sapping winter, it was only a matter of time before nerves snapped. There had been several border clashes in late 1968. On March 2, 1969, shots were fired. Troops on both sides of an uncharted border mobilized for defense.[197]

In theory, the issue was the sovereignty of a pair of small islands in the middle of the Ussuri River: Zhenbao and Qiliqin. But it was about so much more too: it was about whether or not China could stand up to its northern neighbor, about how it could best protect its national security. The first imperative, therefore, was to make it clear to the Soviets that China could not be moved by threat of arms. If the Soviets struck China's river bank, Mao ordered, the Chinese were to strike theirs. It was possible, he feared, that the Soviets and the Americans wanted to occupy both Europe and Asia.[198] In planning the resistance to that occupation, he snapped back into guerrilla mode; he would range across great China again. Invasion was not to be feared: China was too big for the Soviets or the Americans to swallow.[199] Let them enter, the better to strike them. Part of him, as ever, was eager for war: if the third world war came, he argued, it would, like the first and second, be bad for imperialism.[200] Mao would not cower before the latest challenge. The Chinese people had stood up, and they would stand up to the Soviets too.

Beneath the belligerence, however, there was a willingness to dial the tensions down before they burned too fiercely to be quenched. A directive was circulated, ordering that no Soviet diplomatic apparatus in the PRC was to be harmed.[201] It had to be made clear to the Soviets that China would not submit to threats, but equally, it had to be made clear to them that there was room for negotiation. The Soviets' opening position—that the Chinese vacate Zhenbao island immediately or the firing would continue—was met firmly; the Chinese were to let the Soviets shoot, then fire back suddenly.[202] This would show resolution, while conciliatory moves were under way. Even after there were clashes at Xinjiang, at the other end of the Sino-Soviet borderlands, suggesting that the Soviets might try to attack China on two fronts, Zhou would meet to negotiate with Alexei Kosygin at the Beijing airport, as the latter returned to Moscow from Ho Chi Minh's funeral. Differences of theory and principle, Zhou preached, should not be allowed to influence the relationship between two countries or prevent its normalization. An agreement was reached to talk the border dispute out; in the meanwhile, they would try to preserve the status quo at the border, avoid armed conflict, disengage in the disputed areas, and, at Kosygin's suggestion, let the border defense departments talk to one another if something came up. Mao did not trust the Soviets; he remained, as he would have been proud to say, prepared for war, but he agreed.[203]

The negotiations that followed were rancorous. They stopped; they started; they stopped again in recrimination, before stuttering on. The Chinese were determined to appear reasonable, to show that the

Soviets could, if they wished, reach an agreement with the PRC. Of course history entered into the dispute, Zhou said; they were living with the legacies of the unequal treaties made in the days of tsarist Russia. But China was far from being so unreasonable as to demand the return of all the territory it had lost in those treaties.[204] Being reasonable extended to the broader relationship too. It was not necessary, Mao decided, to curse the Soviets every day: "There are times when we can stop for a while."[205] On October 20, 1969, the Soviets refused to recognize that there were disputed territories along the border.[206] Attempts to reach out to the Soviets were resumed by December: it was necessary, the Chinese maintained, to preserve the Zhou-Kosygin agreement, so that the dispute could be resolved peacefully, without fear of any threats.[207] The idea was not peace at all costs. It had to be made clear, for example, that the fact that China had tolerated people living and doing business on either side of the disputed border did not give Moscow license to claim all areas where the Soviets resided as Soviet territory.[208] As long as the two sides were talking, however, there was less risk of a war that would profit no one. If both could at least agree to the idea that discussions were better than violence, if the Zhou-Kosygin agreement could survive, then diplomacy would have served its purpose. There was a return to old patterns of diplomacy here: a refusal to give up on an interlocutor as long as core interests were not compromised. This was not easy—Mao, who could be particularly querulous, would ask the Soviets in May 1970, if their delegation was returning to Beijing to fight; when the Soviets replied they were coming for discussions, Mao would counter that to discuss was to fight. But he would suggest too that the fighting could be confined to dialogue rather than actual warfare.[209] Communication remained open. It was not that the talks would necessarily resolve the border dispute; it was, rather, that the two sides were willing to continue talking regardless of whether or not it was resolved. Even after initial soundings of the possibility of a Sino-American rapprochement, the PRC would repeat to the Soviets that differences of principle should not prevent a normal relationship based on the five principles of peaceful coexistence.[210]

The story of the Sino-American rapprochement has been told so often that it is at once familiar and misunderstood.[211] The message Pakistan sent saying President Richard Nixon was willing to talk with Beijing; the resumption of the Warsaw talks and the backchannel communications to ensure that the relationship could be made to work; ping-pong diplomacy, with U.S. and Chinese table-tennis players showing that it was possible for the two countries to get along; Henry Kissinger's trip to Pakistan and his subsequent, triumphant arrival in China in 1971; Nixon bounding down the tarmac to shake Zhou by the hand in 1972; the Shanghai communiqué and the dawn of a new era—these have become the stuff of myth. And the myth has become so deeply encrusted as to obscure certain features of Chinese grand strategy. First, by the time the rapprochement actually happened, the crisis with the Soviets had been averted. Beijing had been careful to keep trying to negotiate with Moscow even after the first message of interest from Washington arrived. There was no reason to place much faith in the idea that things would work out with Washington; protecting the PRC required being prepared for all contingencies. And it was not just Kissinger who recognized the benefits, in triangular diplomacy, of being closer to the other two sides than they were to one another; it was just that he had the luxury of distance whereas Beijing did not. The PRC could not be as close to the Soviet Union as the United States was, but it would not make the mistake of alienating the Soviets completely.

Second, the idea of reaching out to America was not new. There had been attempts throughout the fifties to reach a modus vivendi with Washington. The advice from Mao's marshals and his famous comment about reaching out to faraway countries when threatened by near ones reflected the same geopolitical principles that had animated earlier attempts. At any time, barring the early years of the Cultural Revolution, the two sides could have reached the agreement to disagree that Zhou and Kissinger arrived at. What America refused to compromise on in Warsaw, Kissinger managed easily.[212] The Sino-Soviet border clashes helped catalyze the rapprochement, but the real change was in Washington, with the arrival of an administration willing to compromise with China. Had Lyndon Johnson, say, been reelected, Mao would probably have continued to reach out to no avail. He benefited from one of those rare, fortuitous moments in which a sensible policy finds a receptive object.

Novel as the Shanghai communiqué was to Kissinger, with its blunt statement of the differences between the two sides, it was typical of Chinese statecraft. All along, the PRC had believed that the specific points at issue between two countries could be overcome if the goodwill was sufficient. Beijing would not compromise on core interests, but barring an infringement of those, it could live amicably with those it disagreed with. This was the attitude that had made boundary agreements with Nepal and Burma possible; it was what had allowed the Sino-Indian relationship to survive until the Tibetan uprisings; it was why the Sino-Pakistani relationship had thrived despite Pakistan's membership in SEATO and CENTO (Central Treaty Organization). The plea to the Soviets—that differences of ideology and principle need not stand in the way of normalized relations—was as good a description of the Shanghai communiqué and the relationship it created as any. The differences were vast, true, but if the relationship was solid, that did not matter. More than anything else, it had been Taiwan that stood between Beijing and Washington, Taiwan that had scuppered the Warsaw talks all those years ago, Taiwan that the PRC knew would have to come up as the Warsaw talks were now renewed.[213] And it was on Taiwan that the biggest breakthrough occurred. The Chinese won American acknowledgment that "all Chinese on either side of the Taiwan Strait maintain there is but one China and that Taiwan is a part of China" and American willingness to leave that position unchallenged.[214] The statement might seem half-hearted—but it was the context that gave it force: the American national security advisor and president were in Beijing. They had come in person, to agree that Taiwan was a part of China, and assure China that they would wind down the American military presence in Taiwan along with the Vietnam War. One of the key threats that had defined the Chinese national security calculus since the Korean War—the one along the coast—was being removed. Kissinger was also willing to facilitate the PRC getting the Chinese seat at the UN. He was moving toward recognition, if not quite there. Assuring Zhou that he concurred with the premier's position on Taiwan on his very first visit, Kissinger declared that the matter would be solved in "the relatively near future," leaving Beijing and Washington with "no conflicting interests at all."[215] This signaled goodwill in a way the high-handed American manner of 1958 had not. If this was to be the tenor of the relationship, the PRC could tolerate some delay in formal recognition and the termination of the U.S.-ROC defense treaty.

The rapprochement came with costs. The PRC had relationships built on the foundation of opposition to America; now, like the Americans, it had to do an about-face. It had long counseled Vietnam not to compromise with the Americans; the Americans were weakening, could be defeated entirely. Mao's advice was to talk and keep fighting.[216]

Now he found himself rejecting Soviet requests to send aid to Vietnam through China, then counseling the South Vietnamese Communists to give Nixon a little face; if they negotiated with the Americans, Mao promised, they and North Vietnam could reach a normal relationship with the Americans. It was best to sign a ceasefire; if they were unhappy with the results, they could always start fighting again.[217]

For a people who had been fighting for what seemed like eternity, this would have been especially galling—not least because of the suspicion that the United States had engineered the coup against Sihanouk, bringing to power a new Cambodian government that was intent on attacking Vietnamese soldiers in Cambodian territory. (The coup in Cambodia, ostensibly, had led to a postponement in the Warsaw talks as Beijing and Washington first fumbled toward rapprochement—but it was just a postponement. Cambodia was expendable if one could get Washington's goodwill.) The Pakistanis, so important to both China and the United States, felt that they had not achieved sufficient support from their partners in the latest war with India; the Chinese would bring this up with Kissinger, only to be told that although the United States did not wish India to attack its neighbors, it drew the line at taking "military measures."[218] This did not bother Beijing unduly: Pakistan had served its purpose, and, like Kissinger, they were probably confident that Bangladesh—the new state created after East Pakistan broke away from West—could be a reasonable partner. Although the Sino-Pakistani relationship would survive the disappointment, Beijing's ties in Indochina were damaged irreparably. But there were benefits too. Favorable balance of power aside—and that balance was significant; China's national security had improved dramatically—one could look forward to a thriving trade relationship. Kissinger promised Zhou most-favored-nation status in trade; that would take longer than anticipated to materialize, but the prospect was there.[219] There was room for technology transfer: the president would approve the sale of inertial navigation systems and aircraft to the PRC.[220] In its quest for a stable economy and modern technology—the underpinnings of a modern, competent military—China had received a major boost.

The approach to the relationship being typical of Chinese grand strategy, the PRC would not fall into the American embrace completely. There would be no repeating the errors of the fifties—understandable and unavoidable although those were—by growing too dependent on a superpower patron. Hence Mao's paeans to self-reliance, his wariness when Kissinger got too warm or when the demands of the relationship seemed to threaten Chinese interests. When Kissinger informed him in November 1973, that the United States would not permit China's security to be destroyed, Mao responded that the Soviets' ambitions were excessive, and contented himself with advising against a Soviet-American nuclear war.[221] But with Kissinger gone, he was irate. The Americans had the gall to tell him he was about to be attacked by the Soviet Union; no one was to make the mistake of believing this. When opposing the Americans, it was easy to fall too far to the left; when working with them, one had to be wary of tilting too far right. On no account was China going to join a military pact sponsored by them.[222] (Jiang Qing, Mao's wife and a member of the Gang of Four, the political clique which did so much damage during the Cultural Revolution, attacked Zhou savagely here; the premier had been too craven, she alleged, in his dealings with America.)[223] Later, when Kissinger offered military assistance, Mao shrugged it off: this could wait, he said, until there had been actual strikes.[224] He was haunted by the idea that the Americans were trying to use China against the Soviet Union; he himself manipulated people so easily that it was only natural to assume that others were doing the same.

The war with the Soviets never came. The Chinese never stopped negotiating with Moscow: when Kissinger gave them news that the Soviets, in a particularly cunning ploy, had suggested a mutual defense treaty to Washington, Foreign Minister Qiao Guanhua would respond that the Soviets had proposed a new mutual nonaggression treaty to Beijing. "Of course," said Qiao, "how we will deal with this treaty will have to be seen."[225] There was a reason Qiao was telling Kissinger about Sino-Soviet relations; it was a reminder to Kissinger that the PRC was not to be taken for granted, that it was more than capable of fending for itself in the rough and tumble of geopolitics. The Soviets were tricky, but that did not mean refusing to discuss matters with them in hope of achieving some sort of modus vivendi. Border talks continued, year after endless year, each side making its proposals and failing to reach agreement; the two sides would rehearse the same positions, practically unchanged, when they met in 1978.[226] Nothing had changed about the disputed border—and this, although the Chinese probably never said as much to the Soviets, was the great accomplishment. The opening to America allowed Beijing to apply some pressure on the Soviet Union. But the purpose of the pressure was to improve the relationship, not to shatter it altogether. The balance of power must not be allowed to become too lopsided.

Stable as things were geopolitically—this was as secure as the PRC had been since its foundation—there was a window of opportunity to focus on economic development, and Deng Xiaoping wanted to leap through it. Deng had been cast into the wilderness during the first part of the Cultural Revolution, but Mao had long maintained that he was different from Liu Shaoqi and could be rehabilitated. Now, as the world spun in China's favor, Deng returned to influence, and launched what would later be called reform and opening. No country in the world, he told Mao, as they discussed international cooperation and trade, could sever itself from the international realm, including America—they were all linked inextricably. China needed to make the most of the coming five years. In a country so large, there was no need for everyone to rely on the center. He put it to Mao in terms Mao would understand: the key was stability, and right now there were fears of chaos. Large numbers of people were doing nothing; it was not that the masses were not demanding work, but that there was no way to give it to them. The most important thing for the next few years was to concentrate on production. And Mao told Deng that he and Li Xiannian and Yu Qiuli were to take care of this.[227] Deng was promoted; he had a platform, authority to push for growth. He could stand before his fellow party members and call for what would become known as the four modernizations: modern agriculture, modern industry, modern defense, and modern science and technology. There were comrades who wanted to cling to revolution, not production; this, Deng argued, was a great mistake.[228] It was time for the PRC to join the modern world.

The forces that would allow Deng to preside over China's economic miracle later were already present, then, in Mao's time.[229] There was geopolitical stability: although the PRC would be prepared for the contingency of war, it was safer than it could possibly have hoped to be in 1968. Trade was flourishing, as the United States, Japan, and Europe came flocking to do business. Exports to the United States went from none in 1971 to about $156 million in 1976; imports from the United States climbed from nothing to over $160 million in the same time. Trade with Japan rocketed during that time too, exports growing from about $281 million to almost six times that and imports going from $594 million to about $1.8 billion.[230] The openness to commerce with the outside world that would become a hallmark of the Deng years had taken hold during Mao's era. And there was the sense that it was time to focus on productivity and profit. This was the beginning of China's economic transformation. It was happening under Mao, at the chairman's directive, and it represented hope for a better Chinese future.

But the dark forces—the political infighting, the ideological fervor, the belief that comrades had to be criticized and exiled for the revolution to last—had never gone away. It was easy enough to start a Cultural Revolution; it was impossible for Mao to stop it. Jiang Qing, Mao's wife, was a true believer in the revolution, as were her fellow members of the group called the Gang of Four: Wang Hongwen, Zhang Chunqiao, and Yao Wenyuan. The China that Deng and Zhou were trying to create was not their China, never would be. Jiang had led the criticism of Zhou for kowtowing to Kissinger; in 1974, the Gang would criticize revisionism and, especially, Deng Xiaoping.[231] Deng, no novice when it came to bureaucratic infighting, criticized Jiang in turn.[232] Cultural Revolution and reform and opening: they coexisted, violently, tempestuously, in the China of 1974–1976. A battle was under way for China's future, between the revolutionaries on one side and the pragmatists on the other.

In this battle, Mao Zedong's position was curious and decisive. The chairman was old now, increasingly given to mulling ideology and leaving day-to-day governance to Deng. Isolated as he was, he had reason to be afraid. What if the Gang of Four turned against him? Jiang Qing was reckless, unwilling to stop at anything; if he came out in full force against the Gang, he might lose. And the technocrats might find they no longer needed him; perhaps there was such a thing as giving them too much independence. The fears might seem exaggerated, but to an old, ill man who had been criticized by his own party before, who had been deposed from power and had had to fight his way back, they would have been powerful indeed. So Mao sought to play a balancing role, letting the factions fight on and warning them not to get carried away.[233] It was a policy that sought to maintain his own primacy, and it threatened all that China had gained.

Thus, in 1974, Mao would tell Jiang Qing not to oppose him on Deng being sent to the United Nations and would urge her to maintain party unity.[234] The very fact that she had to be warned not to oppose him spoke volumes; typically, this had not been a point that needed to be made. He would tell her that she could not go around doing as she pleased, that there was a system.[235] To be warned by Mao and get away with it: that spoke of a certain confidence in one's position. On May 3, 1975, addressing the politburo at Zhongnanhai, he urged his comrades not to go around forming factions like a Gang of Four, but the Gang endured.[236] All his directives, all his pleadings were futile. Jiang Qing knew how to admit to error without ceding power, how to flatter the chairman; the chairman, she would say, was not a man to yield on a point of principle.[237] And still the clashes between her and Deng went on.

In October 1975, Deng Xiaoping stumbled. Liu Bing, the party secretary of Qinghua University (Chinese universities come with party secretaries) had given a letter to Deng to pass along to Mao. Mao had, after a cursory glance, set it aside, only for Liu to send a second letter. At this, Mao was incensed. Had not he, Mao, been in Beijing? Why had the letter not come to him directly? Deng must be told not to get above himself.[238] Mao had been convinced that one of the factions in the party might overpower him and seize control of the country. Here was proof positive that Deng was trying to render him irrelevant.

So Deng was now criticized by Mao too. The object of such criticism, Mao said, was to promote correction of errors, not to overthrow the errant party; he had criticized Jiang Qing the same way.[239] To Deng, it made little difference. After all the effort put into wresting

China toward the modern world, after the shift to focusing on productivity and the signing of trade deals, after fostering relationships with America and Europe, he would find himself held responsible for the protests that broke out at Tiananmen Square in the wake of Zhou Enlai's death. It was Jiang who made the accusation; Mao kept his counsel. On July 4, 1976, Deng was relieved of all his posts, although he retained his party membership. He was sent away to a "safe place," all contact between him and the outside world severed. Hua Guofeng, a marginal figure in Chinese politics thus far, was appointed Mao's successor.[240]

Mao died on September 9, 1976. He had unified China and had, against formidable odds, kept it secure in the Cold War world so hostile to him and his revolution. He had done this by pursuing balance of power politics as shrewdly as any grand strategist of his time, as well as by using a military that had developed dramatically from the guerrilla band he had started out with. He had put China on the path to economic growth—which would be the ultimate safeguard for his diplomatic and military accomplishments. It was as secure as China had been at any point in the twentieth century.

He was responsible for the peacetime deaths of as many as forty million of his own people. He had let loose demons that could ravage all he had achieved. There had been foreign foes to face down, and he had done so. But the greatest threats to China came from within.

3

DENG XIAOPING and SEEKING TRUTH from FACTS

To his task as paramount leader of china, Deng Xiaoping would bring several distinctive sets of experience. The first was his passage to France, in the distant days when the PRC had not yet been founded. If you had traveled, as Deng had, by ship and stopped in at the ports of Hong Kong and Singapore, you would know of the thrum and excitement at the docks, of how the profits ships bear can be a lifeline to an entire country; you would feel, viscerally, the sense of possibility the ocean holds, in a way that someone who has traveled only by land never could.[1] You would see how entrepreneurial overseas Chinese could be, would turn to them for support when you arrived in France.[2] Mao could talk of the need for trade and getting support from the huaqiao (overseas Chinese), but these ideas would compel Deng's imagination with a force only direct experience can generate.

There was, too, a shrewd sense of politics. As a young man doing intelligence work for the CCP, he had changed his name from Deng

Xixian; he knew the value of secrecy and silence.[3] On the great debates of his time, he would appear generally orthodox, saying little and little that was memorable. It was not that he did not have ideas; he would speak when asked to offer a solution, and his time in the southwest revealed a man of some resource and resolve. It was just that he volunteered a minimum of information, steered clear of those long, discursive rambles Mao adored. The caustic wit, which would later be given freer rein, was there, but Deng Xiaoping, spy that he was, believed in leaving no trace.

One core belief that emerged early on was that in the primacy of the party. The country needed to be unified under the party's authority. The China in which Deng came of age was one that had been torn by civil war. Unity and order were needed to make it whole again. One needed to cherish the party, cherish the troops, cherish the base the CCP had founded; conversely, one had to oppose warlords, banditry, liberalism.[4] Those were forces that could destroy the party and, with it, the order it promised; as such, they had to be kept at bay. In this belief, he was a typical party member—and it was a belief that would be violated with complete and reckless abandon during the Cultural Revolution.

With the PRC founded, Deng would be dispatched to the southwest. While Mao was grandly strategizing from Beijing, Deng Xiaoping was working in the provinces. Day after day, as Mao's knowledge of the practical workings of the economy dulled, Deng's was honed: he was everywhere, doing everything, seeing how deep the damage to industry caused by decades of war had run, trying to get agriculture working again. Here he would emphasize the importance of the united front; there were some who had forgotten how large a role it had played in communist victory.[5] But it was Deng too who helped craft the agreement that brought Tibet into the PRC's fold. In its acceptance that Tibet's distinctive laity and domestic culture could endure as long as the PRC retained the rights to foreign policy and defense, the deal was a harbinger of the "one country, two systems" model that Deng would apply to Hong Kong and offer to Taiwan.[6] He was, even at this early stage, coming to the idea that political unity did not have to mean a uniform socioeconomic system, that one could do things differently in different parts of the empire. (Mao, of course, understood this too; it was remarkable how similar the two men were in their flexibility when it came to governance. The problem was that Mao's flexibility sometimes took him too far, sparking fires like those of the Cultural Revolution.) It was a practical idea: whatever worked to sustain the country over the long term, Deng would use. That practicality would later bring about his downfall.

In its dismantlement of central authority and the united front, in its reckless abandonment of all that was practical and functional, the Cultural Revolution represented everything Deng Xiaoping was against. He was purged during those years and dispatched to labor in Jiangxi. Life was simple here. In the morning, he worked; in the afternoon and evening, he studied, read, looked at the newspapers.[7] He did not have much money: two hundred and five yuan per month did not go far with nine people in the family. But the party had its regulations, and he would, he said, adjust to his new life.[8] There was comfort, perhaps, in his son joining him and eventually being transferred to proper medical care: Deng Pufang had been crippled by the Red Guards. It was one more lesson in the dangers of anarchy, of letting young people do as they wished without proper supervision. The chaos the Red Guards had unleashed had destroyed his son's life and wrecked the country he had worked so hard for. For Deng Xiaoping, the political and the personal went hand in hand.

He was, despite all that had befallen him, still ambitious. There were people within the party who still supported him; Mao himself had often pointed out that Liu Shaoqi and Deng were different, implying that the latter could be rehabilitated. And Deng would do all he could to claw his way back into the party's inner circle. He himself had no documents on Lin Biao, he wrote to Mao from exile; all he had was his memories, which suggested that Lin was a bad man, jealous and intolerant. (Lin Biao, whose generalship had helped win the civil war, who had spoken up for Mao when Liu turned against him—Lin had been vanquished in a power struggle with the chairman. He died in a plane crash. But there were those in the armed forces who remembered him fondly.) His own health, he added hopefully, was still good; he could still do some work. He wanted a chance to atone for his errors, return to the chairman's side, and serve the revolution.[9] He knew exactly how to flatter and cajole his way into power.

Summoned back to Beijing for service, he met Mao for the first time in years. "How," Mao asked him, "have you passed the years?"

"Waiting," said Deng.[10]

He had waited a long time, and he was done waiting now; in Mao's last years, he was a veritable dynamo, going everywhere, meeting everyone, doing everything, trying desperately to drag this vast, chaotic country that had been bent on self-destruction into the modern world. It was Deng who argued that China needed, when all was said and done, to embark on the four modernizations.[11] The military budget, he pointed out, was sky high; one needed to keep an eye on the country's economic capacity too. The troops' fighting capacity needed to be appraised realistically; it would not do to deceive oneself.[12] There was to be an emphasis on science, on modernity in military goods.[13] It was the precise drive for military modernization, for balance in the demands the military placed on the economy, that would become the hallmark of his own reign as paramount leader.

Meanwhile, he was doing diplomacy too. He spoke at the United Nations General Assembly in 1974, the face of new China before the world. He made clear to Secretary of State Henry Kissinger that China would not compromise on Taiwan. He told the Okinawans that China supported their cause, that foreign occupation of their island should end.[14] He explained the finer points of China's nuclear policy to Pakistan: China could not support the idea of a nuclear umbrella, because it ceded control to larger powers that would try to control other countries. A no-first-use policy, particularly toward countries that did not have nuclear weapons themselves, was infinitely preferable.[15] He was charming to the Japanese: resolving the Diaoyu / Senkaku Islands dispute, he said, was something that could be put off for a while. The great thing was to enjoy good relations.[16] Insofar as was possible, China would seek to be on good terms with just about every state—and Deng was the person enacting that policy. He was, Mao said, a person some feared, but resolute in getting work done.[17] An ambitious, unquenchable man, finally given permission to do what he thought necessary.

The basic grand strategy that Deng would pursue during his time in power, then, was already in place during Mao's last years. The overarching goal—keeping China secure—would remain the same. The main adjustment was in economic policy. Mao would have agreed with Deng that staying secure required a sound economy; the difference was that Mao did not understand economics, was too prone to wild flights of experimentation and too unwilling to digest the consequences. On the balance of power, their instincts were the same: they sought to stay as close to other states as they could without compromising on core interests. Deng was able to rest easier in his attempts to do so because of the geopolitical situation he inherited from Mao, a situation Mao had played no small role in creating. Both men recognized the need for a modern military and would work hard to forge one.

But Mao had done one other thing. He had left the party torn asunder, with many of its members in the grip of a crazed, destructive ideology. And those ideologues, unhappy with the power Deng was wielding, would seek to oust him again. He had, in an uncharacteristic moment of indiscretion in 1962, made his infamous comment about it not mattering whether a cat was black or yellow (later, he would turn the cat white) as long as it caught mice.[18] Mao's desire for a positive verdict on the Cultural Revolution, Deng's suspected role in turning out angry crowds for Zhou's funeral, and his acting as a filter for correspondence to Mao—all these combined to allow his enemies to oust him from the party again. He had come so close to being allowed to modernize China; now he was cast into the wilderness once more.

He still had supporters within the party, and with Mao dead and the Gang of Four arrested, he would make yet another comeback. But in doing so, and in setting the country back on the course he had charted in those halcyon years of 1974–1975, he would have to engage in a dazzling act of intellectual warfare—and it was this that would make everything else possible.[19]

The Great Reformation

It was deeply ironic that Hua Guofeng of all people would do what Mao, Deng, and Zhou had failed to do: take on the Gang of Four. He had risen to power in alliance with the Gang; when Mao—done with Liu Shaoqi, done with Lin Biao, done with Deng—had anointed him as his successor, he had been a nonentity. Perhaps because he had not achieved anything of note, perhaps because of his sheer insignificance, Hua was able to move against the Gang more effectively than Deng could. Hua Guofeng, whose only qualification was that he looked like Mao, whom the Gang would never see coming, until he arrested them and put them on trial.[20] And there was irony upon irony: it was the neutering of the Gang, Hua's greatest accomplishment, that laid the seeds for his own gradual demotion. For with the Gang's power broken, Deng's allies within the party would start calling for his return. Those brief tastes of modernity had been addictive, and Deng, who still felt he had some work left in him, was eager as ever. The party, with Hua as leader, had won a great victory—in which he, Deng, rejoiced like everyone else.[21] He was a survivor of the Mao era; he was an expert in the art of reassuring flattery. Hua would remain insecure about Deng—how could he have felt otherwise?—and Deng would take care, especially in his early days back, to appear as unthreatening as possible. Hua was confirmed as chairman; Deng made clear he would not be competing for the post. He understood—perhaps it was the experience with Jiang Qing that had driven the point home—that tremendous influence could be exercised without the chairmanship. One could perhaps achieve even more working in the shadow of a chairman, refusing to take credit for good deeds, explaining that decisions were collective, that someone else was in charge when things went wrong. It was not the title that counted, not the trappings of office, but power—and power was a function of support within the party, of having allies in the right places and minimizing enmities.

To shore up support, one would have to convince party members that they were not departing from Mao Zedong thought. Mao himself had been flexible enough in his beliefs to embrace the four modernizations, freer trade, the self-tilled land, and the opening to the United States; Deng too was no ideologue. But the beliefs purveyed over the

past decade or so had resonated with others. Like religious fanati-
cism, they had permeated people beyond the central leadership, and
in doing so had morphed into something almost ridiculous, something
the leadership would be hard-pressed to stop. In Guangdong, Deng
told his economic advisor Zhao Ziyang, he had heard of places where
raising three ducks was socialism, but raising five was capitalism. This
was most strange.[22] But it was one thing to grumble to Zhao in private;
it was another to gentle party members into a more reasonable frame
of mind. They had, after all, believed or purported to believe in Mao
Zedong thought; to ask them to abandon it entirely would be forcing
them to admit that they had been wrong, culpable. It would not do,
therefore, to frame reform as a repudiation of ideology and revolution. Rather, the party must be convinced that Deng's program was a
refinement, a further step along a road that China had already been
following, had been destined to follow. To interpret Mao too literally,
Deng told Hu Qiaomu—hitherto custodian of ideological rectitude—was to destroy the entire system of Mao thought. It was the
essence of the thought that one had to follow—and this could not be
done by focusing myopically on what Mao actually said. Letting
salaries of fifty yuan rise to a hundred or even two hundred would
not turn China capitalist.[23] The most basic tenet of Mao Zedong
thought, Deng reminded his comrades, was to seek truth from facts;
only by doing this could the party safeguard the tradition Mao had
bequeathed to it. And seeking truth from facts, one saw that four
little tigers—South Korea, Taiwan, Singapore, Hong Kong—were
bounding ahead at a tremendous pace, their trade with the outside
world burgeoning, their power growing. Why could China not do
the same? Global conditions favored it: the Western, developed, capitalist countries were interested in strengthening it (for a strong China
would boost their profits); seeking an outlet for their capital, they

wanted to offer China loans. And yet China's heads remained clouded with old, unworkable ideas; they hovered between those and that bright, reachable future. China kept talking about the four modernizations, but it had yet to move beyond empty talk.[24] He was, well before that famous 1978 plenum, fighting to make economic modernization ideologically acceptable to the party.

It was an extraordinary feat—and Deng's capacity to achieve it showed a deep understanding of human nature. True, Mao had been so contradictory on economic policy that it was possible to find just about anything consistent with his thought. But it was Deng, persuasive of speech and indefatigable in spirit, who made the case, Deng who ingeniously set his interpretation of Mao in opposition to that of the Gang of Four. The Gang had caused so much damage, so much suffering, that if they were shown to be against a policy, the policy itself assumed an aura of virtue, nobility. Mao Zedong thought did not occur in a vacuum. It was an augmentation to Marxism-Leninism. It had a purpose: the protection and well-being of the party and people. That that purpose had been thwarted was down to the destruction wrought by the Gang of Four, going back to their association with the Lin Biao affair.[25] Their version of ideology and acceptance of their version of ideology constituted a betrayal of Mao. He, Deng, who had suffered the Gang's evil, was a far better arbiter of what Mao would have wanted. And Mao, Deng maintained, would have approved Deng's policies.

This was, of course, far from sincere. Any vestiges of loyalty to Marx or Mao that Deng might have had were long gone. If capitalism was what it took, he would be capitalist, even if he was too shrewd to call it that. But he could go only so far. There were still pockets within both the military and the party that were fervently ideological, committed to their particular interpretation of Mao Zedong thought. And Mao—Mao with his Great Leap Forward and his Cultural Revolution—Mao had been the party made flesh. To criticize him too roundly, as Deng would admit to President George H. W. Bush in a moment of candor in early 1989, would be to deny an important part of the country's history; it could lead to ideological chaos and political instability.[26] And instability was the one thing Deng wished to avoid above all else; instability could tip into chaos, at which point all hopes of modernization could die. Seeking truth from facts and condemning past errors could only go so far. As it was, there were some people claiming that the party had ceased to exist during the Cultural Revolution; this, Deng argued, was patently false. There had been, to be sure, some organizational difficulties, but the party had continued to exist; it was during the dark days of the Cultural Revolution, after all, that China's global position had been strengthened.[27] People need something to believe in. This the party would provide; it would merely add economic modernization to the canon.

The achievement of the 1978 plenum in committing China to economic growth has long been celebrated. Lost in the celebration is the fact that the plenum only formalized ideas that China had, by 1978, been pursuing for a while and that it would have to work hard to continue to pursue.[28] It was not that Deng waved a magic wand at the plenum to cast China on the road to economic growth; rather, he used the plenum as a forum at which to declare victory and intent. Growth had a purpose: strengthening the country, sustaining the great China that had been so painstakingly put together. As such, the party would pursue growth in its quest for national security.

There were, broadly speaking, two ways of setting China's economic affairs in order: cutting expenses and boosting revenues. Aid recipients would have to be warned that China would be less generous than in the past. Mao had given aid as much as a matter of prestige as of grand strategy; it had won friends in a world where China needed them, but it had also become a matter of face—he would export grain even as China starved. Deng's approach was blunter: China was still a developing country, and till such time as it had developed, it would have to limit its obligations to others. On a trip to Nepal, as he celebrated the friendship between the two countries, Deng would explain that because of the damage wrought by the Gang of Four, China could not offer economic assistance at a large scale. More modest forms of assistance were possible. He would, in principle, let Nepal's planes fly over Chinese airspace, moot a railway in Tibet—but the days when Nepal could ask China to compete with India in providing aid were over.[29] A similar message would go out to other countries. The third world was important, Deng told his colleagues in 1981; assistance to it could take the form of increased visits or people-to-people contacts. But China had its own difficulties, so upping the aid budget was out.[30] The spirit of the Deng era was China first.

There were tougher measures yet. The state, Deng had long argued, was far too bloated: it would have to be trimmed, especially the military. There were too many troops, he announced on March 19, 1979, and it was important to cut them. There would not be a major war for ten years; there was no need, therefore, to be on such heightened and expensive alert.[31] That last point is worth emphasizing. It was not that Deng was a pacifist, bent on peace at all costs; rather, he felt that the geopolitical situation allowed China some breathing room in which it could balance its military expenditure with its economic base. The development of national defense had to be subordinate to economic development; otherwise, national defense would be hollow. The foremost imperative was to cut the number of troops; if this were done, one could use the money saved to make sure that the military was properly equipped.[32] Deng was anticipating an argument that would become popular in a few years: a military can grow too top-heavy for its economy, and that is when decline sets in.[33] Armed forces are meant to keep a country secure. They cannot do so if there is no money left to sustain them.

So there would have to be cuts. Part of carrying these out was instituting a proper retirement system; aged military cadres would have to go. There they sat, these famed heroes of battles of yore, their salaries and perks draining China's economy of its lifeblood. The youngest of them, Deng noted caustically, was sixty-four or sixty-five. Most of the officials at headquarters were already over sixty-five; in five more years, they would be over seventy.[34] This was no way to run a country.

And there were demographics. More than any other country, perhaps, China was haunted by the Malthusian specter: too many people and not enough food. Traditionally, Deng explained to a United Nations official working on population issues, Chinese held that the more children they had, the better; they were a form of wealth. But population growth, once incentivized by the government, had now outstripped increases to productivity, forcing China to implement a one-child policy. The goal was to keep the population from exceeding 1.2 billion by the century's end. Tough as it was, China would have to do it; otherwise it would be unable to develop or offer its people a better standard of living.[35] Population control was intimately connected to the four modernizations—and it was much harder to implement.[36] The West did not require a one-child policy, Deng believed, because people there did not want a high population, thus providing an automatic mechanism for population control.[37] In China, the mechanism would have to be provided by more draconian means. It was an intrusive, cruel policy—and its consequences would go well beyond those Deng intended—but it made a crude strategic sense. The logic was the same as that behind the four modernizations. To be secure, a country has to be well off, and to be well off, it cannot have too many people.

Cutting costs was just one part of the equation. To truly fix its problems, China would have to increase productivity too. Deng's instinct here, whether with agriculture or with trade, was to see what was working and then create conditions to allow it to work better. His mind was racing ahead: he saw possibilities everywhere for removing the stoppers that had held the Chinese economy in check for so long. He would learn from everyone here. There were advisors from Japan, conversations with Singaporean leader Lee Kuan Yew, exchanges with Western economists and intellectuals telling him what would help; above all, perhaps, there were his own observations of China, of the supply chains stretching in surreptitiously from Hong Kong, and of the self-tilled land that had proved productive during the darkest days of the Great Leap Forward.[38] He had the sense, too, to have good lieutenants. Hu Yaobang and Zhao Ziyang, Xi Zhongxun and Wan Li, would all argue for the economic policies that came to be known as reform and opening. Wan Li, traveling in Anhui, would make the case for devolution and a certain autonomy in agriculture. If households could meet the demands of production, why not let them bear the responsibility for it and do as they would with the surplus, even if they did sell it on the market? The household responsibility system, as it came to be called, was in effect the old, self-tilled plot system that had existed even during the dark days of the Great Leap Forward, allowed to grow far beyond the 7 percent Mao had contemplated.[39] Of course, Zhao wrote to Wan Li and Hu Yaobang, one did not want to go too fast with changing production. That could make people uneasy, harming agriculture. One could contract production to the households in poor areas (which needed it most), let the places where collectives were working continue without household contracts, and, in places that were doing well with household production, continue with the experiment to see what happened.[40] Seeing what happened: it was the key to understanding not just agriculture but China's entire approach to the economy under Deng. If a policy worked, it could be persisted with. If it proved unrealistic (like a ten-year plan emphasizing heavy industry that Deng had formulated in the Mao years), it could be retired and China could move on.[41]

Agriculture was just one sector. There would have to be modern industry, international trade, investment, and perhaps most importantly, education for China to grow. Deng wanted to build a shipping industry to rival Japan's on the global market. Chinese ships could be cheaper than Japanese ones (the Japanese suffer from this bizarre idea that top quality should fetch top prices), could compete in the global market, and could get foreign exchange.[42] Foreign exchange, in turn, was crucial to developing the economy, to develop the coal, the metal, the petrol, the electricity that China needed; without those, it could not have its aircraft and its tanks.[43] The economy undergirds security, and developing the economy means reaching out to the world.

So Deng reached out. We have much to learn from you, he told the Japanese, and we need friends to realize our four modernizations.[44] He traveled to Japan in 1978. The peace treaty between the two countries would get the attention, but the commercial deals that followed were of far greater importance to China's future. There was already a long-term trade deal between the two countries, but it was worth only $20 billion, and Deng wanted more. He was not shy of asking for help: China needed capital, scientific assistance. He visited companies, observed techniques of production.[45] In those days, Japan seemed to be roaring back to great power status; more than any other country, perhaps, it provided a model for China to follow. "First: use; second: criticize; third: fix; fourth: create"—this was the path Deng saw for

China—it had worked well for Japan.[46] When Japanese scholars advised China to not focus exclusively on growth rates, but to develop infrastructure and energy (one thought was to raise the prices of coal and petrol while exploring hydropower), Deng paid attention.[47] Japan had done immense, irreparable harm to China in the past; now it would do China immense good.

America too was to become a partner. He wanted to send Chinese abroad to observe and study, he told the Americans in February 1978; and if Sino-American relations were normalized, it would boost the rate of trade between the two countries enormously. He, Deng, would be willing to go to Washington.[48] When the American trade envoy came to discuss textiles in 1979, Deng's vision stretched further. There was a lack of mutual familiarity with one another's markets and economies. To fail to develop trade between China and America, Deng said, would be disadvantageous to both countries. China wanted to open new avenues of trade and improve its solvency. The Americans needed to think beyond textiles; they should take the opportunity to explore other sectors and see what other trade links might be feasible.[49] There was a colossal impatience to the man; China had been dormant too long. Now, commerce would become an important part of the Sino-American relationship—so important that in 1983 Deng could mention technology transfer to Secretary of State George Shultz in the same conversation as Taiwan: such transfers were indicative of mutual trust.[50] By 1986, representatives of the New York Stock Exchange were welcomed to Beijing so that they could understand China better—not just the China of this century but the China of the next. Joint ventures were now possible; so too were sole proprietorships. And if these bearers of foreign capital were wary of China's legal system not being ready for such enterprise, China would work to resolve these difficulties step by step. The risk of investing in

China, Deng assured them, was minimal.[51] American Motors and Beijing Automotive Works would embark on a joint venture; IBM sold China computers and offered training in their use. Some of the technology had military applications, such as spectrum analyzers, which could be used in antisubmarine warfare.[52] This raised concerns in Washington, but trade went on. The opening of reform and opening was crucial in allowing China to catch up with the modern world.

Of course, there was blowback. People like Chen Yun were not thrilled by the new ways—Chen thought that China was going too fast, importing and spending too much—and it was important not to alienate them. Zhao, seeking to counter impressions that trade had created chaos, pointed out how great the achievements were, that problems were inevitable when conducting reform, but they could be addressed.[53] But for all the debate, the overall course toward greater economic linkage with the outside world was not to be reversed. There would be periodic cycles of tightening economic policy, even broken contracts that incensed Japanese investors, but the general trajectory China would follow was clear.[54] It was open for business and eager to make up for lost time.

There was room for economic relationships beyond the powerhouses that were Japan and the United States too. Deng sought greater trade with the French—and was savvy enough to invoke the idea of Europe as he did so (he would later maintain, in conversation with the Greek prime minister, that a strong, united Europe was good for international peace and stability).[55] When Zhao Ziyang told him that the Brazilians were interested in buying food and petrol, he was excited: he was alive to the importance of Brazil and eager to develop the relationship, not just economically, but politically as well.[56]

Above all, perhaps, he was interested in fostering links with the huaqiao. Everywhere he had traveled in Asia, he had seen Chinese; they were thriving economically, but they were living outside the PRC. Surely they could help China thrive too. They had to be reassured that they could keep their citizenship in Thailand, for example, although they were welcome to PRC citizenship instead, if they so wished.[57] They had to be wooed, persuaded that they had a role to play in fostering good relations between the countries they lived in and the country they were from. It would be nice, he told the British, if Hong Kong could encourage private investment in Guangdong; this would ease the pressure of mainlanders flooding into the still-British territory and spur economic growth in the PRC.[58] Guangdong and Fujian, whose people had been foremost in venturing beyond Chinese territory, should use the huaqiao for investment, technological development, the construction of factories; even if the eighty million people there grew rich before the rest of the country, there was no harm done. This was not capitalism. The great thing was to be flexible, to allow them to be economically active. Shenzhen, Xiamen, Shantou, and Zhuhai were to be made special zones, so as to take advantage of their proximity to economic hubs like Hong Kong, Macao, and Taiwan.[59] Taiwan was doing so well just across the strait; trade with that island could be developed.[60] As with agricultural reform, Deng was sailing with winds already behind him. There always had been a healthy underground trade in these places: smugglers and fishermen creeping in along that vast, porous coastline, taking advantage of kinship and clan to conduct commerce despite the government.[61] In Taiwan, as on the mainland, the government authorities had long worried about smuggling; it undermined authority, created political risks. Deng's great insight was that the trade served an important function and that it could, if boosted, become more important yet. Why not take advantage of forces already at work? Commerce with the huaqiao was an important part of Deng's grand strategy; where such traffic had once been seen as threatening to China, it was now seen as a key to growth and thus to national security.

Believing as he did in seeking truth from facts, Deng would take to the road to see how the policy was working. He had, he reported to his comrades in March 1983, traveled from Jiangsu to Zhejiang and thence to Shanghai. He liked what he had seen. Goods in the markets were abundant; the cadres' morale was high. There were new houses springing up; people were happy.[62] Still it was not enough; he was hungry, insatiably, burningly hungry, for more. Ideas and directives flew from him like sparks. Xiamen could do much of what a free port could; its airport could become an international one. Shanghai needed to build large hotels; it should encourage more foreign ventures, more imports. Port cities like Dalian and Qingdao were not special economic zones, but they could serve many of the same functions. Hainan needed to be opened up.[63] That island should, Zhao Ziyang would point out, be courting investment from Hong Kong and Macao, from the outside world. For countries like the United States and Canada, development had begun at the edges. China needed to follow their example; Hainan was a good place to try doing so.[64] That the economic experiments were working was not cause for complacency. It meant only that there was more—ever more—to be done and done swiftly.

The difference between Deng and Mao on political economy was tactical, not strategic. Mao too had grasped the idea that the economy was the final guarantor of national security; it was only that having understood as much, he had little idea of what to do. He would veer into the Great Leap Forward, suggest expanding the self-tilled land, but never expand it as much as needed; he would seek trade, but only in his final years did he allow Deng to exhibit a fervent commitment to it—and he was too proud and too insecure to relinquish full control of economic planning to someone who understood it better. The basic precept driving Deng was the same: the difference lay in his approach to economic policy. He would, cautiously, let what was working work. There would be no utopian schemes—only a persistent, unflagging drive to modernize and grow over the long run. There was no transforming China's economy overnight, but the policies pursued in the seventies and eighties created the conditions that made the miracle years that followed possible. That Deng was able to pursue such a course was due largely to the favorable geopolitical situation Mao had helped achieve. That he chose to pursue it and pursued it successfully reflected his own approach to policymaking.

Looking Outward

All these measures were geared toward fixing China's internal problems. Looking outward, the PRC had two main tasks: recovering lost territories and maintaining a favorable balance of power in its immediate neighborhood and with the great powers. Deng's approach to these tasks was based on a deceptively simple principle, the same one that had underpinned Mao's: differences on specific issues did not have to preclude an amicable relationship overall. His was not so much a willingness to compromise as a refusal to let failure to compromise scupper business. He would not back away from the defense of core interests, but he was willing to agree to disagree, to let matters take their course and see where things wound up over the long run. The "one country, two systems" model, the idea of joint development in contested territory, the management of relations with the United

States—all reflected the understanding that specific issues mattered only so far. It was the overall balance of power that the PRC needed to bear in mind.

Hence his handling of Hong Kong, still in British hands when he took charge. It had to be made clear to the British that sovereignty over Hong Kong was not something China was about to abandon; China was getting Hong Kong back by 1997, and not just the New Territories but the island, Kowloon, everything. To do otherwise, Deng scoffed to the British in 1982, would mean that the current Chinese leadership was like that of the late Qing dynasty: weak of will, like Li Hongzhang, bartering the country's sovereignty away.[65] That would not happen now. But asserting sovereignty did not mean transforming Hong Kong's system. Hong Kong had been good for China; as Zhao pointed out to his British interlocutors, trade and investment across the divide had benefited Guangdong. Plans were being made for a highway between Hong Kong and Shenzhen—proof positive that things were going well.[66] All of which meant that there was no reason to bring about major changes in Hong Kong once the Chinese took over. Like Tibet once upon a time, Hong Kong could retain its distinctive way of life under PRC rule—in this case capitalism. Hong Kong, Deng told the British viceroy, was a part of China, but a special part; the PRC had no intention of destroying what made it special. Nothing would be done to harm investment in Hong Kong; this was a long-term policy. Hong Kong could retain its capitalism while the mainland remained socialist. There was room in the PRC for both.[67] He would make the case directly to Hong Kong's businesspeople too. Nothing would change with the handover, he promised: not the social or economic system, not the law, not Hong Kong's capacity for free trade or its status as a financial center, not its way of life. Beyond troops—and the troops were coming in to defend the country, not to meddle in Hong Kong's internal affairs—China would not be sending cadres to the region. The PRC was recovering sovereignty; it had no intention of harming Hong Kong's stability.[68] In this, one suspects, he was sincere. Deng was a practical man. He knew that governance worked best when the governed were cooperative, and they were most likely to be cooperative if their basic needs were being met. It is difficult to imagine him conducting a policy toward Hong Kong similar to that of Xi Jinping—not because he was a kindlier man, but because the waste, the pointlessness of it, would have appalled him. If the basic interests of Hong Kongers were not damaged, they were unlikely to revolt—and the fruits of capitalism there would be beneficial to the PRC too. In its political philosophy, "one country, two systems" was a descendant of the seventeen-point agreement in Tibet. The same state could contain different ways of being. As long as things worked, there was no reason to change them.

The formula having been worked out, it could be applied to other places. In this too Deng was like Mao: a solution to a specific problem having been worked out, it could be applied elsewhere. Marx, Deng said, never came up with "one country, two systems"; this was something unprecedented in world history (a touch of pardonable grandiloquence here; there was something almost endearing about his pride in the idea, like that of a little boy who had spotted something his elders had missed), which the CCP had come up with as it encountered reality. It could be used with Taiwan.[69] The point was the unity of the Chinese people. (He would be wary of using this rhetoric though: it was all right for the diaspora to use it but better, perhaps, for the PRC to tone it down. Deng was alive to the idea that smaller countries, even the Chinese people within them, might be suspicious of the PRC's intentions; his country was too large to appear unthreatening.) It did not matter what those people's political persuasions were; Communists and those who cursed the Communists could unite on the basis of nationality. The "one country, two systems" formula could be applied to Macao too.[70] It was pertinent not just to Hong Kong or Taiwan, he gushed to an American huaqiao, Chen Shengshen, in August 1984, but to the entire world; wherever there was a global "hotspot," this solution could be used. The world's problems did not necessarily require the use of force. "One country, two systems" offered an alternative.[71]

This did not prove quite as effective as he had hoped. Hong Kong and Macao would return to the PRC fold, but Taiwan was a different matter. He would bring up "one country, two systems" with President Ronald Reagan as a solution to the Taiwan problem in 1984. There was room for peaceful talks across the strait, which could lead to reunification. If the Americans persisted with former secretary of state John Foster Dulles's line on Taiwan, it would, someday, become a flashpoint.[72] When he finally signed an agreement on Hong Kong with British prime minister Margaret Thatcher in 1984, he would urge her to explain the Sino-British cooperation on Hong Kong to Reagan. Reagan, he told Thatcher, had seen "one country, two systems" as a possible model for Taiwan; there was much that the United States in general and Reagan in particular could do to solve the cross-strait problem. He had provided extensive reassurances to the Iron Lady about how China would abide by the agreement and refrain, for fifty years, from any changes to Hong Kong's system.[73] He had a vested interest in showing the world that China would keep its promises. The better the promise of "one country, two systems" in Hong Kong, the more likely the Americans were to pressure Taiwan to accept a similar model.

The problem was that Taiwan, ambiguously protected as it was by the Taiwan Relations Act, did not feel the same compulsion to accept the "one country, two systems" offer. Hong Kong and Macao had no choice; Taiwan had at least a chance of one. Deng was correct in noting that the Hong Kong solution made them nervous, increasing the pressure on them to accept a similar deal.[74] But the American commitment to defend Taiwan, Deng realized, hampered the PRC's outreach with Taiwan's officials: Taiwan would not have to concede sovereignty to the PRC as long as America might come to its defense. Deng would rail to the Americans about this, but to no avail. In Taiwan, there was a fervent debate about how to respond to the "one country, two systems" offer. Wei Yung, a political scientist who worked in the Executive Yuan, would argue that multisystem countries were workable and that this might be where Taiwan's future lay.[75] But old-school GMD officials like Wang Sheng would be skeptical; they had seen too much of the CCP to trust Deng easily. The 1978 plenum, according to the Liu Shaokang, a special ROC government unit responsible for policy toward the Communists, was a menace to the ROC's security. The CCP's rapprochement with the United States, its appeals to the Japanese and Western Europeans for understanding, and its willingness to appear reasonable on the Taiwan question—all these undermined the ROC. The Communists, the Liu Shaokang held, were using the Taiwan independence movement to weaken the GMD. There is no proof of this, but it seems plausible: exploiting local discontent in order to overthrow an existing government structure before taking over had been standard CCP practice in farther regions. The Liu Shaokang was preparing to defend itself against an ideological assault. Students would have to be monitored; they were prone to CCP manipulation. Smugglers and traders were suspect too; the Communists were trying to use their lust for profit to take over the ROC—what else could Deng's proposals for trade, his request that the huaqiao invest in the motherland, possibly mean? Each of Deng's proposed three cross-strait links—transport, trade, and mail—was to be rejected. In particular, trade with the mainland was to be strenuously impeded (although even the Liu Shaokang acknowledged that it would be difficult to stop trade that went via a third party); the Communists were playing shamelessly on the people's lust for profit. Beijing was working to win hearts and minds among the huaqiao; the ROC would have to do the same.[76]

Hong Kong, where the Communists seemed to be so successful, would be an especially fraught battleground. This talk of nationalist sentiment, of a greater China, would have to be countered by reminding the Chinese scattered across Asia that Deng and his cohort remained, irredeemably, communist, with all the dangers that that involved. In its reading of how Chinese grand strategy would seek to work, the Liu Shaokang was shrewd: it knew the mechanisms, the pressure points, the agents of change that Deng would seek to use. Less shrewd was one of its proposals for how to strike back. The ROC would need to win over communist officials; if it could convince a certain number of them that this man Deng was no different from Mao or the Gang of Four, it could bring down this new, dangerous foe. Taipei could work, too, to deepen the contradictions between Deng and Hua Guofeng; there was no way the Communists could stay this united.[77] Given all that had happened in the recent past, the plan was understandable, but it showed how hopelessly dated the ROC's understanding of its rival was. Deng had long moved past this; his problem was not being conflated with Mao, but being accused of having moved too far from Maoism. Taiwan would be vulnerable to the PRC's blandishments; it had had, after all, such a conflicted, tormented identity. On the one hand, it had been told it could not forge an identity of its own, that its destiny remained union with the mainland over which it was sovereign; on the other, now that union seemed to be possible, it was being told that union was unacceptable, that it would have to resist siren calls to the contrary. There were two different visions of how to deal with China: the Liu Shaokang's counteroffensive and Wei Yung's more accommodating position. Jiang Jingguo, who had succeeded his father, Chiang Kai-shek, as leader of the country, would let the two sides argue back and forth, permitting the extension of gentle feelers to the mainland, trying to sound out the possibilities but never committing one way or another. There would be trade, greater linkage, but full acceptance of sovereignty never happened. On a clear day on Little Jinmen, you can still see the words "One country, two systems" winking at you from the mainland: a blandishment, a promise still unfulfilled.

"One country, two systems," Deng would explain to the Burmese, was a form of peaceful coexistence.[78] So too was Deng's other grand idea: joint development, another concept China had invented on the basis of its encounters with reality.[79] There were various points around the globe—and quite a few of them in China's neighborhood—where sovereignty was in dispute; there was no need, however, to let an abstract principle get in the way of profit. Not that Deng would concede the principle; he would simply not let it become an obstacle to getting along. Many maps, he told the Filipinos, showed that the Nansha Islands were a part of China. But there was no need to let the dispute stand in the way of a good relationship between Beijing and Manila. Why not develop the resources in the territory together? One could always discuss a final settlement of the territorial dispute later. The Filipinos were receptive to the idea.[80] He would push his luck on this in 1988, suggesting that with Chinese sovereignty recognized, the regional claimants to the islands could proceed with joint development and refrain from sending troops there. The islands were minuscule; there were no people living there, not much grain; beyond a few hydrocarbons, there was little to claim. Joint development—and China being sovereign had the right to make such a proposal—would be in everyone's best interests and preserve the peace.[81] He would not insist on immediate recognition of sovereignty as a precondition to such development; that would be counterproductive. In its willingness to shelve a dispute and get along with business, Deng's proposal was consistent with Mao's approach not just to territorial disputes, but to foreign relations in general. One could not let specific disagreements hamper the development of a sound overall relationship. And this flexibility was something the world could learn from. China, he explained to the Italians, could insist on recovering the territories that had historically belonged to it, or it could pursue joint development. The latter approach was one that could be used elsewhere: the British and Argentines could try it on the Falkland Islands. "One country, two systems" and "joint development" constituted peaceful coexistence: this was how China would seek to manage its disputes.[82]

Since China was no longer doling out money to third world countries with quite the same largesse, it would have to find other ways of making its commitment to those countries clear. South-to-south cooperation would become the rallying cry; Zhao Ziyang would make speeches about it in Cancun in 1981, when leaders from around the world gathered to discuss poverty reduction in the developing world. The Cancun summit was seen as an opportunity to show that China stood firmly on the side of the third world, against hegemony; there were possible advantages to isolating America. But it was important, too, to sound a positive note, to declare that south-north dialogue was in the interests not just of the global south, but of the developed world as well, and crucial to global peace and stability. China supported global talks and the solution of concrete problems.[83] It believed in economic cooperation among third world countries, in the greater unity of free peoples. Outside hegemony was to be frowned on—whether it came from the Soviets or from the Americans. China remained, he reminded Guinea-Bissau, a victim of such aggression; the Americans still sold weapons to China's Taiwan.[84] It was the interference of the great powers that had set the third world to fighting among itself. The sooner the third world ended such interference, the better. Not that Zhao was above all such interference; if the Americans could see their way toward helping the third world—and China was, he acknowledged to Richard Nixon, critical of the American role there—it would be bad for Soviet hegemony.[85] It was the nature of the interference that counted. Zhao would visit Africa in 1983. He would be unable to give leaders there as much aid as they wanted, but he was able to find common ground in opposing hegemony.[86] It was important that the third world be reassured that China still cared about it.

One tool that came in useful was China's membership in the UN. Here, Deng informed the secretary-general, China would speak out on behalf of the global south; this was consistent with its duties. It took its responsibilities as a UN member seriously, and it would speak for the third world because it was against hegemony, for peace. He would not claim leadership of the third world; this would be presumptuous. It was simply a matter of making sure that these newly independent countries were not victimized again, of preserving international stability.[87] He would call for a fairer trade system, one that could bring more benefits to the global south, to those still impoverished. China advocated openness on trade; it would, ultimately, benefit both developed and developing countries to let emerging markets grow.[88] China's foreign policy, Deng said, had three planks: opposing hegemony, protecting world peace, and strengthening unity and cooperation with the third world.[89] And despite the changes wrought in

China's circumstances by the American willingness to be reasonable, he would not abandon the idea of seeking good relations where possible. Hence the joint-development proposals made to the Philippines and Japan; hence too the persistent attempts to achieve a rapprochement with India. Why continue to squabble over a few thousand square miles in the high mountains? It seems unlikely that he offered to swap the western sector for the eastern one—that would have undermined Chinese national security—but he was willing to keep negotiating.[90] One gained nothing by shutting talks down. And one gained nothing by assuming that negotiations with one country closed off negotiations with another; despite the talks with India, he would continue to celebrate the Sino-Pakistani friendship, telling the Pakistani prime minister that China remained concerned about Pakistan's stability.[91] You needed as many cards as you could get to maintain a favorable balance of power.

A similar pragmatism marked China's relationships with the great powers, although there were limits to how far it would go. It would try to remain closer to the major powers than they were to one another—Beijing voiced skepticism about Washington's attempts to reach arms control agreements with Moscow for a reason; that fear of being left out in the cold, of larger powers ganging up on it remained intact—but certain core interests had to be protected. Good relations with other countries were important, but they would remain good only if other countries were clear on what China would and would not compromise.

The relationship with the United States illustrated the problem best. For all Henry Kissinger's smooth assurances, the American commitment to the ROC remained intact when Deng took power, and Washington would need to know that this was unacceptable to Beijing. Now that they were talking to one another, the Americans kept wondering what normalization would take. Deng would explain to American secretary of state Cyrus Vance that the United States would have to meet three conditions: withdraw its troops from Taiwan, renounce its defense treaty with the ROC, and sever diplomatic relations with it. To ask the Chinese to repudiate all intention of using force to recover Taiwan, as Washington was doing, was intolerable. Not that China was dying to use force; it was simply that Taiwan was an internal matter, and the PRC reserved the right to deal with it as it saw fit.[92] Until such time as the Americans adopted the appropriate attitude toward Taiwan, there could be no normalization. President Jimmy Carter was, of course, welcome to Beijing, but Deng could not visit Washington as long as there was an ROC diplomatic mission in town. The problem dogging Sino-American relations was not a diplomatic one—on diplomacy, on the global balance of power, the two countries had, as had been the case when Kissinger visited, interests in common—but a political one.[93]

Deng would make it to the United States eventually. The Americans would meet the three conditions and relations would become normal, although Washington's policy on Taiwan was never quite what Kissinger had promised. Deng was incensed by the Taiwan Relations Act (which among other things, provided ambiguously for the United States to come to Taiwan's defense in the event of an attack), by American weapons sales to Taiwan—but he would not permit anger to kill the relationship; even as he denounced the Taiwan Relations Act to the Americans, he would call them his friends; friends ought to pay attention to a problem like this one.[94] There would be warnings from Zhang Wenjin, a Chinese diplomat: the act constituted interference in China's internal affairs. The Americans kept saying it was a concession to internal politics, but this was a major problem for the PRC. How would the Americans feel if, citing special concern, the Chinese were to launch an Alaska Act or Hawaii Act? The United States and the Netherlands were the only two countries to have continued selling weapons to Taiwan after the establishment of diplomatic relations with the PRC. Sino-Dutch relations, Zhang warned, had suffered as a result.[95]

But the key principle in dealing with the Americans—as in dealing with everyone else—was not to let specific problems get in the way of the overall relationship. "I say this," Deng said to Nixon as he concluded a litany of complaints about the Taiwan Relations Act and arms sales, "because you are our old friends."[96] There was so much else to discuss between the two sides. Trade was an issue, with agricultural imports (Hu Yaobang would explain to Nixon not to hope for too much here) and imports of technology, including defensive weaponry, on the agenda.[97] Taiwan was, however sensitive, however emotional, just one strand in a larger web of interests. China and America had their differences, as Deng acknowledged to an American delegation, but those differences had to be judged in a larger context— in which context, nurturing the Sino-American relationship was of key importance.[98] Trade and scientific exchange with America, after all, were necessary to China's four modernizations. Geopolitics, too, drew them together. The invasion of Afghanistan had brought the Soviets far too close to Xinjiang; the PRC would stand with America against the threat.[99] Progress on the Korean peninsula would demand similar cooperation. Deng had kept Kim Il Sung informed of the progress on normalization; Kim expressed approval of the progress, hoping that Deng would use his time in the United States to introduce Pyongyang's plan for an independent, unified, peaceful Korea.[100] When he visited the White House, Deng would propose a new push for peace on the Korean peninsula. Talks between the two Koreas should include not just the governments but parties, people; the United

States, China, and Japan should all be encouraging the two Koreas to negotiate.[101] Relationships are never purely bilateral; they are enriched and encumbered by all the other connections the states involved have. From the Soviet Union to Korea, Japan to Vietnam, Chinese interests demanded a decent working relationship with the United States. To sacrifice those interests purely because of continued disagreements on Taiwan would have been folly. It was a point Deng would make when Reagan swept to power, questioning the one-China policy. It was important, Deng impressed on then vice presidential candidate George H. W. Bush in August 1980, that Reagan understand the overarching importance of the Sino-American relationship, its significance as an organizing piece in the global order.[102] Reagan, Deng explained to his comrades at an enlarged meeting of the politburo standing committee, would have to be told that China viewed the relationship from a strategic perspective.[103] He would echo the point to the Americans in 1982: one had to view the relationship from a strategic angle, respecting the interests of both one's own country and the other.[104] The stakes were too large for pique.

The same thinking underpinned Chinese relations with Japan and the Soviet Union. The aid, investment, and trade with Japan were simply far too valuable to jeopardize; one could agree to disagree. Back in the Mao era, Zhou had maintained that there was no need to discuss the Diaoyu / Senkaku Islands dispute; Deng would follow the same tack. It was an issue that could be left to future generations to resolve. For now, the important thing was to have a good relationship. It was the same approach that had marked Mao's attitude to border disputes, the same refusal to let specific disagreements overcome general bonhomie that had made the Sino-American rapprochement possible and that would allow the PRC to move past the Taiwan Relations Act. He wanted not just contact between the governments, he would explain in 1982, but contact between the peoples—and contact that would go beyond just the economic. He was concerned, not that Japan would go militaristic again, but that there were a few people within Japan with outlandish ideas about militarism; it was just something worth flagging.[105] Hu would reassure the Japanese about China's own intentions: it educated its people, he said, that they should not seek revenge on Japan. He hoped that the Japanese would educate their citizens against militarism. This would be in the interests not just of the two peoples, but of the entire world.[106] Zhao would sound an early note of caution: Beijing was all for developing Sino-Japanese relations, but it could not tolerate revisions of history that minimized Japan's cruelty in the war (a change here from Zhou Enlai's casual gratitude for taking down the Nationalists). The Taiwan issue too remained a problem.[107] Despite Tokyo having severed diplomatic relations with the ROC, there was a lingering sympathy in Japan for Taiwan's plight. The textbooks troubled Deng. They were, he explained, things that would poison the next generation; they could thus kill the hope of Sino-Japanese relations improving with the passage of time.[108] There might be lingering distrust—which could fester, dangerously, as time went by—but Beijing's general approach to Japan had much to commend it. It deferred a dispute, allowing the two sides to profit in the interim.

With the Soviet Union, the issue was not so much avoiding a dispute as terminating threats to national security. The invasion of Afghanistan, Soviet support for the Vietnamese invasion of Cambodia, and Moscow's stationing of troops in Mongolia meant that China felt threatened, encircled by its northern neighbor. Hence the cooperation with the Americans in Afghanistan and the combination of skepticism and curiosity about the Strategic Arms Limitation Talks (SALT) between Moscow and Washington. The Soviets, Deng told Nixon, were basically social imperialists.[109] He was well schooled enough in balance of power politics, too, to reach out to the West Germans: China and West Germany had a neighbor in common in the Soviets, with Soviet troops poised at the gates of each. There was no harm in sounding out Bonn, seeing how the negotiations were coming along; there was room perhaps for cooperation against Moscow's menace.[110] You amass your pieces on the great global chessboard and take help wherever you can get it.

But the door to rapprochement with the Soviets was never closed. It would not do to become too dependent on the Americans, and although Beijing did not enjoy as intimate a relationship with Moscow as Washington did, there was no reason to eliminate the possibility altogether. Deng refused to sever trade with the U.S.S.R.; that would only alienate them, and besides, it would be bad for business. China would, as he owned to the Japanese, keep talking to them after the 1969 border clashes; these talks had stopped after the Soviet invasion of Afghanistan, but had now resumed.[111] The relationship would work best if they understood what made full rapprochement impossible: their policy on Indochina, Mongolia, and Afghanistan. In 1985, Chinese official Li Peng met President Mikhail Gorbachev in Moscow and laid out what it would take for Sino-Soviet relations to improve. The Soviets would have to abandon the idea that the Chinese were a younger brother in one big family. China was an independent country. (Remember Chairman Mao: We the Chinese people have stood up.) The Soviets should compel Vietnam to withdraw its troops from Cambodia. It was for the Cambodians to decide what was best for them.[112] The significant thing, as ever, was that the two sides were talking to one another. They were willing to make the relationship work. By 1987, Zhao was telling the Bulgarians that China was pursuing a complete normalization of its relationship with the Soviets, although the Cambodian issue stood in the way.[113] It was nice to be able to tell the Americans that Gorbachev was coming, even though, Deng confessed, they did not know what would come of it. Relations would not go back to what they were in the fifties, Deng said, but he did want an improved relationship. Bush would pronounce himself delighted that the Soviet leader was coming to Beijing, while noting that the American watchword in dealing with Moscow was caution.[114] It was a neat little play, performed with the utmost courtesy and to everyone's satisfaction; the point had been to get across to the Americans that China was not wholly reliant on Washington's goodwill, that it had other potential partners in the new world order. Even reassurance can bear an undercurrent of menace if need be. When Gorbachev visited in 1989, the Soviet policies that had bothered China had been remedied, and even Vietnam had announced that it would withdraw its troops from Cambodia—so Deng was more than eager for a rapprochement. There was trade to build up, a border to be negotiated where troop reductions would help.[115] With Beijing's conditions met, there was no reason to continue quarrelling: a better Sino-Soviet relationship made for a better balance of power. It was telling, after Tiananmen, that horrified although the Soviets were, they would refrain from criticizing Beijing. Dead students were sad, but it would not do to meddle in the PRC's internal affairs.[116]

Using Force

There was one exception to this generally defensive foreign policy, and it came early in Deng's tenure: the war with Vietnam.[117] There had long been border clashes, some by land, others over disputed rocklets—but in 1979, the conflict moved from sporadic clashes to all-out warfare. The Vietnamese, so the official central Chinese notification for war had it, were engaged in nationalist expansion, which was the same as regional hegemony. They were doing so with the support of the Soviet socialist imperialists; they were attacking the huaqiao and Chinese traders in their country and had invaded their erstwhile comrade in arms Cambodia. They were invading China's land and killing its troops; they were doing so in concert with the Soviets to the north, undermining the four modernizations. China would therefore fight—a limited war, to protect its own borders, one that would be followed by withdrawal.[118] To the UN secretary general, Deng would explain that it was opposition to aggression: great powers did not have a monopoly on invading their neighbors and trying to exert unjust control.[119] Assessing the great victory, the General Political Department would tick off many achievements. The war had brought the plight of the Cambodian liberation struggle to the world's attention; it had isolated the Soviets who had voted against a UN Security Council resolution calling for the Vietnamese withdrawal from Cambodia. It had made clear that the polar bear, as the Soviet Union was creatively dubbed, would not dare to send troops to China; the Soviets' strategic center was in Europe, and besides, they now knew the Chinese were prepared. A defense pact with Moscow, Vietnam would now know, was impotent. And finally, the war had made clear that China was a reasonable, responsible country, bent on opposing hegemony.[120] The list was long, but it ignored one brutal fact: the Chinese had been summarily defeated.

This does seem to have been a departure from grand strategy. The usual openness to keeping on talking—one that marked even relations with the Soviet Union—was absent in dealings with Vietnam; Beijing, it seems, refused to talk to Vietnam unless Vietnam withdrew its troops and agreed to a Cambodian government that would include the Khmer Rouge and Sihanouk.[121] With the Soviets, there had been conditions for normalization but not for talks; it would have been far more in keeping with the tenets of Chinese grand strategy if conversation, at least, had remained open. Deng, as human as any leader, would try to justify the defeat as a strategic victory: it had shown the hollowness of the Soviet commitment to Vietnam and shown Cambodia that it was not alone. And yet, all the war had done was to show that Vietnam, standing alone, could defend itself against China as surely as it had against the United States and France. Deng's was an ex post facto justification, designed to put a brave face on the matter. He had miscalculated; his troops had not been up to the task. In China's continued, futile insistence that Vietnam evacuate Cambodia, in its hopeless pleas that Southeast Asians resolve their disputes peacefully, there was more than a touch of frustrated impotence. It was reminiscent, in more than one way, of the American debacle in Indochina: Hu would find himself urging the Cambodians to unite; only once they created a united front, he explained, could they count on getting world sympathy. Vietnam, he promised, had overestimated its strength in Cambodia as surely as the Soviets had in their Afghan misadventure; the Vietnamese too would be defeated by righteous struggle.[122] But things did not turn out that way. China could not achieve the outcomes it desired in Southeast Asia. Even after the Vietnamese had announced that they would withdraw their forces, Deng remained dubious that they would do so.[123] The intervention was a reflex action, with unexpected consequences, far removed from the cold-blooded planning and reasonability that were typical of the man and the time. Only later, once the policy had proved bankrupt, would China resume talks with Vietnam. For all the rationalizations that would follow, the simplest explanation was probably the truest: Deng had made a mistake. Even the best of grand strategists have a hard time sticking to grand strategy unwaveringly. Being human, they behave inconsistently, yield to policy impulses far removed from what they planned to do. Deng Xiaoping had a plan that involved avoiding military entanglements. Vietnam was proof that even he could lose sight of long-term goals.

One thing the war showed was that the PRC had not renounced the use of force as an element of statecraft. (The point seems banal, but given how often the PRC would insist that it was a peaceful country and given how often foreigners would believe in its noninterventionist rhetoric, it is perhaps worth emphasizing.) Going forward—and the debacle of Vietnam underscored the need for this—it would seek to modernize its armed forces; the navy engaged Vietnam out among the Spratly Islands in 1988.[124] Deng believed in active defense: defense that was not merely a holding action but incorporated a counteroffensive. War was a protracted affair—and China had rich experience of this, from its war against the Japanese to its engagement in Korea. But it would need to modernize its forces to remain secure.[125] He would tread carefully here; men with guns can be unpredictable, and there were pockets within the troops who remained fervent fans of the Gang of Four. But he would not stop: there had to be reform. The PLA would have to rid itself of factionalism, undergo political training.[126] It would have to be reminded that it was the party—Deng's party—that exercised authority over it.

Cutting troops, as Deng wanted to do, did not mean weakening the military. It meant, instead, that the PLA would become a more streamlined, technologically advanced, and thus effective fighting force. China would need a proper air force: this was the first key to national security, and where the bulk of investment was to be focused. Without air support, your navy, your ground forces, everything was vulnerable to enemy attack.[127] Naval power was to be developed too, though Deng was content to confine it to the near seas. China did not need a blue water navy; it did not seek hegemony and therefore had no need to project power beyond its neighborhood. Active defense demanded a navy capable of defending interests in the immediate vicinity, no more, no less—and that is what Deng would pursue.[128] Such a policy would have helped reassure China's Southeast Asian neighbors too that the PRC was not becoming a territorially adventurous power. One of the best guarantors of security, as Deng's China saw it, was a secure neighborhood; Hu Yaobang would assure the Filipinos in 1982 that even as China rose, it would not be aggressive. It had suffered oppression itself and would not inflict the same on other people. Its constitution would demand as much.[129] Military capabilities were not to be pursued for the sake of capabilities; such pursuit could jeopardize the very security those capabilities were meant to provide. The country's needs would determine what type of means it should possess. Given China's geostrategic situation, as Deng read it, there was no reason for either needs or means to be infinite.

Not that China would give up on older forms of warfare altogether. Hu Yaobang, in particular, was aware that modernizing weaponry carried its own financial burden; the PRC could not, he explained to Somalia, abandon people's warfare altogether. The creation of a patriotic spirit, training people in martial matters, making sure that they could launch guerrilla war and respond when the country is invaded—these would remain important to the Chinese way of warfare.[130] That militiarized culture, the notion that everyone had a stake in national defense, would not go away just because China was entering the twenty-first century. As it entered the new world, China would bear old ways and means with it.

Perhaps the clearest demonstration of what Deng's grand strategy was for came with the Tiananmen Square massacre.[131] Reform and opening had been meant to protect the state. It had not been a prelude to democratization. He remained as convinced as ever that the state required stability, to which democracy was inimical. This conviction, it is worth emphasizing, was not one all party members shared. His acolytes had been willing, even eager, to move toward some form of democracy. The students had thronged to the square to commemorate Hu Yaobang, who had passed away and who had spoken out in favor of political reform. One of Zhao Ziyang's great mistakes, politically, would be to speak movingly of his former comrade, of what Hu had contributed to the party.[132] But in the students massed on the square, Deng saw only a threat to China's stability and thus its security.

Deng Xiaoping did not like young people. He was wary of the dangers of youth protest: it was a group of protesting students, after all, young, innocent, asserting their rights to participate in the political process, who had rendered his son paraplegic and driven him into exile. There were things young people did not understand, he explained in 1979—about the history of the party, of the revolution, of the bitter suffering that had been life under the Gang of Four; they had not been through what he and his cohort had been through; they could not know the complexities of life. They needed to be educated, trained to see that their interests and difficulties had to be judged in the context of what suited the country as a whole. Of course one wanted democracy. But democracy without centralized control at the top was useless. There had to be an organizing power with paramount authority—and this, it had to be made clear to the young malcontents, was the party.[133] It was an old man's grumble, but it was a heartfelt one; he would put all the resources at his disposal into making sure that youth did not run wild again. When the first student protests happened in 1986, he was quick to realize the stakes. This was not some lighthearted jape; it was a rabble, and rabbles could do great damage. The students were acting up, Deng told his colleagues, because the cadres were not making their authority plain; their attitude was too indecisive. Even then, the beliefs that would shape the response to the 1989 protests were clear. China could not have Western-style democracy. China could not consent to the termination of the party's authority. China would do what it had to, fearless of criticism from the outside world. What hope could China have if it sat back and let chaos fester?[134] Deng was honest, brutally so, with Secretary of State George Shultz: China had been through the Cultural Revolution and this could become a new Cultural Revolution. It threatened the four modernizations, for one could not have those without political stability.[135] He genuinely believed this. Everything he had experienced, from his early years as a revolutionary to his suffering during the Cultural Revolution, pointed ineluctably to the importance of stability. The party guaranteed stability; absent stability, one could not have economic growth, the four modernizations that were crucial to national security. To let the students protest as they wished would be to jeopardize all that Deng had achieved and all that he hoped to achieve in years to come. (It is one of the unfortunate features of the Sino-American relationship that perfect honesty almost always meets with polite disbelief. Deng was rationalizing, American intellectuals thought, justifying the party's position; that instability truly horrified him as much as he said it did, that he would invoke the Cultural Revolution, was just political posturing. It was nothing of the sort. Deng was saying exactly what was on his mind; he had known, from his earliest days, that China needed a strong state.) The 1986 protests would dissipate without much harm done, but Deng was primed for 1989. When the students took to the square next, they would be killed.

Of all the mysteries that continue to surround the Tiananmen Square massacre, the most puzzling perhaps is why it took Deng so long to summon the tanks. He was clear, as early as April 25, 1989, that the student protests could not be tolerated: chaos had to be stopped. There could be no hesitating out of fear of criticism, domestic or international. These protesters wanted to topple the CCP, destroy its economic policies of reform and opening, its four modernizations; they wanted to take a China with a promising future and transform it into a China without hope. They were like the perpetrators of the Cultural Revolution; the only thing they feared, Deng said, was the absence of chaos. "We still have a few million troops," he observed. "What are we afraid of?"[136] The personal and the political had always gone together for him; now they were coming together again. He had had to fight so hard to drag China into the modern world, had had to overcome being purged and purged again, had then had to combat the opposition of diehard ideologues. To lose it all now because one was afraid to do what was necessary was unacceptable.

So the troops went out, killing the young. In the aftermath, there were two things Deng would do extraordinarily well. The first was standing firm in the face of all the criticism he was receiving from foreign quarters. What China did to govern China was none of the outside world's business. When President George H. W. Bush wanted to send a special envoy for frank discussions, Deng was willing to welcome Brent Scowcroft to Beijing. But the basic principle to communicate to Scowcroft was simple: China would not tolerate any interference in its internal affairs.[137] When Bush's letter hinted that the responsibility for worsening Sino-American relations lay with China, Deng was adamant: it was the Americans who were responsible for the deterioration. They had upped their interference in

China's internal affairs; the sanctions they had had placed on China after Tiananmen harmed China. He hoped this situation would improve soon.[138] Even at this juncture, Deng knew better than to close off the possibility of improved relations. One would tell the offending country what one considered unacceptable; if the offender altered its behavior, one could go back to amicability. The funny thing was that he had not miscalculated. The world revolved, realized it needed China as part of the international system. Bit by bit, life returned to normal.

Standing down foreign critics was the easy part. There remained, within the party, a faction that believed that the protests could be attributed to reform and opening; the abandonment of Marxist-Maoist orthodoxy had led to the student protests. The case being proved, surely the party could now proceed to undo reform and opening. Here too, Deng would prove a formidable fighter. Tiananmen, he argued, did not prove that the entire strategic direction the country had chosen was wrong; it highlighted only the need to educate people better. The past decade had seen a rise in people's standard of living; reform and opening had had definite accomplishments, which one could not wish undone. There was still not enough of it; China had to go further, faster, with the development policies that had brought it so much success of late.[139] He had taken military action at Tiananmen for a cause: to secure China, which meant, as he had spent the past decade and a half arguing, securing reform and opening. To abandon the economic reform program would be to render the steps taken to deal with Tiananmen meaningless. There was a grand strategic goal; it was in pursuit of that goal that Deng had used force at Tiananmen. He would not lose sight of it now. Even in his long-awaited retirement—and the institution of a retirement system was something he considered one of his greatest accomplishments—when Jiang Zemin had taken over, he would not let reform and opening come undone. When news came to him that other party leaders wanted to roll back the economic reforms, he would take to the road, traveling south—to Shenzhen, to Shanghai—to trumpet the benefits they had brought. People here had become rich. Did they not have a stake in the maintenance of reform and opening? While the ideologues fought it out in Beijing, Deng, aged child of the revolution, knew that there was a China beyond the imposing halls and bureaucratic bickering of the capital, a China of flourishing markets and bustling trade, where he could find support among cadres and workers who were finally growing rich.[140] He would emerge victorious from this final march: a charming, invincible sprite of a man, who would bring reform and opening to China by any means necessary.

4

JIANG ZEMIN, HU JINTAO, AND THE VIRTUE OF DULLNESS

THE PROTESTERS HAD FALLEN OR SCATTERED, but China had yet to be made secure. The events of Tiananmen Square exposed the wounds of the state: the uncertainty of what the party stood for; the dependence of the civilian government on military power, and the potential danger that power posed; the restive murmurs of citizens in Beijing and beyond. Meanwhile, the world was changing around the PRC in terrifying ways. Communist regimes were tumbling away; the West, triumphant, preached the gospel of capitalism and liberal democracy. China would have to decide what it meant to be a socialist country and whether it wanted to continue being one. It would have to find a way of making itself whole. And it would have to do so in a world that was suddenly uncertain. Deng Xiaoping had issued his directives, but this was not enough; each passing moment brought the possibility of a different course, a possibility that had to be considered and responded to. The decisions to secure a state cannot be made just once; they must be made again and anew if the state is to survive.

Into this maelstrom stepped Jiang Zemin and Hu Jintao. These were technocrats, colorless men really, especially when compared with Mao Zedong or Deng. Jiang was not even supposed to have been in the position he found himself in after Zhao Ziyang's ouster; Hu seemed bent on making a virtue of blandness. And yet, in their wooden, unobtrusive way, they would weather trouble in the Taiwan Strait, riots in China's far west, financial crises, and an unpredictable United States. Luck had something to do with this, of course, but so too did grand strategy. As the old certainties faded around them, China's leaders seemed to realize both what responses change would require, and, perhaps more importantly, what had not changed, what had to be kept from changing. They would keep steering the country in the general direction Deng had set, persisting with reform and opening, and they would do the ideological work this required. They would continue to seek a balance of power in a world that for all the talk of uncontested American strength, they saw as multipolar. And they would continue to try to modernize the military, render it fit for the twenty-first century. There would be no bold, imaginative leaps of the kind that might have been required to deal with the problems piling up: the growing bulk of state-owned enterprises and corruption, the poison creeping into the waters and winds that would threaten to choke the life out of the country. Theirs was a conservative grand strategy (despite adjustments, the Jiang and Hu years were bound by a single grand strategy, a common blueprint for what China needed), stolid, not prone to adventure. But stolidity, although it bodes ill for creativity and boldness, can minimize disruption, thus allowing continued success. The PRC endured, even thrived, which had been far from certain when Jiang took office as general secretary of the CCP.[1]

The Importance of Ideology

A strange void had opened up in China with reform and opening, a nagging, spiritual hunger. Deng Xiaoping had opened the path to riches. There would be no more mass starvation. People could live in growing comfort; indeed, if they were enterprising, they could dream of making fortunes. But the price, whatever Deng's claims to the contrary, had been faith in the old verities of Maoism: of equality and heroic struggle, of the Chinese people standing up to fight a common foe. The pursuit of these ideas had led to great suffering and mass death, but they had, when all was said and done, given people something to rally around. In their absence, one was left longing for something to believe in.[2] Chen Yun had fretted about the ideological weakening of the party back in the Deng years, but it had been an abstract problem, not easily addressed; besides, China was too busy getting rich to grapple with the matter. Now Jiang found himself with a party confused about what it stood for and with a population that might well lose trust in its leadership.

Several responses to the situation were possible. One was to abandon reform and opening altogether: 1989 had demonstrated the perils of the program, and abandonment would satisfy the diehards longing for a return to the romantic fervor of Mao's time. (Deng would object, of course, but one could wait him out; age was not on his side.) One could also consent, as other socialist regimes were doing, to democratization and the possible termination of the party's authority. The emphasis Deng had put on warning that China would remain socialist suggested that at least some in the party were suspected of wanting such change. And finally, China could just muddle along.

All these options were open in the years following 1989. What Jiang chose to do was straightforward: he would continue to pursue Deng's path while bringing ideology back into fashion. There were ideas of human rights, democracy, and freedom floating around: what if these entered the party and created ideological chaos? There were some forty-eight million members of the CCP now—many of whom had entered the party's ranks during or after the Cultural Revolution; untempered by experience as they were, they would be vulnerable. They would have to be educated in ideological rectitude, in the ways of Marx and Mao, in the development of Marxism that was reform and opening, for it was from ideology that the party drew its strength. The party would have to continue with the traditions of criticism and self-criticism that produced unity. It would have to avoid revisionism.[3] There were party members who paid no attention to politics, to ideological work; while the mainstream trends within the party were good, the danger of corruption could not be underestimated.[4] This would have to change. There would have to be proper education for the young: on the China that was, its socialism, its culture, so that they could understand how difficult it was to transplant Western ideas to Chinese soil, how vulnerable they were to Western propaganda.[5] (There was a shift in emphasis here: Deng had talked much of education in his early years too, but he was mostly focused on science; it was after Tiananmen that educational efforts focused on cobbling together a more politically oriented curriculum.)[6] And there were, beyond the party members and the patriotic students, the ranks of China's faithful: men with long beards who could get guns from Pakistan, women wearing turquoise beads who kept alive the hope that the Dalai Lama would return, lost souls searching for meaning, drawn to house churches or the Falun Gong. More than Mao or Deng, Jiang understood that this was an expression of the deepest needs of the human soul. Mao would have insisted that people could be swept along by the tides unleashed by a great man; Deng, caustic and impatient, would have had no time for superstitious nonsense getting in the way of business—they would have tried to co-opt religion, but only because it made for easier governance. Jiang's musings on the subject reflected a sense that religious belief was a response to spiritual hunger. Religion, he explained, had existed a long while; it was beyond the state's power to eliminate it. Far better to bring it into harmony with socialism, to make clear that although the rights of the religious were respected, they were rights granted by the state. Education would be the main weapon: in a multiethnic, multireligious country, the government must ensure that the peoples stay united, socially stable, in one country. Religious autonomy was to be safeguarded, in China's fashion, for since there would be believers, it was foolish to alienate them. But believers, like nonbelievers, were to be educated in patriotism, socialism, and Marxism. The state would have to be wary of foreign religious entities; they could be agents of empire, intent on bringing the CCP down and China, so recently put together, with it. The party would have to take charge of religious work.[7] Jiang said this in December 2001, but he was following a train of thought that had exercised him for a long while; years earlier, he had spoken of Xinjiang, of the power of religion there. There were dangerous forces at work in that far-off region, foreign preachers seeking to split the territory from the motherland. This could not be permitted. The cadres—and they were to hail from all ethnic groups—had to remember that they served the government. Religious and nationality (the CCP's term for ethnic groups) policy would have to be made to work; there would have to be effective propaganda, proper education on Xinjiang's history, on how it was, irrevocably, a part of China. The constitution provided for religious freedom, but there was freedom for both believers and nonbelievers—and no freedom to separate from China. No foreign religious forces would be permitted to interfere.[8] There would be religious autonomy but with Chinese characteristics. One must monitor what those imams in the mosques were saying, make sure that the church pastors were properly licensed. Belief could be as dangerous as weaponry, which meant the party must remain paramount over it. In the PRC, there could be no religion without regulation.

The ideology Jiang preached was Deng's. He had, back in 1988, made his loyalty to Deng's ways clear; he spoke of the liberation of thought, of seeking truth from facts, of the need to deepen reform, of Deng's heroic contributions to China—all of which, naturally, were augmentations to the Marxist tradition.[9] Since he was claiming to persist with Deng's course, it was necessary too to stick with Deng's interpretation of Mao. Deng had explained that there was a science to Mao Zedong thought, that it offered the country a key to the future. Deng, in teaching China how to value Mao, had said that the chairman's achievements came first in consideration, the mistakes of his later years second. So Mao would be remembered as patriot and strategist, revolutionary, hero.[10] Jiang was doing nothing less than constructing a communist canon for China. There were great thinkers, holy books—Marx and Engels, Mao and Deng—around which the country could congregate. In a sense, it did not matter that belief in Maoism had worn thin, that these were tired shibboleths that held no meaning for a tired people; it mattered only that they be repeated, be given lip service. Belief was something performed, rather than felt, a test of political fealty. Jiang himself was an agnostic on such matters; Joseph Prueher, commander of the U.S. Pacific Command and later ambassador to China, would recall Jiang telling him that he would be glad to use any system of government that allowed him to maintain stability in his country of 1.24 billion.[11] But as interpreter and custodian of China's revolutionary canon, Jiang became one with it. Hu Jintao, his eventual successor and a man who similarly understood the uses to which ideology could be put, would later quote him in the same breath as Deng, speak of Jiang's "three represents" (and most people had a hard time remembering just what the three represents were, so mind-numbingly dull was the idea that the party represented "the development trends of advanced productive forces," "the orientations of an advanced culture," and "the fundamental interests of the over-whelming majority of the Chinese people") as part of a tradition that included reform and opening.[12] It was a measure of Jiang's success as a politician: ideology had legitimized him among party members, to the point where Hu would have to claim his mantle. In a curious way, ideology had become more important than before. The importance was on the surface, in things said rather than done, but considerable all the same.

The advantage of invoking Deng's version of ideology, of course, was that it allowed reform and opening to continue. This was important: effective governance was not just a matter of telling people what to believe, but of showing them that they were, on balance, better off with the CCP in charge than without. Deng had emphasized that it would be important to follow the basic line of the program for a hundred years. Now, with Deng's views as lodestar, the party would take reform and opening to a new phase, vital to China and to the cause of modernizing socialism.[13] The recent past had made clear that falling behind economically rendered a country passive, vulnerable to outside control; were development to slow, the consolidation of the socialist system and China's long-term stability would suffer.[14] Allowing what worked to continue working, remaining open to global trade—these were the keys to China's future. Indeed, Jiang would take reform and opening further, for he would seek to use them to pacify China's often restive minority groups. Uighurs and Tibetans were people too; surely, if well fed, they too would be quiescent. Hence the emergence of the Western development policy: it was Jiang's initiative, but it was, in essence, an expansion of reform and opening, taking the policies Deng had found to work wonders on the east coast and applying them to China's Inner Asian reaches. Jiang saw economic links being forged between the booming coast and the minority districts, new markets being opened, especially in the borderlands where trade with neighbors offered a fair prospect. They needed capital, technology transfers, and investment.[15] The tacit bargain being offered was the same as that which the CCP had struck with the majority Han: economic benefits, if uneven, in exchange for political obedience. Later, when violence flared in Xinjiang, Hu's response would reflect the official mind's basic understanding of how to keep the country together: he would call to suppress the violence ruthlessly but also speak of the need to guarantee the standard of living there. Functioning markets, water, electricity, heat: these are as much part of counterinsurgency as police work and brute force.[16] (It was telling, perhaps, that a new wave of violence in China's far west began after the financial crisis of 2007–2008 had begun to make its effects felt. At the time, pundits were proclaiming that China had secured itself against the financial crisis, but Hu was warning his fellow officials that the PRC was in for a hard time. Wandering China's streets, seeing the stalled construction projects and the slouched shoulders of people who had once walked with swift purpose, hearing the young complain about the difficulties of finding employment, it was impossible not to sense that there had been damage. The question was how deep it ran.) The goal, Hu declared, was to bring Xinjiang's gross domestic product per capita up to the level of the rest of the country by 2015.[17] The tone on the violence was stern, uncompromising—and yet, one of the notes struck was of poverty alleviation. In Tibet, Hu explained, one had to work to improve the backward conditions and educate people against the separatist nonsense the Dalai Lama purveyed. The solution to separatism was further development.[18] These were far from the only counterinsurgency measures of course—there would have to be better policing, work to make sure that these separatist ideas did not spill over into other territories; in Tibet, one could even contemplate negotiations with the Dalai Lama if only he stopped spouting these ideas of Tibetan independence—but Hu was driven by a simple idea: the economy mattered, which meant continuing with Deng's ways.

Not that economic growth was without costs. The environmental toll was immense. More immediate were the problems posed by the changing nature of economic success. As the economy grew, so too did the power of state-owned enterprises. The stories of small entrepreneurs finding success and fortune that had been the life force of the eighties gave way to a different tale: that of large, well-connected firms using their ties to government officials to squash competition. Income inequality grew; the Chinese economy became one afflicted by crony capitalism.[19] Both Jiang and Hu recognized the problem, and they knew it was existential. Corruption could eat away at the ties holding governed in loyalty to government; it could, left unaddressed, bring the party down. The government would have to take effective measures to remedy the situation.[20] There would have to be law, and the cadres would have to be schooled in it. Deng had told China that it needed law; party and government would now strive to realize that goal.[21] Hu would try to invest effort in improving the lot of the peasants; the state would have to make sure there was room for the rural population to participate in the economy.[22] It was a question of self-preservation. But the sheer size of the party made it tough to police all impropriety; besides, if they were serious about moving against corruption, Jiang and Hu might well have had to move against party members whose support they needed to stay in power. For all the considerable effort they would pour into the task, there was one central conundrum they could not overcome: how to devise a system of law to govern the party when the party itself was the ultimate arbiter of what the law said. In his diagnosis of China's problems—the lack of a moral center, the disenchantment corruption could create—Jiang was unerring. His solutions, like Hu's, could go only so far.

There was one other challenge reform and opening posed for the PRC. One of the goals had been to integrate China's economy more closely with the global one. This brought immense benefits, but it also rendered the PRC vulnerable to shocks beyond its borders. When the Southeast Asian financial crisis struck, China stepped in to prop up the financial system. It would cut the amount banks had to keep in reserve, so that the money could go to finance and investment banks; this would boost the stature of Chinese banks on the world stage. China, Li Peng reassured foreign officials, would keep the renminbi stable.[23] These measures also helped sustain domestic demand.[24] It was, although no one knew it at the time, a trial run for a financial crisis that would find China even more deeply entwined with the global economy.

The 2007–2008 financial crisis, Hu Jintao warned, would have an influence on China too; the government would have to take appropriate measures to protect its national interests. It would have to look to the security of its foreign exchange assets. It would have to maintain a steady, swift pace of growth—not easy given the role finance played in the modern economy. The financial crisis would harm China's exports; there would need to be readjustment designed to boost internal demand and consumption.[25] There would have to be a turn to emerging markets and the markets of developing countries.[26] China's fellow BRICS (the acronym stands for Brazil, Russia, India, China, and South Africa, which would join in 2010) could come in handy here too; Hu, at one of the many gatherings those countries held, would suggest that they had a role to play in combatting the financial crisis and reforming the financial system.[27]

And he was swift to lecture the Americans on what needed to be done. Faith in the market had to be restored. The developed economies bore the most responsibility for the current mess. But the solution was not to abandon the ways that had brought economic growth. International society must resist protectionism in trade or investment; progress should be made with all due haste on the trade negotiations which the World Trade Organization's members had started on in Doha, Qatar, back in 2001. There needed to be deeper cooperation on supervising global finance, greater exchanges of financial information. The international monetary system should be diversified. The developing world, which was not at fault in this, should be helped to the greatest extent possible in weathering the storm; aid to countries there should be maintained and even upped. (Tellingly, he spoke of Africa. That mantle of protector of the third world was not to be abandoned lightly.) Meeting the UN's development goals and overcoming the financial crisis: these were responsibilities common to the entire world.[28] Well before Donald Trump rode to power on a mantra of "America first" and Xi Jinping found himself playing defender of global capitalism, a Chinese leader was speaking earnestly of the need to keep world trade flowing. It showed how deeply the PRC had bought into Deng's ideas about how to safeguard China's national security: wealth was the answer, and wealth depended on continued reform and opening. And reform and opening meant stable relations with the outside world. Beijing had always had to pay attention to diplomacy; its security depended on the balance of power. Now, as it sought to manage its diplomatic relations, it would have to pay attention to questions of trade and economics to a greater extent than before. Commercial considerations would go hand in hand with geopolitical ones, for both were critical to national security.

Braving the Post–Cold War World

There were many lessons to learn from 1989, but the one that the Chinese leadership took was simple: the Western world was bent on bringing about political change in the socialist world. This was not as outlandish as it might sound. The revolutions of Eastern Europe had been cheered on by the West; in China itself, Tiananmen had brought sanctions and condemnation.[29] China had watched the socialist countries taking advice from the West—and the results had not been encouraging. In 1990, Jiang would meet with Kim Il Sung in Shenyang and mull over the way the world was going. There were doubts about the future of socialism, now, what with relations between the Soviet Union and the United States improving and the march of revolution in Eastern Europe. There were some who thought that the cordiality between Moscow and Washington would lead to world peace, but Jiang knew better: this was a naïve point of view, he said, for the weakening of the Soviet Union relative to the United States was rendering the world unstable. Before one knew it, the Iraqis had invaded Kuwait, and the Americans and the Western Europeans were in the Gulf War. "What events will happen in the world after today," he mused, "is hard to predict." What he did know, he told Kim, was that the G7 was taking an interest in politics. In 1989, those countries (Canada, France, West Germany, Italy, Japan, the United Kingdom, and the United States) had supported the changes in Poland and Hungary and agreed to sanctions on China. Now they talked of protecting democracy, encouraging the global wave of democracy; there was even talk of continuing change in the Soviet Union. To Jiang, this talk of democracy was nothing but a pretext for meddling in the internal affairs of other states and imposing the West's political and economic model on other countries. (It was astonishing how accurate this reading was: there *were* Western policymakers and intellectuals who thought that democracy would soon take over the entire world, simply because it was better. It was just that the rest of the world did not necessarily see it that way.) The year 1990, as Jiang had recently told Kissinger, was the 150th anniversary of the first Opium War— that tortured conflict that marked the beginning of China's invasion by foreign powers. Of the seven countries sitting in judgment on his, six were participants in the international force that had invaded China during the Boxer Uprising (back in 1900 when Chinese citizens had risen against the Western powers carving them up). In the invocation of those old evils, one could see what was troubling Jiang: the notion that political reform would be used to carve up China once again. This was not to be endured. China would keep aiming to relate to the West on the basis of the five principles—and one of those principles was noninterference. Of course, socialism was having a hard time, but China, Jiang assured Kim, intended to stick with it.[30]

The gospel of the end of history and the embrace of liberal democracy, then, did not gain much traction in Chinese officialdom.[31] Jiang would remain suspicious, for the rest of his tenure, of foreign attempts to westernize or split China; talk of linking trade rights to human rights or of China's forthcoming liberalization served only to exacerbate such fears. Nor did Jiang buy the idea of the unipolar moment, which Americans were so swift to proclaim at the end of the Cold War.[32] To Jiang, the end of the bipolar order meant the emergence of a multipolar one—an era in which the avoidance of major war was possible but one rife with contradictions, with territorial disputes and religious conflict.[33] The Americans were, as Jiang would later explain, indeed a superpower. But there were other powers in the world: the European Union (increasingly willing to assert its independence), Japan, Russia. In a world like this, there was room for China to pursue a balance of power, a need to pay due attention to powers other than the United States.[34] (Interestingly enough, Li Peng had mentioned that the world was multipolar, not bipolar, when meeting Mikhail Gorbachev back in 1985.)[35] It was a very different reading of what the end of the Cold War meant from the American one, and it would define Chinese grand strategy for decades to come. As far as China was concerned, it had survived, in Tiananmen, a concerted attempt to overthrow the state; there would be more challenges in the years ahead, and the state would have to rise to them. The diplomatic balancing it had undertaken during the Cold War could continue in the post–Cold War era, although of course, there were new challenges to be confronted. The basic precepts of Chinese grand strategy would remain the same as they had in the Cold War; the strategic environment was different, and yet, in key respects, it was the same. The world the PRC was trying to survive in was still hostile, although that hostility could, as before, be ameliorated. Of all the major powers, it was the PRC that found least need to alter its grand strategy with the end of the Cold War.

Like Mao and Deng before him, Jiang would judge his relationships with other countries as a whole, rather than issue by issue. The idea remained to give voice to specific disagreements without letting them destroy the entire relationship—as long as that relationship served China's overall interests. This was evident from the earliest days, when Brent Scowcroft showed up in Beijing as President George H. W. Bush's special envoy. Scowcroft's task had been to remonstrate with the leadership for the Tiananmen Square massacre; Jiang reminded him that the two countries had much in common in a changing world. Good relations between them augured well for world peace and development. Economic cooperation could fuel growth in the Asia-Pacific region. On trade, on technology transfer, there were mutual interests: China was a vast market. True, the Taiwan issue remained unresolved, but this need not be an obstacle to improving relations. It was important that Scowcroft keep the larger strategic picture in mind.[36] Scowcroft would be castigated for clinking glasses with the CCP leadership, and yet it is difficult to imagine what else he could have done. Jiang had a point: the Sino-American relationship was larger than Taiwan, larger too than murdered students. There were deals to be struck, a new world order to be plotted. For the United States to sacrifice the broader relationship because it could not conform to etiquette would, by Jiang's lights, have been folly. He was fortunate in having an interlocutor who saw it the same way.

The trouble with the Americans was that one never knew what they would do. They would preach realpolitik one day and human rights the next; they did not act rationally, consistently. That they had gone ahead with the Taiwan Relations Act while recognizing the PRC was proof of this—and yet, somehow, China never gave up on the idea that there was a readability, a logic to American actions. When the Americans failed to live up to these high standards, Beijing would get angry. Then, the anger would die down, and China's leaders would try, once more, to find common ground with the Americans in pursuit of larger mutual interests. Nothing illustrated the point as well as the third Taiwan Strait crisis.

Strictly speaking, the crisis should never have happened. Jiang appears to have believed that there was an understanding between the mainland and Taiwan that a move toward independence would not happen. Beijing would talk of the 1992 consensus on there being one China; while Taiwanese would later claim that it had been made up, the understanding in the PRC seems to have been that it was sincere. But Lee Teng-hui, Taiwan's president who was running for reelection, was a different breed of politician: charismatic, popular, intent on claiming that Taiwan's people were not just mainlanders in exile, but had a destiny, a nation of their own. Lee was skilled at having it both ways: he would imply that his ROC was the superior China but that Taiwan was Taiwan, something distinctive. He was well connected in the U.S. Congress, and saw himself as every bit the equal of Jiang. He was, in sum, everything that would drive a Chinese leader wild with fury.

Lee's presence alone was bad enough. But it was compounded by the vagaries of American policy. Jiang did not trust the Americans. In essence, he pointed out, there were two sides to American policy toward China. On one hand, he suspected, Washington did not wish to see China strong, united, developed; it would continue to use whatever it could—trade, human rights, the Taiwan and Dalai Lama issues—to put pressure on China. On the other hand, the sheer size of the Chinese market meant that Washington had a basic interest in developing trade and economic cooperation with the PRC.[37] He wanted, he assured President Bill Clinton at the Asia-Pacific Economic Cooperation meeting in Seattle, a decent relationship. Despite the end of the Cold War, the world remained an unsafe place: the Chinese and the Americans had common interests. America had spoken of the American need for a strong, stable China; Jiang approved of this. But the Taiwan issue continued to dog the relationship. The Americans would have to abide by the one China policy they had supported for so long, enshrined in so many communiqués. The PRC was willing to negotiate with Taiwan on the basis of the one-China principle, to pursue reunification by peaceful means. (He gave a similar message on the Dalai Lama: if the Dalai Lama would just accept that Tibet was part of China, the PRC could negotiate anything with him.) But any attempt to create two Chinas or one China and one Taiwan would be intolerable. If Taiwan pursued "Taiwan independence," if it got support from the outside world in doing so, there would be chaos in the Taiwan Strait—and that, Jiang warned, would harm everyone: people on either side of the strait, the Americans, and the broader Asia-Pacific region.[38] In the grand scheme of things, Clinton needed to realize that Taiwan was just one part of the Sino-American relationship, but he needed to realize too that there were things the PRC would and would not stand for. This much had been made clear, repeatedly, and Jiang's China believed that the United States would not grant a visa to Lee Teng-hui. But the executive is the executive and Congress is Congress; in 1995, Lee found himself with a visa to come speak at his alma mater, Cornell.

This the PRC could not accept. To signal its displeasure, it took two tracks: diplomatic and military. The PRC's ambassador to the United States was summoned home; visits to Washington by senior defense officials were called off. In the summer of 1995, it began testing missiles and conducting military exercises uncomfortably close to Taiwan's ports. And a curious thing happened: the United States did nothing. Just why remains a mystery—some suspect it was to let the Chinese vent their anger in a contained way, although this seems dubious given what was to come—but the fact that nothing was done sent a message to the PRC. American inaction meant acquiescence. At some fundamental level, the Americans must have accepted, finally, the PRC's position that Taiwan being a part of China, Beijing could deal with cross-strait matters as it saw fit—at least to the point of testing a few missiles. This conclusion reached, testing missiles again in 1996, with a view to deterring Taiwan from reelecting the intolerable Lee Teng-hui, would have seemed unproblematic. Then, suddenly, the Americans decided that they had to respond. How was China to deal with such a people? What had first met with silent inaction now saw the United States sending the aircraft carrier *Independence* from Subic Bay to a point two hundred miles east of Taiwan. It was never in the Taiwan Strait during the missile testing, but it was close enough to weigh heavily on the official mind in Beijing. It did not help that at the time, communication between the PLA and their counterparts in the U.S. Pacific Command was virtually nonexistent (one thing that would come out of the crisis would be an attempt to create such communication). A second U.S. aircraft carrier, the *Nimitz*, began making its way to the theater from the Persian Gulf; meanwhile, the United States put Aegis cruisers, with the capability to intercept PRC missiles, off the Taiwanese cities of Taipei and Kaohsiung. (There were no strong guarantees on missile interception at the time, but that fact was not advertised.)[39] It was terrifying how swift and uncompromising the American response was; what was even more terrifying, perhaps, was that it was utterly unpredictable. Having tested a few missiles, the PRC stopped.

Emotion, not grand strategy, informed the PRC's behavior here. Responding to Lee's invitation by recalling the PRC ambassador to the United States was out of all proportion to the problem. (Henry Kissinger, meeting with Bill Clinton to try to reset U.S. policy on China, said that he had never seen "such potential for disintegration of relations," that they were convinced the United States could refrain from giving Lee a visa again.[40] Perhaps the Chinese leadership was right in its idea that there was no such thing as a former official.) Lee's visit had, of course, been provocative, but it could have been dismissed as just a man giving a speech at a university. The willingness to recall an ambassador suggested the PRC was not keeping Taiwan in perspective, as it had long been hectoring the United States to do: as one point in a larger strategic picture. Taiwan was a trigger point; it awakened emotions in Chinese officialdom that might lead it to depart from grand strategy. Indeed, the whole desire to take Taiwan back was, at a certain level, emotional rather than strategic, for by this point, Taiwanese independence did not pose much of a threat to the PRC. It was one thing when the island was governed by a man intent on taking back the mainland and waging low-intensity war against the CCP. What sat across the strait now was a quiet democracy, willing to do business with the PRC. Granting it independence might have made it more pliable, susceptible to the same blandishments and threats that other small states in the region were. The whole military effort demonstrated how wide the gap in mutual comprehension was. Jiang thought it would deter Taiwanese from voting for Lee; instead, the man swaggered triumphantly to office, on the back, as it were, of PRC missiles. From start to finish, the endeavor was completely counterproductive.

With the first fierce emotional reaction out of the way, however, there would be a return to grand strategy. After the crisis—after the shelling and recrimination, the carriers and the election—Jiang and Clinton sat down to talk on June 27, 1998. The Americans, Jiang acknowledged, did not support Taiwanese independence, but they had not come out in support of peaceful reunification either. The differences between China and America on the issue were not of the here and now, but of the past—and yet the past was inescapable. The PRC, Jiang made clear, was willing to be reasonable on the matter. Taiwan could stick to its own ways after reunification, maintain its own executive and legislature, even its own troops; the PRC would not dispatch troops or officials there. The island could participate in the central government's conferences. In the meanwhile, China was promoting official contacts, economic and cultural exchange across the strait. It advocated three links: direct postal services, shipping, and transport. Just to reassure the Americans, Jiang declared that there would be no harm to their economic interests there once the Taiwan issue was resolved; indeed they would be better protected. (The assumption, of course, was that the issue would be resolved correctly, on the terms Beijing wanted.) American officials could continue to come and go. This would be best for the Americans over the long term. All that was needed was an acceptance of the one-China principle: China and Taiwan could then proceed to peaceful negotiations. Such negotiations, said Jiang, offered the best way forward on Taiwan. If, on the other hand, the Americans did not make their support for Chinese reunification clear, this notion of Taiwanese independence would only take deeper hold, exacerbating the problem. Back in Seattle, he reminded Clinton, he had spoken of the need for creating a safe, peaceful, stable world for the twenty-first century. Last year, the two sides had agreed that the relationship between China and America should be one of strategic partnership. Taiwan should not be allowed to impede the development of such relations.[41] It was both threat and request.

For China needed the United States. The signal achievement of reform and opening was China's accession to the World Trade Organization, and this would not have been possible without American support. Looking back, in 2002, Jiang would observe that the accession was as significant politically as it was economically. It was a mark of all that China had accomplished, of the economic strength reform and opening had brought. The PRC's output had surged; no one could look on it as small or insignificant; the pace of its growth, the massive potential of its markets, exerted a powerful attraction on every single country around the globe. The moral of the story, of course, was that China's new economic policy, with all its openness to the outside world, was to be persisted with—not least because of the threats of hegemony that endured in the post–Cold War world. This remained true despite the fact that Jiang felt that China's enemies might seek to use accession to the WTO against it. As Jiang saw it, the Americans had reached an agreement with China about letting it into the organization because it was too strong economically for them to be able to do otherwise, but it would not do to be naïve about their overall strategic objectives in dealing with China. They would, he believed, seek to do what the West had long sought to do with erstwhile socialist countries: use economic liberalization to foist "so-called political liberalization" on the PRC; it was the standard Western ploy of westernizing and splitting a socialist country. Had not Clinton said as much when he mused that WTO accession meant that the Chinese would be unable to stanch the information revolution, thereby bringing about social and political change?[42] Such political change, as the Chinese saw it, would only bring chaos and destruction—which was, of course, consistent with the American goal of keeping China undeveloped, disunited, and unstable. Beijing's plan, therefore, would be to exploit the opportunities this latest milestone in reform and opening brought while remaining vigilant in its dealings with the outside world. There was a way of making globalization work for China, one that involved economic change without political liberalization; it was not the way the Americans had in mind, but Jiang felt it was feasible. However one felt about American rhetoric, it was important to keep talking to them.

But before accession came the NATO bombing of the Chinese embassy in Yugoslavia on May 7, 1999. At one level, this was useful: if one wanted to keep the state together, nationalism could provide the requisite glue. Jiang was all for patriotic demonstrations among the young. The students were to be supported in their patriotic protests—although one must be careful, of course, to ensure that patriotism did not slide into instability.[43] "It was kind of funny," recalled an American official, treated to one such demonstration outside the United States consulate in Shenyang. "They were trying to burn a U.S. flag, and they couldn't understand why it was taking so long to burn. They just kept holding a lighter to it and clicking. They didn't seem to know that you need kerosene to make it burn fast."[44] What they lacked in skill, however, the students made up for in enthusiasm. And enthusiasm was something China needed.

But at another level, the bombing was a disruption to Sino-American relations—and one that China was determined to handle without jeopardizing the long-term goal of accession to the WTO. Jiang would later recount the sequence of events. He had been discussing China's participation with Clinton since Seattle. The Americans had kept upping their demands; China had refused to bow its head. When the embassy was bombed, it was China that ceased talks with the Americans. On May 14, Clinton called China—he had called China—to say he was sorry and wanted to resume talks. The current atmosphere, Jiang shot back, was unfavorable to discussion. On August 18, Jiang said he was willing to resume talks, but Clinton would have to write a formal letter of apology. And Clinton delivered. The letter came through on August 27. The Chinese central authorities decided they could go ahead with talks; it would help to stabilize the Sino-American relationship and would be in China's basic interests. On September 1, Jiang replied that he was willing to talk—and asked that America extend unconditional, long-term normal trade relations to China. The two countries finally started talking again in Auckland on September 11, 1999.[45]

Two things are notable about this résumé of events. First, Jiang was careful to emphasize the collective nature of decision-making: the central government had approved these maneuvers; Zhu Rongji was named a key player. Jiang was not going to stand out from the crowd. Second, for all the anger at the embassy bombing, the incident was kept in strategic perspective. Anger was to be expressed righteously, but anger could not be permitted to get in the way of long-term security. Channels of communication with the Americans were kept open. It was made clear to the United States that there was a specific problem and that this problem could be addressed. Once that was done, China was more than happy to play its part as a responsible member of the international community; this was, after all, good for China's economy and thus its security. Pique could not be allowed precedence over long-term interests.

A pattern had emerged. A crisis with the Americans—and such crises were the result of misperception more than ill intent—would provoke anger, fierce recrimination; then there would be a return to prudence and a calm pursuit of long-term objectives. The same pattern would be evident when a Chinese F-8 collided with an American EP-3 in international airspace on April 1, 2001. There had long been American flights over the international waters off the Chinese coast, and there had long been Chinese protests about such flights. Sometimes, the PLA would send jets out to intercept or harass the American flights, and the Chinese pilots would behave with varying degrees of professionalism; they tended to be more professional in the East China Sea than in the South China Sea.[46] (Why this would be the case is difficult to say: it most probably had to do with different ideas about rules of engagement and discipline in different military districts; it is possible, too, that there was some idea that the Americans cared more about Japan and its safety than about Southeast Asia.) The F-8 broke apart and tumbled into the water; the Chinese pilot, Wang Wei, was never found. The American crew was forced to land on Hainan Island. The first bit of luck both sides had would be in Hainan. There, the authorities cleared a runway for the distressed American aircraft, when, as Joseph Prueher, now ambassador to China, would observe, "they could have parked trucks there instead." Knowing that the crew was unharmed had a dramatic influence on the way the Americans would approach the negotiations.[47]

The initial reaction on both sides was anger. The Chinese maintained that the American aircraft had caught up with and rammed the fighter deliberately; they demanded an apology and reparations. Prueher, who knew something about such matters, pointed out that it was impossible for the slower EP-3 to catch up with and ram the faster F-8; an apology and reparations were out of the question. The Americans were incensed at irresponsible conduct in international airspace, which was what had led to the whole incident in the first place. Attempts to locate the senior Chinese leadership were unsuccessful; most were planting trees for Arbor Day. (Jiang himself was absent for most of the crisis, on a trip to Latin America.)

Very soon, however, tempers calmed. Prueher, after a chat with Kenneth Lieberthal, a former official on Clinton's National Security Council, who happened to be in Beijing at the time, was willing to try a "change of tack." Secretary of State Colin Powell was willing to let the ambassador try one; Powell's support, Prueher would later recall, was crucial to the eventual outcome. While continuing to refuse reparations and a formal apology, Prueher would avoid blaming the Chinese for the incident and focus on how to secure the crew's release. "Our goal and the Chinese goal was the same: to get the crew out," he remembered.[48] The Americans decided that it was possible to express sorrow for the Chinese pilot's death and for the Chinese failure to hear the U.S. plane's call, without apologizing—something they were intent on avoiding. The Chinese decided it was possible to construe such expressions as an apology despite the Americans saying they were nothing of the sort. A letter from Prueher expressing those sentiments could serve to save face and quash need for further escalation. The bid to host the 2008 Olympics was still pending; the vote on China's WTO membership was yet to be taken; and when all was said and done, the Americans were China's biggest trading partner. There was so much China needed America for; it could not afford to sacrifice all its interests in order to make a point about a dead pilot. It was important, as Jiang would have said, to think of the larger strategic picture.

The whole episode could have gone very differently. The crew could have been denied a clear runway in Hainan. A more nationalistic government—or a more nationalistic mob—could have mistreated, perhaps killed, the crew, and then insisted it was America's fault; at that point, Washington would almost certainly have felt compelled to take more serious steps. That this did not happen owed something to the American willingness to climb down without climbing down; it also owed something to China's willingness to keep the issue in perspective. The same was true of the embassy bombing and the Taiwan Strait crisis. Beijing could have opted to refuse the American apology for what had happened in Yugoslavia; it could, had it wanted to see just how dangerous things could get, have continued to test missiles in the Taiwan Strait, perhaps even engaged the Americans militarily. (This would have been suicidal, but it is astonishing how often governments and people in the throes of nationalistic fervor make suicidal decisions. Nationalistic sentiment in the Chinese population, certainly, was running high: a government more responsive to public pressure might well have felt obliged to do something violent and stupid.) In all its dealings with the United States, the PRC would do its best to keep face, but it would not escalate the situation to a point where conflict damaged larger interests. Life would be allowed to go on.

Even before 9 / 11, then, the PRC's basic policy on the United States had taken shape. China did not trust the United States, but it wanted decent relations with it. The September 11, 2001 terrorist attacks on the United States would provide an opportunity for some adjustments; they did not alter the general substance of Chinese policy. (The impact on Washington's policy toward China is a different matter: George W. Bush's administration had been talking of the China threat, talk that would diminish, although not entirely disappear, as the focus shifted to terrorism.)[49] The attacks, Jiang thought, had shown the Americans that the main threat to their security was not China; they would also help China in its attempt to quench the East Turkestan terrorist movement (the campaign for Xinjiang's independence). The PRC's task, as ever, was to stay calm, watchful, not aspire to leadership. A balance would have to be struck between fighting terrorism—which China wanted—and keeping hegemony—meaning the United States—at bay.[50] There seemed to be room for the cooperation the Chinese had long wanted too: the Americans had asked Beijing for help; it was in their own strategic interests, now, to get Chinese support and assistance. Jiang had talked with Bush in Shanghai on October 19, 2001; they had agreed on the importance of developing a cooperative relationship. This, Jiang noted, marked progress from the rather unstable relationship of the recent past. It also gave China a chance to try to set the terms of counterterrorism. They were all for it, but any military action would have to avoid collateral damage—there were memories, perhaps, of the Belgrade bombing at play here; the last thing one wanted was an accidental American attack on Xinjiang, which shared a border with Afghanistan—and be under the auspices of the UN (this last was a theme that would become important when the Iraq War of 2003 came to the Security Council).[51] One needed, after all, to balance opposition to terror with opposition to hegemony, which was where Beijing's ties with other powers would come in useful.

Since the Deng-Gorbachev meetings of 1989 and the subsequent dissolution of the Soviet Union, Beijing had been strengthening cooperation with Russia and Central Asian countries; there was so much more to the international system than just a North American colossus. In the wake of 9 / 11, China's ties to its Central Asian neighbors would suddenly seem farsighted; one could build on these relationships, try to ensure a reasonably secure neighborhood. It would not do to leave the Americans unchecked on China's western frontier. Enemies of the state moved back and forth across the high mountain passes there; they might make common cause with the Americans over human rights, religious freedom, and democracy. The American presence alone was enough to make the PRC uncomfortable; Xinjiang was geostrategically crucial, and although it was true that relations were better, there was something a little discomfiting about having so massive a military power so close. One could not eliminate the American military presence in Central Asia altogether, but one could at least try to constrain it by creating a regional balance of power. It was the same idea that had animated Mao and Deng: China would seek to be closer to all powers than they were to one another.

The entente with Russia created a force that would balance the United States. The border dispute, Jiang noted on a visit to Moscow in July 2001, had essentially been solved. China would not forget how much the Russians had supported China in its time of need. With the end of the Cold War, both countries were adapting to a changing environment, and in this new world, strategic interest called for a stronger relationship. He spoke out against the expansion of military pacts—was this an attempt to show Moscow how sympathetic Beijing was to the Russian position on NATO? It would certainly have played well with his hosts—and against arms races. There would be trade and exchange; they could cooperate on resources, transport, and flights. The development of China's far west needed foreign assistance; Russian traders were more than welcome to come help with that great task. Both Russia and China were members of the UN Security Council; as such they could cooperate to make sure that international relations remained democratic (which is to say, not unilaterally decided by the Americans) and that global issues were addressed in a manner consistent with their interests.[52] In the wake of 9/11, Jiang would talk about developing the strategic partnership between the two: there was scope for trade, work on border stability, and military cooperation, especially when it came to technology.[53] It did not matter that trust was still nonexistent, that in the borderlands where Jiang was inviting Russian traders, suspicions of Russian imperialism remained strong, that in the farther reaches of Russia's wild east, locals would grumble about their land being sold out to China. Friendship is something ritualistic, performed; you must go through the ceremonies and motions to create it. Proclaim friendship often enough, and it just might be forced into existence.

Perhaps the most tangible expression of this newfound spirit of partnership was the Shanghai Cooperation Organization. It had evolved gradually, this little Central Asian club, beginning simply as a conversation about how to reduce troops along shared borders. Now, it could be of tremendous influence not just for the interests of the six countries involved, but for the entire region and Eurasia. The gulf between global north and south was wide, creating a deep contradiction for the world in its quest for peace and development. The dangers

of terrorism (tellingly, Jiang was using the word before 9/11), separatism, and extremism showed no sign of declining. In a world like
this the SCO was necessary. It could promote regional trade, which, in
true Dengist spirit, was good for everyone. Its members could cooperate
on fighting the three forces China would keep coming back to: terrorism, splittism, and extremism.[54] Restive local Muslims constituted
a transnational problem, more easily solved if China had goodwill
from regional partners. The forum could also, Jiang said, promote
multipolarization—by which he meant the dilution of American influence.[55] The official SCO declaration calling for an end to foreign
presence in Central Asia would come much later, in Hu Jintao's time.
Hu would praise the SCO for its achievements and celebrate its capacities to combat terrorism, separatism, and extremism. Regional
affairs needed to be left to the people of each country in the region
(a dig here at the Americans, who were always preaching the gospel
of human rights and democracy); China opposed outside interference in internal affairs. The SCO countries could not always be in
one another's business: that would get in the way of pipelines and
railways, cooperation on the Internet and information. And there
was so much to gain. This was the old Silk Road, Hu recalled; trade
and investment were in everyone's interest. SCO could help with
everything, from banking to a better food policy.[56] Later, Xi Jinping, Hu's successor, would pick up on the theme of the Silk Road,
the visions of profit it conjured. But it was the geopolitical calculus
that showed how little Chinese grand strategy had changed. The idea
of limiting outside influence in the region was as old as the Bandung
declarations Zhou and Jawaharlal Nehru had championed ages ago.
The Sino-American relationship was far better than it had been
then, but there was no reason to let the Americans sit that close to
China's borders.

Beyond Central Asia too, Jiang sought to improve relations with neighbors so as to limit American influence. Early in his tenure, he moved to restore diplomatic relations with Indonesia, establish formal diplomatic ties with Singapore, and normalize the relationship with Vietnam.[57] China needed good relations with bordering countries: this would help with promoting modern socialism, with opening up to the outside world, with maintaining internal stability. It was not an easy task. The legacies of colonialism in Asia ran deep. There were disputes over territory at both land and sea, which could flare up. It was in the natural order of things that smaller countries would be suspicious of a behemoth like China; Beijing's task, therefore, was to work to eliminate the idea of a China threat. The five principles of peaceful coexistence that underpinned agreements China had signed with India and Burma had become a global norm. (Jiang omitted to mention that the five-principled relationship had ended in war with India, and that Burma, in a state of civil war, was a place where Beijing was working with every possible side; it had been able to broker the unsteady peace between the government in Rangoon and the ethnic armies in the Shan state precisely because it had strong ties to both.) China could champion a peaceful resolution of disputes: on the South China Sea in particular, it could maintain that it was sovereign but avoid squabbling and focus on joint development. As far as the disputes between the neighbors went, there were some it could remain aloof from, others it would have to be more active in dealing with. For one could not allow regional peace and stability to be upset, permit the emergence of regional hegemony. All these calculations were haunted by the specter of American interference. The United States might not be a neighbor, Jiang pointed out, but it was a key player in the security of China's neighborhood. Good, stable relations with Washington were in Beijing's interests. The PRC would therefore try to cooperate with the Americans on matters of common interest; where there was a clash—American interference in China's sovereign rights and security, in particular on Taiwan—it would not back down.[58] Stable relationships with smaller countries in the Asia-Pacific region were good in and of themselves; they also served the purpose of denying the Americans an excuse to get more involved in regional politics. Not that China would abandon claims to disputed islands; it had always known how to be assertive. Even before Xi Jinping, China maintained that it would negotiate with Southeast Asian countries bilaterally, not en masse at the Association of Southeast Asian Nations (ASEAN); there would be occasional forays into contested waters, followed by statements on China's sovereign rights. But for the most part—especially when judged against what was to come—Jiang and Hu sought to avoid needlessly antagonizing neighbors.

Even on Taiwan, Beijing could move to a calmer policy, a policy that sought to conciliate reasonable people there, instead of terrifying them with missiles. One would be hard put to find a Chinese leader who would admit that Taiwan was a neighboring country, and yet this was how Beijing had to treat it: there would be negotiations, trade, but a careful avoidance of the use of force; the American commitment to it, ambiguous although it was, left little choice. The coming to power of the Democratic Progressive Party (DPP), hitherto the main opposition party in Taiwan, was appalling, but Hu Jintao would not repeat the error of 1996. The Guomindang might have lost the election, but it had more in common with the CCP than the DPP did, and the great thing about dealing with a democracy was that the party out of power today could come to power again tomorrow. Lian Zhan, chairman of the GMD, would go to China for the first talks between the heads of the CCP and GMD in sixty years. "Grandpa," chanted the children at Lian's old school in Xian, stepping forth with arms extended, "you've come back."[59] Hu was warm, flattering; he knew that there was a good deal of pressure on the GMD not to come. He mentioned the common understanding of 1992, the agreement, between both sides, that decried the notion of an independent Taiwan. The mainland had changed: it had modernized, he told his guest. And Taiwan's accomplishments were not to be underestimated; they were the pride of all the Chinese people. There was much the mainland had to learn from the island, and the economic exchange across the strait had been of immense benefit to all. The two economies, Hu noted, were now deeply intertwined: it made sense for them to join hands and pursue joint development. It would revive the entire people.[60]

But ranged against this glorious vision were the separatist forces of Taiwan independence; these had not only harmed cross-strait relations, but had created political chaos on the island. There was an implicit reminder here: good relations with the PRC were good for the GMD. Mainland China could offer the GMD power, a political future, which it might not have if left to stand alone in a Taiwan that believed it had an identity that was not Chinese. One rules through local chieftains; those chieftains have to be promised benefits; this was what Hu was offering Lian. The way forward, Hu suggested, was negotiation on the basis of the 1992 consensus. There should be deeper economic cooperation; links should be forged between the people on each side of the strait, with the Taiwanese traders having a particularly important role to play. Dialogue should continue. There were some problems that could be resolved, some that would have to wait; the important thing, as in all China's relationships, was to just keep talking.[61]

The fires of third world unity and anti-imperialism could still be stoked. Jiang remembered the stories of the fifties and sixties, of men like Nehru—for stories are told selectively—and Gamal Nasser, Tito and Sukarno, Julius Nyerere and Kwame Nkrumah, who did much for the cause of freedom from the colonial world. China had been very helpful at the time, giving them money and supporting their revolutionary activities. Now, with the Cold War over, the Western world was bent on westernizing and splitting the third world. The West spoke of democracy and human rights; it tried to foist a Western multiparty system on developing countries. And the countries at the receiving end of this policy would find their economy suffering, religious and ethnic conflicts exacerbated. It was for China to stand with these countries and insist on noninterference. The countries of the global south had common interests. China had relied on them when its human rights record was being criticized at the United Nations; now China would stand by them too.[62] Hence Jiang's courtship of Latin America: it would serve common interests, from boosting wealth to democratizing international relations. There should, he declared, be attempts to promote mutual understanding and trust, cooperation on issues like UN reform and international security, which would help multipolarity along. And of course, he wanted trade. In 2000, trade between China and Latin America reached $12.6 billion; things could only go up from here. China welcomed Latin American investment and would encourage its own entrepreneurs to invest in Latin America.[63] The web of globalization stretched farther and farther each year; there were old strands to be strengthened and new ones to be forged. Hu would continue with Jiang's Latin America policy: visiting Peru, he spoke of increasing political trust, deepening trade cooperation, and collaborating on issues like food safety, climate change, and financial safety.[64]

The pursuit of mutual interests brought Jiang to Africa in 1996. China and Africa, he declared, were among the earliest places where human civilization developed. They shared a history in fighting colonialism, in having suffered foreign oppression; they supported one an-

other in national liberation. He promised all-weather friendship between China and Africa, and he promised mutual noninterference: it
was not for Beijing to tell African officials what to do, to set political
conditions on aid. (There was a touch of empathy here: Jiang's country
knew what it was like to be lectured on its internal affairs, and it was
something he would instinctively avoid in his dealings with smaller
countries.) There should be joint development, growing trade, and
collaboration on the international front; China would do its part to
ensure that Africa was respected in the global arena.[65] Here too, Hu
would follow Jiang's trail.[66] They were harkening back to Mao's tradition of statecraft, one that gave smaller countries due importance.
(As in the Mao era, high policy was one thing; it was another, harder
task to get everyone from across China's diplomatic and business
communities to avoid big country chauvinism.) Power was diffuse, multifaceted, not confined to Moscow or Washington. There was money
to be made, support to be won from Kenya and Peru, Brazil and
Ethiopia. The smaller, forgotten countries too had a role to play in
the global balance of power; their friendship could bolster China's
national security.

The Chinese Way of Warfare

The emphasis on diplomacy, on the pointlessness of dragging conflict with the Americans too far, did not mean China would neglect
military power. Defense was not something to be compromised on.
The world was not peaceful, Jiang observed; witness the Gulf War.
And as that war made clear, there was a revolution in military affairs
under way. Electronics had become crucial, whether in aircraft or missiles. There was much to learn from the events in the Middle East:
the Americans were able to triumph so quickly, Jiang argued, because

they were able to knock out the Iraqi communication systems almost immediately. China should research this, pay attention to technology. Not that it was going to abandon the emphasis on the role of people in warfare altogether; it was simply that it would have to catch up with the modern world too.[67]

The basic function of military power had not changed: it remained active defense. And it was the precept of active defense that would continue to determine just how far budgets and capabilities must extend. China did not seek hegemony abroad; its military did not need to be capable of invading another country. The weaponry Jiang wished to focus on developing therefore needed to focus chiefly on defense. This was particularly important because although China needed to invest in modernizing its forces, it had only so much that it could invest at a given time. Military expenditure had to be kept in proportion to the overall budget. As much as in any other sector, there would have to be efficiency in military spending.[68] The country would support and strengthen military development, but according to need and capability.[69] Like Deng before him, Jiang was wary of bankrupting the country by spending too much on defense. To do so would be self-defeating. Military power has a purpose: it is to contribute to the security of the country. Pursued without attention to the country's overall needs and circumstances, it defeats the object. This did not mean ignoring military needs; it meant thinking of them in the context of the overall health of the state and in terms of the revolution in military affairs unfolding abroad. The broader strategic landscape around China was changing; the Americans, the Russians, the Japanese were looking ahead to 2010 and 2020 as they modernized. China too would have to look to the future. And looking to the future meant continuing to cut the number of troops; around the globe, Jiang argued, this was what countries were doing. Deng had done great work on this, but still there were too many men at arms; China would just have to cut more.[70] It was not the number of soldiers, but modern weaponry that would determine future contests. A twenty-first-century military would need to invest in these rather than in just personnel. One thing on his mind as he thought about modernization was Taiwan. If there were suddenly to be a local war because the Taiwanese declared independence, he observed in 1993, a PLA without modern technology would be powerless to prevent it and thereby preserve the unity of the motherland. Of course, if China were well prepared, the Taiwanese would never dare to take such a step—proof, if any were needed, that in a rough-and-tumble world, it was always best to be prepared.[71] And being prepared meant having the latest in technology.

This did not mean neglecting personnel altogether. It was important that the soldiers be schooled in obedience. The PLA would have to be subject to stronger political education—on the meaning of socialism, the difference between socialist democracy and that of the Western parliamentary system. The troops would have to unite with the politicians, with the people, and among themselves; this, Mao had assured China, was the key to victory. (It was natural that the chairman would make the assurance and natural that Jiang would invoke it: splits within the military and rupture in civil-military relations had long meant civil war and carnage.) The military leadership would have to be steeped in Mao Zedong thought and Deng's notions of socialism with Chinese characteristics; only thus could it truly comprehend its role in the state—that role being subordinate to the party's leadership.[72]

The emphasis on training underscored the fear that the CCP could never quite escape: the risk of a military coup. Hosting Jiang in Hawaii, while head of Pacific Command, Prueher would find himself "poked in the chest, but in a nice way." "Admiral," asked Jiang, "what are you trying to do with the PLA?"

"Well, I'm trying to build trust between us so as to avoid a miscalculation," said Prueher.

"But for there to be trust there must first be understanding, and for there to be understanding there must first be communication," said Jiang.[73] It was vintage Jiang and it was perfectly true—and yet behind the whole questioning, there was a nagging anxiety: his troops communicating with the Americans, without the party, without him as organizing channel. The Americans were used to such exchanges; Jiang, coming from a place where keeping the state whole was a challenge, where soldiers grown too powerful had turned into warlords and thus broken the country, was not. Great China was still fragile. It was important to remember and remind all necessary that the party was paramount over the military. Western enemies, bent on westernizing and splitting the PRC, were testing the PLA: they whispered temptingly of the troops' "departification" and "depoliticization." China would have to strengthen political training in the troops, make sure the men with guns were properly versed in ideology. Only thus could they hold firm to the precept that they were subject to the party's authority. They would also have to be given incentives to obey the party. This involved a tacit deal, in which the party would preach unity between troops and people and the troops had certain rights— legitimate interests—that the party had to protect.[74] In 1998, Jiang would call for the PLA to sever itself from the business empires it had spawned.[75] But the call rang hollow. The military's entrenchment in the Chinese economy remained strong.

Hu too would emphasize the need for the military to remember that it was under the party's control. One of the most famously humiliating moments of his tenure would come when U.S. secretary of defense Robert Gates was visiting, and the PLA tested a stealth fighter—apparently without Hu's prior knowledge. He would call for modernization, informatization, highlight the need for a navy and an air force that met twenty-first-century needs. It was in his reign that China would take steps to keep up with powers moving to militarize outer space, even as he decried that militarization. The goals, of course, remained defensive, and this was understandable, even necessary. In 2004, he would remark the need to protect China's sovereign airspace and seas, and warn of the need to prevent the success of the Taiwan independence movement; this was still very much a look at close quarters. The dynamics of warfare had changed: one needed to look to outer space and the security of the electromagnetic field as well.[76] It did not matter that war seemed unlikely in the here and now. The attitudes of other powers were changeable, and although they were reasonably well disposed to China today, one wanted the capacities to make sure one could deal with them if that changed tomorrow. No responsible Chinese government could have done otherwise. But it was also a way of appeasing hawkish voices within the Chinese state, both military and civilian. And because of China's geography, because of its vastness and the countries around it, military modernization would only exacerbate the suspicions of its neighbors. How could one assure them that the capabilities being acquired were purely defensive, that they would not be used for offense? Where did the line lie, especially out at sea? Active defense sounded good, but to a smaller country, the risk of it becoming offensive could never be discounted. One moves, stumbling and uncertain, to make sure one is ready for defense; the diplomatic tone shifts, and before one knows it, the world is talking, terrified, of a China threat. It had been a problem since Mao's day; with China more powerful, it would remain a pressing one for Jiang and Hu.

Part of what kept the problem manageable during their time was their sheer blandness of tone. Jiang and Hu had gone about grand strategy quietly, not altering much, trying, when possible, to be conciliatory. They sought simply to keep China on the course Deng had set—continue with reform and opening, seek a balance of power in a multipolar world, modernize the military, and keep China whole. There was something dull and uninspiring about their ways. But dullness can be a virtue—and it was a virtue that would shine all the brighter in the days of Xi Jinping.

5

XI JINPING AND THE INSECURITY OF POWER

I N 1969, Xi Jinping went to work in the Shaanxi countryside. In the later telling and retelling, the story would acquire a certain romance, like that of a monk who finds enlightenment through his wanderings. The princeling whose father had been denounced by the Red Guards; the boy, not yet sixteen, volunteering for rural labor; his willingness to work almost without rest; his capacity to eat whatever bitterness came his way; the bugs that feasted on him; the enormous loads he carried up the mountain paths, inspiring the villagers' approval; the way the villagers came to see him off when he finally left to go resume his studies—all this would become the stuff of legend.[1] It was not that he had not suffered during the Cultural Revolution; these were the Mao years, after all, and he would remember how the Red Guards had denounced him. But it was those seven years of rural labor, so the story went, that allowed him to understand the Chinese countryside and its people, to understand the basic condition of China. And they gave him his true vocation: doing real work for the people.[2]

Xi Jinping: heroic monk who had spent seven years in the wilderness, anointed by the people to bring light to China's darkness.

Lost in this telling were the harsher lessons the Cultural Revolution had to teach. Different people would respond to the trauma of those years in different ways. Xi, ripped from a comfortable existence and plunged into criticism and loss (his half-sister died during those years), seems to have come away with the insight that stability was both important and ephemeral, dependent on the whims of the strong. To make certain that life stayed stable, one could not rely on others; the only guarantee of stability was to protect it oneself. Until such time as one was in a position of power, it was important to maintain a low profile—this was crucial to surviving. But once one had attained power, it was important to assert oneself, to make sure that potential sources of danger did not survive. Governance could not rely forever on compromise between different, competing factions, for compromise can come unraveled. One must act resolutely to quell competition.

He rose through the ranks of the Communist Party, seemingly as quiet as Jiang Zemin or Hu Jintao. (He would express a liking for *The Godfather*: perhaps there was something of Don Vito and Michael Corleone to him, hiding his strength, encouraging potential foes to underestimate him—until the time was right to strike.) He worked in Fujian and Zhejiang: coastal provinces, booming thanks to reform and opening. He saw firsthand the benefits trade and openness brought; he saw too the corruption that came with wealth. Every now and then, one would have to make peace with corrupt dealings, but it was a cancer to be fought.

He inherited the China of Jiang and Hu, and it was here, perhaps, that the sense of vulnerability instilled by the Cultural Revolution came in. Look at China from the perspective of Jiang or Hu, and you see a country doing rather better than you might have thought possible even a few years ago. It has its problems to be sure, but these can be tinkered with; there is political stability and the country continues to grow. Shift your vantage point ever so slightly, just enough to incorporate a more intense awareness of how easily stability can be upset, and the fault lines and pressures are what impress you most: the disenchantment with cronyism among the Chinese people, the smog hanging thick in the air, the Americans muttering about war with China from across the narrow seas. Seen in this light, China is suddenly imperiled—and the peril demands an immediate response, before things get worse.[3] It is a curious paradox of the Xi era: on the one hand, China has come of age as a great power and never been stronger or more feted in recent memory; on the other, this is as insecure as it has felt since the late sixties.

It is in this paradox that the grand strategy of Xi Jinping is rooted. He pursues the same goals as his predecessors did, but with greater urgency and vigor. China has to be made secure once again. This would require internal strengthening: here, to continued growth, an anticorruption struggle, and ideological work, Xi adds a cult of personality—something not seen since the days of Mao. It is no longer enough to have the party move in the direction one wishes; he must formalize his authority, by writing "Xi Jinping Thought" into the constitution. Abroad, China must maintain a balance of power. Xi too tries to remain closer to other powers, large and small, than they are to one another; like Jiang and Hu, he links commercial and geopolitical considerations in an attempt to shore up China's strength. Here too he goes further than his predecessors: China, he suggests, can be a model for others to follow. (Deng, of course, had mentioned the transferability of "one country, two systems" and "joint development," but those were specific ideas, just parts of China's overall approach to the world; Xi's notion that socialism with Chinese characteristics could be a beacon for other countries was far more all-encompassing. Not, he would clarify subsequently, that China would export that model; that would have been going too far.)[4] And what has become most pronounced in Xi's reign is the quiet but persistent use of force. Jiang and Hu were reluctant, for the most part, to use military power; there were exceptions, to be sure, notably in the Taiwan Strait, but armed force was not generally the tool they turned to. Xi, by contrast, will do anything from setting up a naval base abroad to using armed fishing boats, although he too has the idea that force can be dialed up or down. There is a hustle and muscle to his grand strategy: pursuing national security means actively pursuing it, not just letting things continue on the same course. But intensity can be self-defeating. The assertive vigor that Xi brings to his task has undermined Chinese national security significantly.

Defining and Defending National Security

Xi's conception of national security became clear at the party plenum in 2013, when he announced the establishment of a new National Security Council. Security and social stability were essential to uninterrupted reform and development, he said. The country needed a single, unified structure that could meet the needs of national security.[5] Experts would compare the new organization to its American counterpart—but there was a crucial difference, one that showed just how different the Chinese definition of national security was.[6] The Americans, young, confident in their own institutions and national cohesion, had formed their National Security Council to deal with an external threat: the Soviet menace. Rich, prosperous, surrounded by three oceans and two harmless neighbors, the United States could afford to distinguish between problems within and without. Xi does not have that luxury. His is a country that has never been able to take its own integrity for granted and that is ringed by potential foes: his concept of national security must comprehend both internal and external threats, and the ways the two could coalesce to bring great China—great China which had only recently been put together—down. The internal and external factors affecting national security, said Xi in his first speech to the NSC, had become far more complicated. Pursuing national security with Chinese characteristics means thinking broadly: there must be security of sovereign territory, military affairs, economics, information, environment. A country has to be rich to have strong soldiers, and its soldiers must be strong to protect it.[7] One cannot afford to ignore anything when planning for national security; there are so many different pieces that come together to keep a country safe. Keeping track of them all requires centralized decision-making—with Xi firmly, perhaps even immovably, in charge.

Domestically, what troubles him most is corruption. It has infected both party and military, and it is something that threatens the very foundations of the CCP's power. The party, Xi explains, comes from the people. It serves them; its strength derives from them. Bereft of the people's support, the party can do nothing. And it is this very base, this strength that corruption risks eroding. There will be no more tolerance for corruption, no further tolerance of the idea of "policy above, countermeasures below."[8] That last phrase highlights one more reason corruption troubles Xi: it allows for the creation of alternative centers of power within the state. To amass money is to amass influence; were an official to acquire those, he or she could begin to drag the state in directions different from those set by Xi. That contest could drag great China apart again.

So Xi is ruthless in his campaign against corruption. The first essential is to burnish a common ideology, as Jiang and Hu had done.

"Only when the thought and will of the entire party is unified," Xi argues, "can the thought and will of all the peoples of the entire country be unified"—which, in turn, he sees as the key to realizing the full strength of reform. There must be homage in the party to the great saints and tracts communism has produced: to Marxism-Leninism, to Mao Zedong thought, to Deng Xiaoping's socialism with Chinese characteristics, and to the three represents. For common ideology is the beacon that guides officials away from corruption; it gives them the semblance of a code to live by, quashes any defense based on the idea of not knowing better. China is to be a country of law; its constitution is to be strengthened.[9] There must be clear standards in which everyone is schooled, leaving no excuse for corruption.

Jiang and Hu had said much the same; the difference is how far Xi is willing to go. If the law is to carry credibility, it must govern both weak and strong. Xi's anticorruption campaign, therefore, purports not to balk from taking on the popular and the powerful. The names of the rich and famous began to adorn newspapers: tigers, taken as trophies in the hunt for the corrupt. Bo Xilai, the charismatic party chief of Chongqing, whose housing policies had made him so popular and who had done so much to foster nostalgia for Mao, was one scalp. (Charisma and popularity, one cannot help suspect, were in part what worked against him.) Zhou Yongkang, erstwhile head of the security services, found himself brought low. Even the ranks of the PLA were not safe: Xu Caihou, Gao Xiaoyan, Guo Zhenggang; here they were, these erstwhile military heroes, suddenly dragged into the limelight, accused of stealing from the people.[10] There will be no hesitation, no mercy in rooting out corruption. Some questions linger. Is the motive truly anticorruption, or is it simple political bloodletting, of the sort Mao had practiced? The answer being a bit of both and there being no truly independent body that can investigate Xi and those closest to him, there will always be doubts about the legitimacy of the enterprise. But such doubts weigh little with Xi. The campaign, even if greeted with a touch of cynicism, has been reasonably popular; corruption is so pernicious a problem that any attempts to address it will gain some support. For Xi's part the calculus is simple: to save China, you have to move against the corrupt, and if you do not move against them today, you might not have the chance to tomorrow.

The risk, of course, is blowback. Xi has identified himself so deeply with the anticorruption campaign that officials uncertain of their future might move to block him. It is particularly dangerous to target soldiers; these are armed men and women who could lash out violently, perhaps even seize power in a coup.[11] So Xi seeks to inspire loyalty to himself, by creating as formidable a cult of personality as China has seen since Mao's day. He drops into pork bun restaurants unannounced, to huddle with the masses. He and his wife are immortalized in songs, adoring if a touch saccharine.[12] Young soldiers, who might follow the siren call of their superiors in revolt, are to be reminded that there is the law—and Xi is the embodiment of it. He mingles with the people, as he did during the Cultural Revolution, because he wishes only to serve them; he will fight on their behalf against the powerful who have robbed their wealth, as tirelessly as he carried those loads in Shaanxi. He is protector and defender of the law, of the people, of China; he is Xi Jinping. It is a very different model of governance from that of Deng, Jiang, or Hu. Deng's character was unquenchable, but he preferred to work in the background; he had personal experience of how destructive a cult of personality could be. Jiang and Hu would not talk about themselves often; they strived to be unmemorable because being too prominent would get in the way of the work (which is one reason we hear fewer stories about their past than Xi's). Jiang's attempts at expressing himself—playing the erhu, for example—made for better comedy than inspiration. For Xi, personality is a tool to be used; it can advance the work of governing this vast, uncertain country that is pulling itself in so many different directions. His glory and that of the party and the Chinese nation have all become one.

None of this means abandoning the economic reform program that began with Deng. Xi's China remains committed to world trade, to profitability. Greater urgency about security does not require undoing the policies that have contributed to that security; it only means that certain adjustments, supervisions, have to be added to the mix. Both government and market have a role to play in the working of a healthy political economy; both invisible and visible hands, as Xi puts it, have their uses.[13] Some of this is straightforward: the state-owned enterprises still need to be reformed; China could use a better tax code; the *hukou* system, which makes labor mobility so difficult, can be relaxed. Some of it is clumsy, born of worry. The capital controls imposed suddenly or the abrupt eviction of Beijing's migrant workers do little to inspire confidence; they are the knee-jerk reaction of a government terrified by how much wealth is leaving the country or a migrant underworld that seems impossible to contain. Attempts to gauge and serve debt prove Sisyphean: there is always more credit extended, always one more person with shadowy government connections guaranteeing a project that cannot possibly pay. Of course, some of these problems—debt, taxation, income inequality—are far from unique to China; they are, as Marx might have said, an inevitable product of the capitalist system, and China, like most capitalist countries, will have to live with them. (Communist countries, for that matter, have had to live with them too.) But in a country where the party has staked its legitimacy on the promise that people will grow richer, they are troubling. One could, of course, move to dismantle the Dengist project altogether—but no serious Chinese policymaker would contemplate this. Far better, instead, to pay greater attention to the workings of the economy, to make sure that there is sufficient state regulation and initiative. Getting rich is glorious; the government will just have to do its part to make certain that riches and glory continue to flow without disrupting order.

The Balance of Power

Not just money is at stake. Money, as Deng had seen all those years ago, guarantees security—and the world beyond China's borders is far from stable. That old arc of instability, which had terrified Peng Dehuai in the run-up to the Korean War, still exists on China's eastern front. There are American forces perched in South Korea, Japan, the Philippines, Thailand. Taiwan is free of the American military presence, for now, but the Americans retain an ambiguous commitment to its defense. The Americans speak of a "pivot to Asia," which, for all their denials, is easy to interpret as an attempt to contain China or worse; it does not add credence to their denials when their policymakers and intellectuals discuss a coming war with China. The pivot turns out to be more talk than substance—among American allies there were grumbles about President Barack Obama's policy of retrenchment even before Obama's successor, Donald Trump, pulled the United States out of the trade pact that was the pivot's most crucial part—but talk can be worrisome; if nothing else, it suggests aspirations and possibilities that China must guard against. In the region itself, there are forces working against China. Japan continues to hold the Diaoyu / Senkaku Islands, denying Chinese claims and stoking nationalistic fires with their leaders' visits to the Yasukuni shrine. Tiny rocks and islands scattered across the South China Sea remain disputed—and countries like Vietnam are not shy about pushing their claims, their mobs not hesitant to kill ethnic Chinese. All of them look for support to the American behemoth, which is still uncertain about how far it will go to contain the PRC. Look outward from Beijing at a map of the world, and there is a disquieting sense of being locked in, with hostile forces ranged against you. Xi's China is not just a rising power inspiring fear in an established one, nor one whose sole ultimate purpose is the revival of lost glory.[14] It is a country uncertain of how durable its power and integrity will prove; it will do all it can to make certain of them. The grand strategy it pursues is, at heart, defensive—and all the more implacable for that. And because it is a massive country, that defensive policy can look suspiciously aggressive.

In trying to defend the state he is in charge of, Xi Jinping will use all the tools at his disposal. The first is diplomacy: an attempt to reason with both the Americans and those who seek their support against China. Second, there is money; one can offer it and deny it to get states to modify their behavior. And finally there is the use of force, for one cannot shy away from doing what is necessary.

The most basic task is to communicate what China will and will not put up with. China is bent on peaceful development, Xi promises; it, like the rest of the world, needs peace to develop. But no country, he warns, should hope that the PRC is going to barter away its core interests. Sovereign rights and security, development interests—these are not going to be compromised on.[15] If the rest of the world wants peace, it will have to be as reasonable as the PRC. In reaching out to the Americans, therefore, he has suggested a "new model of great power relations." As Xi first outlined the model, it is trite enough: mutual respect, cooperation on areas of common interest, and enriching the people of both countries, as well as those of the world as a whole;

Sino-American relations, as Xi observed, could facilitate world peace. He listed the achievements the bilateral relationship boasted: trade, environmental cooperation, Strategic Economic Dialogue, cities joined in friendship, the students each country sent to the other. The two sides needed to build on all this, strengthen the relationship.[16] It was nothing more or less than the kind of relationship the Chinese had demanded since Mao; the call for "mutual respect" harkened back to the five principles of peaceful coexistence. This did not stop American pundits and policymakers from parsing the phrase for hidden meaning and cunning traps, over and over again, but in essence, the model is simple. First, Beijing will cooperate with the United States where cooperation suits its interests. Nothing brought the point home as clearly as the climate change agreement, which Beijing pursued vigorously. Xi knows—knows with a cold, terrifying certainty—that the smog, the emissions could smother party and China. Early in his tenure, he had talked of the need for a revolution in energy: in the way it was produced and distributed, the resources tapped to get it. And he had pointed to the need for global cooperation in that quest.[17] Almost overnight, China has become one of the major users of green energy.[18] A meaningful climate agreement with Obama could only bolster China's national security. Xi would therefore pursue that agreement.

The other side of the new model—and there is, again, little new about it—is implicit in the idea of mutual respect: China would be vociferous in protecting its interests. If the United States were to menace it, say on the Korean peninsula or out on the South China Sea, Beijing would do all it could to protect its interests. The Americans are excluding it from the economic architecture of the region; Beijing will propose its own trade pact as an alternative to the Trans-Pacific Partnership, design its own Asian Infrastructure Investment Bank to offer an alternative to the World Bank. It is surprising how effective this proves: even the British, for all their talk of the special relationship with the United States, are willing to sign up. Since talking to Washington can go only so far, Beijing tries to pick apart that web of alliances and partnerships that is Pax Americana in the region, a web that threatens to tie China down. Asians, Xi says, are best suited to solving their own problems.[19] There is no need for outside— American—interference. It is whispered, as it was in the days of Bandung, to countries like South Korea and Japan: would it not be easier to solve regional problems without the Americans ever present? What need have people of a common region and heritage for outside interference?

The problem with this approach is that in a time of crisis, Asian countries continue to rely on that American guarantee of security. Beijing had spent so much time and effort wooing Seoul since the nineties.[20] There were stronger trade ties; there was cultural exchange, with South Korean soap operas immensely popular in the PRC. There was even room for condemning the old enemy, Japan, together, when Tokyo seemed to downplay its role in World War II. Besides, every now and then, South Korea seemed unhappy about playing host to the American military. Here, surely, was an American ally ripe for picking away. And yet when the North Koreans tested their missiles and the Americans offered a Terminal High Altitude Area Defense system (THAAD), the South Koreans accepted it despite Beijing's threats and blandishments. As Beijing sees it, the system will spy on the PRC as well as North Korea; it would be foolish to just accept American assurances to the contrary. The South Koreans, surely, should understand Beijing's concerns. Yet the South Koreans stood firm. And they did so despite Chinese tour groups boycotting their country, despite Beijing ceasing to air South Korean television shows and doing all that it could to make clear that THAAD would hurt the South Korean economy. The unhappy truth of it is that South Korea is more worried about what Kim Jong Un might do to it than about Beijing's ire; the latter is troublesome, the former a mortal threat. Only after a year of failing to shift South Korea's stance did Beijing cave to the inevitable and "reset relations." The reset was short-lived; the ban on tour groups was reinstated almost immediately.[21] Pique and pragmatism were still at war. But it was important, Beijing appeared to realize, to keep talking.

The bigger problem was Kim Jong Un. Kim is a client, ostensibly a friend; this does not mean he will desist from missile testing if Beijing asks. Threatening him with sanctions or denying him vital resources could trigger a refugee crisis that would bring a flood to China's northeast—home to its own ethnic Korean population. Worse, it could bring the North Korean state down. Troublesome as that state is—and there are some in China who think that with its unpredictable leader and its nuclear weapons, North Korea is a more immediate, more existential threat to the PRC than the United States, that some form of cooperation with the United States in the event of a North Korean collapse might be necessary—it remains a buffer zone on a sensitive frontier. With the Americans so active in the Asia-Pacific region, that is something hard to give up. Invading North Korea and changing the government, although tempting, could set off another Korean War. And potential successors to Kim backed by Beijing have a way of being found assassinated. It is astonishing how limited the leverage one has over a client state can be. Let the client state figure out that it is needed, and it will do as it pleases, regardless of its patron's imprecations to prudence and decency.[22]

Changes in South Korea and the United States did little to help. Moon Jae-in came to power in South Korea talking of reaching out to the North—which means reaching out to China too. Donald Trump, meanwhile, has been talking about charging the South Koreans for THAAD. His defense team denied this would happen, but the mere talk was sufficient to get the South Koreans to start thinking about alternatives to the American alliance. Just how far Seoul will go remains to be seen. Much depends on whether Moon and Xi can actually get Kim to act more amicably, and that seems a poor hope indeed. Thus far, at least, there has been little sign that Kim will re-sign himself to denuclearization. Sooner or later, this runs the risk of frustrating South Korean patience and marking an end to attempts to reason with Pyongyang. Given all this, Beijing's decision is stark, if devilishly difficult. Does it fear the American presence on its border more than it does a nuclear North Korea bent on terrifying the re-gion into instability? There are no good choices here. Asia for the Asians can be a difficult place to be.

Emotion can overpower grand strategy too. Deng Xiaoping had been almost dismissive of the territorial dispute with Japan; there was no need to allow such matters to get in the way of business. But the dispute had never been resolved; that, coupled with the oft-told sto-ries of what Japan had done to China in World War II, meant that new leadership could always find ways of squabbling. It was almost inevitable that the assertive and swaggering Xi Jinping and the effort-lessly patronizing Japanese prime minister Shinzo Abe would clash over the stretch of sea and rocklets that lay between them. Meanwhile, Liu Xiaoming, China's ambassador to the United Kingdom, would, in an almost comical reference to Harry Potter, describe the Yasukuni shrine as a horcrux, containing the darkest parts of Japan's soul. The Japanese would hit back by pointing out that China had launched an arms race, which was what the dark wizard Voldemort had done—and from there the whole matter went on. For a year, the two sides groused about one another, their ships risking war at sea, till Abe and Xi met at the G-20 summit for the most stilted handshake in history. There was room, they decided, to ease the tension. Japan and China, Xi said, were important neighbors: good relations between them were good for both, as well as for the region. China's basic position on improving the relationship had not changed: they should take responsibility and be alert to crises, work to expand the good and minimize the bad between them. There could be dialogue to keep the East China Sea stable.[23] For all the warships and fury, Beijing's diplomacy was still based on the idea that having been dialed up, tension could be dialed back down too. Things had not reached the point where one wanted a war with Japan. It was best, therefore, to continue talking, even if the talks went nowhere. One would not compromise on core interests, of course, but as long as those were not bartered away, there was no harm in seeking dialogue. But that earlier burst of anger would rankle with Tokyo, give ammunition to those who argued that in the long term, there was no reasoning with Beijing.

Taiwan too would prove hard to manage. Xi had invested enormous time, energy, and prestige in his dealings with the renegade island. He had gloried in the achievement of the three links (direct postal services, trade, and transport), had shared his vision of further profit and economic cooperation to come. He had met with the GMD honorary chairman, spoken of how they could work together to restore the Chinese nation, of how they needed to nurture the cross-strait relationship on a peaceful basis. To be sure, he acknowledged, the relationship had problems—legacies of a troubled past—but these should not be allowed to get in the way of fostering good relations, cooperative exchanges between the compatriots across the strait.[24] The Taiwanese needed to understand that China, of which they were unavoidably part, had been good for them; why was this so hard to understand? And yet somehow, as 2015 drew to a close, those impossible young people who claimed a separate Taiwanese identity were on the verge of powering the Democratic Progressive Party, with the hated Tsai Ing-wen as potential president, into office. In his last desperate attempt to keep the Guomindang in power, Xi Jinping met with Ma Ying-jeou—and in that attempt demonstrated just how poor China's understanding of Taiwan remained. Xi had thought that meeting Ma would give the latter face, credibility, which he could campaign on. Here, Ma's electorate would realize, was a serious man, who could meet another serious man and thus deliver good governance. What Taiwanese saw instead was a leader suspected of being too close to Beijing proving he was too close to Beijing as he tried to rescue himself from a raft of failed policies. They saw too a giant that already exercised too much economic sway over them trying to influence the results of their election. They had heard Hong Kong's citizens complain of how "one country, two systems" had meant a steady diminution of their autonomy, had heard tales of people abducted from that territory for holding views Beijing deemed unacceptable; they knew how easily an agreement based on "one country, two systems" could give way to one country alone. Tsai Ing-wen was voted into office, and peaceful reunification remained, at least for the moment, a distant dream. Xi Jinping cared deeply about Taiwan—so deeply that he did not understand it.

Farther south there was better luck. China had long insisted that it would deal with the Southeast Asian countries one to one in addressing the South China Sea disputes, as opposed to going through the Association of Southeast Asian Nations (ASEAN). It made it simpler to achieve a balance of power. If one could reach a deal with one country it was easier to point to it when dealing with others, an example of how reasonable China could be, of what could be achieved if Beijing could only find a similarly reasonable negotiating partner, and of what could be lost if it failed. Vietnam—perhaps because of the memory of Chinese aggression—was implacable, but the Philippines was a different story. China had been uncompromising in warding Manila and its citizens off from the territory between the two, and the Philippines, believing in international law, had taken China to The Hague. China had been incensed; this was none of the World Court's business. The verdict came in favor of the Philippines—and then something remarkable happened. Even as the Americans were gloating about the triumph of a liberal world order and international law (this was particularly ironic: Washington had never ratified the United Nations Convention on the Law of the Sea, the treaty that lay at the heart of the dispute; both Beijing and Manila were parties), the Philippines' president Rodrigo Duterte announced his own pivot to China. It was unclear quite what his statement of "separation" from the United States meant: the U.S. military base would stay there. But suddenly trade deals worth $24 billion were being signed between the two countries, with more to come. Beijing would promise to buy bananas from the Philippines, help with ports and railways.[25] A cynic could be forgiven for suspecting that there might be something for Duterte in it personally. Later, Duterte would claim that Xi had signaled his willingness to go to war over the South China Sea; this seems unlikely, but the two sides did initiate a dialogue about the territorial dispute. As long as they were talking to one another, as long as their economic links continued to strengthen, there was room for an understanding based on "joint development" of the sort Deng had once floated. Money was a tool—it could be used to induce negotiation.

Behind the economic blandishment and the willingness to be reasonable, there lies a growing military power. The PRC declared an Air Defense Identification Zone over the South China Sea in 2013;

the United States sent fighter planes right through it. The American resolve is tested, the measure of their commitment, their strength taken. There are air and naval forces to be modernized: aircraft carriers and submarines to be acquired, a military base in Djibouti to be set up, anti-access and area denial capabilities to perfect.[26] And there is always people's warfare: older, less expensive ways of tilting the battlefield in one's favor. The fishermen have always strayed into the East and South China Seas and the waters beyond: why not arm them, allow them to assert themselves when they come into conflict with foreign pretenders? Why not dump earth into the sea, as others were doing too, to raise islands where there were none, and militarize the new creations? Such policies do not achieve much in the conflict with Japan. The Japanese coastguard is more than capable of dealing with the fishermen; those waters are too well protected to allow for land reclamation. But in the South China Sea, such measures can alter the strategic landscape, slowly, inexorably. The Americans do not quite know how to respond to this. Barack Obama was a cautious man, unwilling to enter a conflict he could not see a sensible way out of. He was willing to run freedom of navigation sorties through the troubled waters, but he would not do more. And since freedom of navigation operations do not really stall the island building (it would be another matter, of course, if the Americans blew the islands out of the water), there is no reason for Beijing to worry about them too much. The limits to where Obama would go had become clear; so too had the possibilities China could pursue in its maritime near abroad. The United States would talk about China's destruction of the liberal world order. It would not do anything effective about it. Simply put, Beijing cared more about the theater than Washington did, cared in ways Washington could not fathom. China needs a place to break through the islands that confine it to the near seas. For it is beyond the seas that markets lie, the minerals that sustain the Chinese economy, the lands where China gets food from now and will get food from in the future. The United States might say it guarantees freedom of navigation, but Xi knows better than to rely on such promises. Goodwill can change tomorrow; to rely on it for access to the high seas is a risk he is unwilling to take.

In the election of Donald Trump to the American presidency, there lies both danger and opportunity for China. The danger: he is reckless; he is unpredictable. He tears away from the Paris agreement on climate change and denounces the international trade system, both of which China had done yeoman's work for and which it has a vested interested in sustaining. His secretary of state threatened to block China's warships from the islands land reclamation had created. To top it all off, after winning the election he took a congratulatory phone call from Tsai Ing-wen, as radical a departure from established policy as any since Reagan's day (and Reagan had threatened to undo the Sino-American rapprochement by restoring normal relations with Taiwan); he then went on to suggest that it might be time to retire the one China principle. This was absolutely outrageous. It would have to be made clear that, as China saw it, the one China principle was the foundation of the Sino-American relationship and all the commerce associated with it, that the principle was integral to the modern world order.[27] Nothing would come, at least immediately, of the dalliance, but it was not pleasant while it lasted. Then too, Trump might rip up the old American alliances that have become part of the fabric of East Asian security; this was something Beijing had long wanted, but the implications could suddenly make one careful of what one wished for. What if Japan, bereft of the defense alliance, went nuclear, with no sensible partner to counsel the warmongers in Tokyo to prudence? A Japan like that could be a dangerous foe; there was no telling what the rest of East Asia would do. Trump's rhetoric and belligerence could upset the strategic environment in ways Beijing had not begun to grapple with.

Once one has had time to recover from the latest Twitter blasts, however, the opportunities Trump poses become clearer. One is that he might be corruptible. Give him and his family the trademarks and business deals they seek, and he might just find that America's core interests are more easily compromised on than one might suspect. It is remarkable how swiftly such trademarks came Trump's way after the inauguration.[28] He remains, of course, eminently unpredictable, but for the moment at least, he is pliable. In Florida, Xi assured Trump that China is peaceful, that it wants to be a partner to the United States, that it welcomes American participation in China's humungous, if rather vague, economic initiative, One Belt, One Road. It is willing to work with America to protect world peace and stability.[29] Trump would hail Xi as a "good man" and celebrate a trade deal, which, experts gripe, comprised mainly promises that China has made before.[30] He tweeted praise for the "King of China" after the party congress of 2017; on his own visit to Beijing, he was almost cloying in his praise of Xi.[31] There were no guarantees, of course. Like Duterte and Kim, Trump would remain unpredictable, now fawning, now lashing out in his National Security Strategy about how "China and Russia want to shape a world antithetical to U.S. values and interests."[32] Rhetorical flourishes aside, the National Security Strategy's portrayal of China as a competitor was little different from that which the Obama or even the Bush administration had articulated. The sheer changeability of the new president gave Beijing room to hope that that portrayal might change. For all the worries that the Tsai call had triggered, this is as smooth as the Sino-American relationship has been at any point since 2013.

The other opportunity was simple too. With turmoil in the American polity, the rest of the world might look to China for leadership. There is a touch of schadenfreude in Chinese press coverage of the distress Trump had brought to American political life.[33] Someone has to take charge—why not China? It is Xi who rises to declare that the Paris agreement on the environment will be upheld, regardless of what the Americans said. It is Xi who gives a stirring speech at the 2017 Davos World Economic Forum in favor of globalization and free trade. "There was a time," he recalls, "when China also had doubts about economic globalization, and was not sure whether it should join the World Trade Organization. But we came to the conclusion that integration in the global economy is a historical trend. To grow its economy China must have the courage to swim in the vast ocean of the global market.... Whether you like it or not, the global economy is the big ocean you cannot escape from."[34] He had spoken in Indonesia in 2013 of the maritime Silk Road; he had talked of the trade that could create a glorious future for Southeast Asia, of China's proposed investment bank to support developing countries, of the responsibility China shared with Southeast Asia for regional stability. It was time, according to Xi, to abandon the ways of the Cold War; they could work together to resolve their territorial differences and contribute to the stability of the region.[35] (Indonesia, as an aside, had a simple way of dealing with Chinese fishermen who poached its waters: destroy their boats.) In the darkness of Trump's protectionist rhetoric and general recklessness, that maritime Silk Road sparkles all the brighter. Almost overnight, the PRC has gone from being a spoiler of the liberal world order to serving as its foremost champion.

To the north and west, the strategic landscape looks friendlier for China, although there is no taking it for granted. The Russians, Xi enthuses in a speech in Moscow, are a friendly neighbor; the sound relations that subsist between them are not only good for the two countries, but for the global strategic balance, for stability and peace in the world.[36] With the United States and Europe placing sanctions on Russia in the wake of the Crimean crisis, there is a window in which to reach out to the Russians; Beijing can be closer to both Washington and Moscow than they are to one another. It can finance Russian gas exploration in the Arctic or build pipelines connecting the two countries; it can even dream of alleviating its drought by bringing in water from those massive Russian lakes. Xi advocates, as have Chinese leaders before him, letting the people of each country determine their own path, noninterference in internal affairs; these are ideas that will appeal to his audience.[37] Not that China could buy Russia completely. There are limits to what money can get, and the Russians will always do things their own way. Even as relations between Moscow and Beijing warmed, Russia was cooperating with Vietnam on gas exploration in the South China Sea—the resources in question were ones the PRC claimed.[38] There is no such thing as a permanent, all-weather friendship. Neither Beijing nor Moscow expects theirs to be one. It is a partnership of convenience, designed to balance against the American menace. Were the convenience to disappear tomorrow, the relationship would suffer accordingly.

The Shanghai Cooperation Organization has, by and large, been a useful forum, and Xi continues to preach the "Shanghai spirit." The partners in that organization would work together for the stability of their shared region; Afghanistan is of particular importance to that cause, and the SCO should, Xi says, support national reconciliation in that country. (A hint here: the Americans have not been up to the task.)[39] Hu Jintao had invoked the Silk Road. Since anything Hu could do, Xi could do grander, China would spearhead the creation of a new Silk Road Economic Belt, which, coupled with its maritime counterpart, became "One Belt, One Road." New projects abound along both belt and road: a troupe of Terracotta Warriors sent to Istanbul, railway projects in Southeast Asia, assistance with building ports in countries like Pakistan. The road and the belt could stretch across Asia and Africa to Europe, stabilizing and enriching the places they touched. China was to spend about $150 billion each year in the participating countries.[40] Truth be told, it was more concept than reality, a label with which to cover all the different deals—some good, some bad, some still unrealized—that came with a growing economy. But labels can be helpful. They sound bold, ambitious, and create excitement, even if the substance behind them folds and crumbles when touched. Since Beijing is committed to economic relations with these countries anyway, it does not hurt to have an appealing slogan.

One component that is of particular geostrategic importance is the China-Pakistan Economic Corridor. It annoys the Indians, who maintain that the corridor stretches through Indian territory, thereby undercutting Xi's attempts to reach an understanding with that particular neighbor. It annoys the local Baluch along the southern end of the corridor too; they signal their displeasure by abducting and killing Chinese workers sent to Pakistan. But the corridor is crucial: the Gwadar port the Chinese were helping to build and run is the closest point of maritime access Xinjiang has. Were the Americans ever to succeed in blockading the Chinese coast, it is the Karakoram Highway that is China's best link to the sea. The Pakistanis are not easy to deal with. Money invested there has a way of paying badly; they are always asking for more, and the security they provide for workers is appalling. But a country cannot choose its neighbors; cursed as it is by geography, China has to placate the North Koreas and Pakistans of the world to remain secure. And there are farther worlds to continue to reach too. Xi travels to Tanzania to celebrate Sino-African friendship, to Mexico to deepen trade and economic cooperation with Latin America. He preaches the Silk Road spirit to the Arab League, calls on fellow BRICS to do their bit for the world economy and humanity.[41] For all the ambition and grandiloquence, for all the talk of restoring the great Chinese nation, Xi Jinping continues to court support among smaller countries. Their importance is not to be underestimated; they still have a role to play in shaping a balance of power favorable to China.

The Perils of Grand Strategy

Xi Jinping, then, is pursuing a grand strategy similar to that of his predecessors. The goal remains keeping the state intact: this, in turn, requires political cohesion, economic growth, a favorable balance of power, and strong armed forces. What has changed is the intensity he brings to the project. To remain a great power, the conclusion seems to have been, China will have to act like one. The state remains ever vigilant to threats—and because its power has grown, it is both more willing and more able to do something about them. Great power does not easily translate into a great sense of security.[42]

Several problems bedevil Xi's approach. The first is that his use of military power has undermined the larger strategic goal it was meant to achieve: a stable neighborhood. Countries like Japan and Vietnam have not backed down when threatened by fishing militias and aircraft carriers. Instead, China's forcefulness seems to have spurred their quests for military power. Absent the threat in the East China Sea, Japan's government would have had a much harder time passing the security bill (or the "war bill" as demonstrators called it), or initiating a conversation about abandoning the pacifist clause in the constitution. Tokyo would start seeking support from others concerned about

Chinese power: Southeast Asian countries, Taiwan, India, and Australia. Vietnam's military spending rose steadily, as did its military cooperation with the United States. Here was a country that had been at war with the United States, courting its former enemy in an attempt to contain and defeat the current one. Taiwan's new leader, Tsai Ingwen, would quietly invest in boosting military power. She could not count on the United States in the age of Donald Trump; if Taiwan wanted to keep the democracy it had worked so hard to build, it would have to secure the means to protect it. Beijing's diplomacy and economic offerings have been countered by the fear its military demonstrations provoke. The surge of military spending that those around China have embarked on suggests that they are far from resigned to Chinese dominance. And this means that the PRC's security environment is becoming ever more dangerous. Across China's neighborhood, smaller countries are banding together, summoning in help not just from North America (where military spending is also on the rise), but from India too, all with a view to keeping the colossus firmly penned in. Such attempts might fail, of course, but they make Beijing's attempts to avoid containment much harder.[43]

To deal with that growing danger, Xi will feel the need to increase his own security spending still further—not just in the aerospace and naval sectors, but on those old home fronts the PRC has long worried about: the borderlands like Xinjiang and Hong Kong, where foreigners can stoke local grievances in an attempt to bring China down. (The decision to ban "abnormal" beards in Xinjiang suggests that Beijing feels far from secure in its grip on that region.) One will need more missiles and sensors, more plainclothes police and neighborhood spies to keep the country whole. The risk is that there will come a point of "imperial overstretch" at which the burden security concerns place on the economy becomes too great to bear.[44] This will not necessarily entail a collapse in Chinese power, but it does cause that power to be diminished. The functioning of the state will suffer, and in China, that always raises existential fears.

It does not help that the rise in military spending comes as economic growth, long overstated, slows. An aging population always means slowing growth, but each new day brings the discovery of another loan that cannot be repaid, another state-owned enterprise that is not delivering what it promised. Xi has tried to rein in the credit that fueled the boom in the housing market, but it is not easy; shadow lenders emerge to do what banks will not. No one quite knows how far or how deep China's debt crisis runs—which, of course, makes it all the more terrifying. And there is the credit extended to foreigners: the investment in Pakistani infrastructure, the loans to Venezuela, the money being poured into the One Belt, One Road fund. These are not the types of debts that will be repaid. (So dire does the situation get that one goes so far as to sue Venezuela in an American court in hope of recovering some money.)[45] They look grand; they buy friends of sorts, it is true, but over time they add to the strain on the state's finances. There was a reason Deng pruned the PRC's foreign aid budget: every little bit helps, and his stance was China first. Xi Jinping has reversed that policy. The reversal brings China to a position of leadership, but leadership can be an expensive pastime.

And then there is the Chinese state: this sprawling conglomeration, where local authorities still try desperately to maintain their little fiefdoms. One can send out orders about curbing pollution, but how can they be enforced all across China's expanse? One can declare that the state will be in charge of religion, but there are only so many illicit house churches one can break up, only so many truck drivers with pictures of the Dalai Lama on their windshields that one can stop out on the lonely mountain roads of the Tibetan plateau. And given all the resentment it has triggered, one cannot be sure that the state will continue with Xi Jinping's campaign against corruption. Since the campaign is bound inextricably with the person, its sustainability is too; there has been no long-term institutionalization. As Xi approaches a time when he should, by the norms Deng set, be contemplating a successor, the future of Chinese grand strategy is remarkably tenuous.

This is challenging enough. To top it all off, China itself seems to have turned against Xi: the air, the water, the land. Soil pollution poisons the food; the state tries, desperately, to stop factories from dumping pollutants into the commons, but it is difficult to police—the land remains awash with mercury and heavy metals. There have been attempts to cut emissions—trying to shut down factories, limit driving—but city alerts and mask purchases showed little sign of abating in early 2017. A series of bad decisions on water management, going back to the Mao days—the enormous dams, deforestation, the killing of the pikas, those keystone mammals whose burrows allow groundwater to recover—all compounded in Xi's time to create water stress and drought.[46] Xi would revive a grandiose scheme from Mao's days: transferring water from south to north. That the plan would only exacerbate the problem, that China's water crisis could not be solved without regulating demand and attending to the ecosystem as a whole, that southerners were grumbling about a distant government stealing their water—none of this altered Beijing's plans. Over the long term, if things continue on this course, the country will be parched. It was rivers that had cradled the Chinese civilization that Xi sought to restore. What will he and his successors do when they run dry?

CONCLUSION

NONE OF THIS is to fault Xi. He is the product of a particular environment, and the grand strategy he is pursuing is part of a tradition that has, for the most part, served the PRC well. There can be few jobs more difficult than that of paramount leader of China: the surrounding world invariably alive with danger, the extent of the state, its integrity, and its stability forever uncertain. For an outsider, it is easy to observe that the PRC is far more secure now than it used to be. To a Chinese leader, that is far from sufficient as reassurance. The Korean War and the tussle with the Soviet Union, the Cultural Revolution and Tiananmen Square, the Taiwan crises, the American flights going by that vulnerable coast—they are all burned in on the Chinese official mind. And behind them there are the lessons of a farther past, of Opium Wars and the warlord era, reminders of how complacency in a dangerous world can lead to dismemberment and despair. National security cannot be taken for granted. That the PRC was cobbled together is remarkable. That it has endured, both self-inflicted damage and hostility from abroad, is even more so. Luck has played a role, of course, but so too has grand strategy—often unarticulated, but usually there to shape decisions. We should see the policies pursued by the PRC's paramount leaders in the round, with all their virtues and their faults.

The ideas and forces that would underpin PRC grand strategy were evident from the state's genesis. Most important, perhaps, was the idea that there was a Chinese state of which the CCP was the rightful governing party. This seems banal, perhaps, but for a group of bandits dismissed by the outside world as either incompetent peasants or a gang of communist thugs, this was revolutionary—all the more so given how many different pieces China had been broken into at the time. One has to understand oneself, one's place in the world, to know what one will and will not defend. This the CCP did. And having defined its goal as statehood, it would use different categories of power to achieve that goal. There was diplomacy, both with great powers and with ethnic groups beyond the area the state controlled, with rivals as well as potential friends; Mao would court the Soviets and the Americans, the Japanese and the Tibetans. Even Chiang Kai-shek could be talked to—as long as he realized he was talking to the representatives of a Chinese state. There was the recognition that the state would need to provide for those it controlled. Delivering economically was a key to governance; the loyalty of the peasants would depend on their getting a decent living. Diplomacy and socioeconomic policy alike would have to be backed up by military power. The way military power was exercised would have to suit the nature of the state, its strengths and its capacities. Hence the focus on guerrilla warfare; it was what was needed at the time. When the nature of the state changed, the tools it employed might have to change too—though it would try to keep what had served it well. In either event, it would not shy away from the use of force. It had fought its way into existence, whether out on the Central Plains or in the mountains of Tibet. The state was forged, to a great extent, by war.

Once forged, there was room for compromise at its edges. At the margins, the state could give and take. Goodwill was what mattered. One could cede territory to Pakistan or Burma. One could leave maritime territorial disputes unresolved and continue with business with neighbors. The status of territory counted less than the overall relationship and its contribution to Chinese national security. But that room for compromise went only so far. That Tibet and Xinjiang, Hong Kong and Taiwan, were inalienable parts of China was a given. In that insistence one detects a departure from grand strategy. The geostrategic importance of Tibet and Xinjiang as buffer zones was evident when they were first taken and remains evident now. But Taiwan shows where grand strategy shades over into emotion. It was one thing to insist on Taiwan being part of China when it was run by Chiang Kai-shek, intent on taking back the mainland. Taiwan today is an entity unto itself—and one more useful to China in that capacity than as yet another province in which it must suppress rebellion. In purely grand strategic terms, the easiest way of gaining a pliable Taiwan is to offer it independence and treat it like the Philippines—incline it to China's will with suitable economic offerings and the occasional threat. In the failure to consider such a policy or in the heavy-handedness with which Xi approaches Hong Kong, Xinjiang, and Tibet, the blind spots of Chinese grand strategy become evident. We the Chinese people have stood up, Chairman Mao had said. It was important to keep them standing. That meant insisting on what China took to be its right; it also meant compromising, giving up a little bit of territory for the greater security of the whole. But that last precept is something not taken as far as it might be.

Even when agreeable compromise could not be reached, the PRC was fine with letting talks wind on. The point of diplomacy was not to reach a specific agreement; it was to maintain a decent working relationship, because decent working relationships kept the state alive. The United States, refusing to recognize the PRC; the Soviet Union, with which the border clashes became so fierce; the Taiwanese, intent on staying apart from the country that claimed them; Japan, unapologetically clinging to the Diaoyu / Senkaku Islands and sending its leaders to the Yasukuni shrine—the PRC would not abandon communication with them altogether. There were exceptions, to be sure, notably during the Cultural Revolution and in Deng's dealings with Vietnam. But by and large, the PRC's practice has been to keep talking, even in—especially in—a crisis.

Geography gave the PRC many neighbors. This could be a curse, often enough, but it could also be of help: the more players there were, the easier it was to achieve a balance of power favorable to Chinese national security. Situated as it was, China sought to be closer to the great powers than they were to one another. Even while leaning to one side, Mao's China would try to achieve a modus vivendi with both the United States and the Soviet Union; only thus could it be reasonably certain that the two superpowers would not conspire to carve it up. Smaller powers too had a role to play, and the more of them there were, the better. It was willing to talk to Vietnam, Cambodia, and Laos, to seek decent relations with India as well as Pakistan. The insistence on addressing disputes in the South China Sea bilaterally rather than through the Association of Southeast Asian Nations reflects China's understanding that dealing with multiple actors is better than dealing with a bloc. One can play them off against one another, shore up little bits of support and understanding that add up over time. The search for further friendships—in Africa, the Middle East,

Latin America—reflects not the type of ideological contest that animated the Soviet Union and the United States, but a deceptively simple insight: it helps to have all the friends you can get.[1] There was a reason Chinese courtship of the world beyond Moscow and Washington survived the Cold War; it was never just about competition with those two capitals. There was a reason too that the type of support the PRC would give to countries across the globe changed from one era to the next. The support was calibrated to its larger grand strategy; it was meant to serve the Chinese state. Beyond China's near abroad, it was never a simple reflex action to keep the Soviets or Americans out; indeed, one could use mutual friends to reach out to an uncomprehending rival. It was, rather, a gathering of friends to make sure the future was friendly.

Because attitudes change and friends are unreliable, it was only responsible to back diplomacy with force. It was always going to be hard in China, with its outlaw bands and citizens' militias, its revolutionary leaders who were guerrilla warriors, to demarcate the civil and military spheres cleanly. The party would have to be perpetually vigilant, always ready to assert its leadership over the PLA. This would involve allowing the army a certain role in the political and economic life of the country; it would also involve defining the limits of that role. Education would be crucial: soldiers would be reminded over and over again that they were subordinate to the party. The relationship between the party and the military remains a difficult one. It will require maintenance and unceasing attention by Xi and his successors.

Two sides to the Chinese way of warfare would emerge. The first was the quest for a modern military, one that had the latest weapons and could stand up against the superpowers. The extraordinary rise of Chinese naval power is rooted in the CCP's early battles along the coast. Defeat to the Nationalists at Guningtou was a lesson in the importance of sea power; with the Americans patrolling the Chinese coast, interest in warships and the airpower that accompanies them could only grow. Since China had gone to war with superpowers in the past, it was only sensible to be prepared for such war in the future. So nuclear weaponry, sensors, missiles, and aircraft carriers would all have to be obtained. Not that one was planning on using them in combat; the strategic precept remained active defense. It was just that guaranteeing defense required a formidable arsenal (one that could also be turned to offensive purposes). As a superpower, the definition of defense would expand: the PRC would be far more active globally, not least because it felt that growing portions of the world were vital to its own survival. With great power comes great insecurity.

But the old belief in the value of people's warfare never went away either. It was a struggling band of guerrillas, after all, who won the state. It was volunteers from China's villages who fought the Americans to a standstill in the Korean War, despite Stalin's dismissiveness of their skill in the air. If danger threatened, it was the people who would defend China, no matter what the cost. There was a time and place for modern weaponry. But there was a time and place too for fishermen militias, for people sailing into contested seas and pushing, gradually, against adversaries. Again, the goal was defensive. These were seen as Chinese waters; besides, letting potential enemies in them today was only a recipe for a larger-scale invasion tomorrow. A modernized military and people's war would both be part of China's military strategy. With both, there remained the idea—and this related to the diplomatic tack of never severing communication—that tension could be dialed up and down. Because one would be willing to keep talking, one could engage in clashes along the Amur River or in the East China Sea. One could signal displeasure by testing missiles (Taiwan) or even by invading a country (Vietnam). In the worst extremity, one could always adjust the use of force and avoid a larger war that would only harm Chinese security. "War," Carl von Clausewitz said famously, "is the continuation of policy by other means." The use of military power was meant to serve the larger policy. It could be recalibrated if need be. This is a risky, imprudent strategy. It assumes that the other parties involved will be as rational as the PRC in calibrating force to larger goals. But that assumption has been one the PRC has made since its inception.

The greatest variations came in the economic realm, with Mao's wild experimentation, the laissez-faire policies of the 1970s, and then the emergence of income inequality and dud loans that challenged China from the 1990s to today. But there was, throughout this, an unwavering belief that the economy was one plank in the larger architecture of national security and that it would have to be treated as such. The economy, like everything else, was meant to keep China safe. This was the idea that lay at the heart of Mao's misguided Great Leap Forward: the only way of ensuring that China could stand up against the larger superpowers was by outstripping them economically. And this was the idea that lay at the heart of Deng's reform and opening: one needed to get China's economy functioning in order to keep it secure. The fruits of that policy would ripen in the Jiang and Hu eras. China's astonishing growth brought in a new tool of statecraft: economic diplomacy. Beijing could offer loans to win friends, or threaten to cease business if a foreign country's policy ran counter to its interests. Mao, of course, had tried the former, with some success, but China had not had the heft, the impact, it does today. It was Deng's economic stewardship that put the PRC in a place where it could use economic power to its full potential.

Problems were inevitable. No grand strategy is perfect—and China's geopolitical circumstances were such that life was always going to be difficult. Some of the problems were intrinsic to getting rich. To get rich is glorious, but in a capitalist system (and for that matter, in a communist one), there are winners and there are losers. There is incentive to cheat, exploit, steal—and one is better equipped to do that the closer one is to power. The state was bound to get entangled in the economy; since its officials were only human, they would take advantage of that entanglement. The insistence that there was only one legitimate institution of power would make it virtually impossible to tackle graft, for the party would have to be cop, judge, and enforcer all in one. Income inequality and corruption represented the dark side of the success.

Abroad too, success came with the seeds of failure. As with corruption, these failures were, to an extent, inevitable. If China succeeded in becoming powerful enough to be secure, its sheer size would terrify its neighbors, who would seek support from abroad. Mao had pointed out that smaller countries would fear large ones—and in this he was not wrong. Xi took charge of a country that places like Burma and Vietnam were already eyeing with suspicion. But because he too felt suspicious—and this was natural—and because he was not prepared to sit still and do nothing, the tone of Chinese grand strategy shifted. It became more assertive, strident; there were more Chinese ships in the near seas; there was more pressure on neighbors. This would exacerbate the insecurity in smaller countries—and in doing so create the very insecurity Xi had been trying to avoid. He himself could not understand this. Did they not see that China was merely defending itself and its core interests? That incomprehension has brought his country almost full circle. The world China faces today is not quite what it was in the early Mao years, but it is as unfriendly as it has been at any point since the late 1960s. As grand strategies go, Xi Jinping's is not a bad one. In a world turning hostile, it is prudent to strengthen control, to shore up support, to make sure that China has the means of protecting itself. At a very fundamental level, Chinese grand strategists have been successful in the goal they set—and this success was by no means certain. To stick to the principles that underpinned that success makes eminent good sense. But it is one thing to pursue them when weak, another to pursue them when at China's current size and shape. The latter inspires fear, and fear resistance.

Success also undermined the physical foundations of China. Corruption, geopolitical upheaval: in a pinch, one could find a way out of these. But civilization had emerged around rivers; what was one to do if they vanished? China could prepare to fight the Americans, but choking skies and land unfit for food production were enemies of a different kind. Environmental change has led to state collapse before—in China and elsewhere. It can do so again. Human beings are animals; like animals, they require suitable habitat, a friendly ecosystem in which to function. Take those away, and the mores and norms that allow states to function crumble swiftly. Without food and water and basic well-being, the PRC's long-term future could be bleak indeed. This existential problem too is a product of success, a result of economic growth. One needs a strong economy to stay secure. But the demands that economy has placed on natural resources are simply too massive.

Some sort of change, as Xi has recognized, will be necessary. And it is worth noting that environmental strain and income inequality are far from being exclusively Chinese problems. Much of the rest of the world is afflicted with them (there was a reason the idea of sustainable development goals emerged; it was a tweak to modernity, one that sought to balance the benefits with a greater amelioration of the costs). The current travails of the United States should remind us that they are not exclusively the product of a democratic deficit either. They are problems endemic to a certain way of doing business, which was once seen as the path to modernity. It remains to be seen if Chinese grand strategy can adapt to dealing with them.

Such success as there has been feels, now, strangely wanting. The purpose of grand strategy—in China's case at least—is to secure the state. That in itself is an accomplishment. But what is the purpose of the state? If it is meant to provide happiness, then the PRC's success has been mixed at best. The millions slain during the Mao years, the students slaughtered at Tiananmen, the activists rounded up in the post–Cold War era—they all show what happens when grand strategy is untempered by humaneness. The Chinese leaders responsible believed such measures were necessary. This is understandable, but untrue. One did not need to launch the Great Leap Forward to up China's productivity. The students at Tiananmen could have been given more time to disband. Even if one dismisses Western-style democracy as unsuited to China's circumstances, some of the arrests and imprisonments seem gratuitous. Between utter chaos and the state they created, there lie several shades of light, which, vision clouded by fear, China's leaders were unable to see. The past, real and imagined, hung as heavy on them as it does on us all; it bent them toward certain futures and rendered others unthinkable.

Meanwhile, the Chinese dream has somehow stalled. Roaming China, there is a sense of unhappiness, discontent, an inability to believe in a better tomorrow. There is, as many Chinese mourn, nothing left to believe in. Life on a day-to-day basis is richer and safer, but precarious. Aircraft carriers are all very well, but one cannot breathe the air. Economic influence might be spreading, but the land itself is poisoned, and people cannot trust the food they eat. For a country that has a coherent grand strategy, China has far too many people moving abroad. There is too much Chinese investment in Boston or San Francisco real estate to suggest a citizenry that feels secure. The capital controls hint at a broader problem: a lack of faith in China. How Xi and his successors will address this remains unclear. But if PRC grand strategy is to serve the ultimate goal—satisfying its citizens—it needs, perhaps, to pay a little less attention to security and a little more to compassion.

Mao Zedong took a broken colossus, made it whole, and stood it up on its feet. Deng dragged it to reason and strength; Jiang and Hu nurtured the still-wounded giant and ensured that it continued to grow. Now, as Xi Jinping emerged to take mastery of it, great China strode the world, a behemoth whose time had come. But though the colossus was whole, it still felt fragile. It was hobbled by the memories of how difficult safety had been to achieve, and it was terrified that it would fall apart again.

AFTERWORD

I was in Taiwan in the winter of 2019–2020. It was a good place to observe firsthand the limitations of Xi Jinping's grand strategy. The oppression of Hong Kong, rooted in Beijing's insecurity, had made a deep impression on the Taiwanese electorate. Tsai Ing-wen, the incumbent president, harped on China's Hong Kong policy over and over again, as she campaigned against her relatively pro-Beijing opponent, Han Kuo-yu. Beijing's characteristically cack-handed attempts at interference—disinformation and public threats—only served to convince Taiwan's voters that any chance of salvation lay with Tsai and her Democratic Progressive Party. What should have been a close election became a landslide in favor of the incumbent.

All this was predictable. Less predictable was the course of the virus that one was just beginning to hear about. I remember looking out at Yangmingshan Mountain and thinking it would be best to get home before all hell broke loose—never realizing that hell would chase us all the way to Boston.

The coronavirus pandemic was perhaps the finest natural diagnostic test for a country's weaknesses. No country could escape infection entirely, but the nature of its response spoke volumes about its preexisting conditions. Was the country, like Taiwan, equipped with a competent, centralized healthcare system and a populace that took public health seriously? Was it, like the United States, a torn electorate where notions of freedom trumped concerns about overall welfare? Or was it, like China, a country that had both a hurt, wounded nationalism and a certain facility with brute force? Answer those questions and you would answer how a country dealt with the pandemic.

If the brute force allowed China to keep shutting cities down long after the rest of the world had given up on containing the virus, it was the nationalism that would become the abiding feature of the country's conduct. The seeds, one suspects, had been sown in the Deng era, when the party decided that patriotic education was necessary. But as with most such seeds, they were never meant to sprout into the wolf warrior diplomacy foreign ministry officials like Hua Chunying and Zhao Lijian practiced by Twitter. It was one thing to stand up to the Americans when they were telling China off or to tell the world that China would brook no interference in its internal affairs. It was quite another to perpetuate conspiracy theories about COVID-19 on social media or to insist on anal swabs for diplomatic visitors. Wolf warrior diplomacy marked as dramatic a departure from grand strategy as China had made since the days of the Cultural Revolution.

Three things about this departure were notable. First, it was pointless. There was no conceivable object to be attained by the diplomacy Zhao and Hua were conducting; a historian almost wanted to clap Zhou Enlai on the shoulder in sympathy. Second, it was counterproductive. There had already been a backlash against China; the belligerence of China's diplomats, coupled with its obfuscations on COVID-19, made that backlash worse. It would have been unthinkable in 2018–2019 for relations between Australia and China to deteriorate as much as they did, and unthinkable for German chancellor Angela Merkel to say that perhaps she had got China wrong. Even Philippines president Rodrigo Duterte, who had seemed quiescent, spoke out against China. Diplomacy had been a crucial part of China's grand strategic arsenal. With that part failing, the balance of power Beijing had so delicately managed faltered.

The third notable feature of wolf warrior diplomacy was that it seemed to be happening in spite of Xi Jinping. As the backlash against China sharpened, Xi would call for a more "lovable China"; the fact that he had to make the call showed how far beyond his control the beast had ravaged. He would continue to try to drag China back to a more stable diplomatic footing—the proposed arms limitation talks in his virtual summit with Joe Biden on November 15, 2021, were an example—but there was a fragility to his grip on power.

This might seem astonishing. At its plenum in 2021, the CCP's central committee passed a much-heralded resolution about how Xi was at the core of the party; his authority was trumpeted from Zhongnanhai to every news outlet in the world. And yet there had been a backlash against Belt and Road, Xi's pet campaign. The fight against global warming he had championed had been going against China, as new coal plants popped up. Resolutions are necessary only when the truth they proclaim has been called into question. It looked like an attempt to project unity and wrangle contending factions together—an attempt born of desperation, the long-term success of which was uncertain.

How this had happened would await the opening of Communist Party archives, some distant day in the future. But regardless of what was going on, China's broader problems had not gone anywhere. That racking up of debt, exacerbated, perhaps, by the pandemic and the subsequent need for stimulus, had become untenable, as Evergrande's bankruptcy would prove. The land and water and air turning against China would not be patient with bureaucratic wrangling about the best balance between environmental needs and economic growth; the pause and reversal in the fight against global warming will come back to hurt China (and the rest of us) with a vengeance. There were some successes, too, to be sure—the pandemic had been brought under control; relations with Russia and Japan remained on an even keel (even if the latter were sympathetic to Taiwan)—but the costs and the challenges were mounting.

Just how successful Xi Jinping's attempts will be to bring back lovable

China remains uncertain. But he could start by recognizing that nationalism and defensive xenophobia do not go well with grand strategy; they cannot be bottled up again once they have been let loose. (A look across the Pacific to the woes of the United States would be telling.) Patriotic education might make for good propaganda. It makes for bad history. And that means bad grand strategy.

NOTES

Abbreviations

DXN1   Zhonggong zhongyang wenjian yanjiu shi, ed., *Deng Xiaoping Nianpu*, 1904–1974, 3 volumes (Beijing: Zhongyang wenxian chubanshe, 2009).

DXN2   Zhonggong zhongyang wenjian yanjiu shi, ed., *Deng Xiaoping Nianpu*, 1975–1997, 2 volumes (Beijing: Zhongyang wenxian chubanshe, 2004).

FMPRC   Archives of the Foreign Ministry of the People's Republic of China.

MZDN1   Zhonggong zhongyang wenxian yanjiu shi, ed., *Mao Zedong Nianpu*, 1893–1949, 3 volumes (Beijing: Zhongyang wenxian chubanshe, 1993).

MZDN2   Zhonggong zhongyang wenxian yanjiu shi, ed., *Mao Zedong Nianpu*, 1949–1976, 6 volumes (Beijing: Zhongyang wenxian chubanshe, 2013).

SMA   Shanghai Municipal Archives.

Introduction

1. For studies of contemporary grand strategy, see Avery Goldstein, *Rising to the Challenge: China's Grand Strategy and International Security* (Stanford, CA: Stanford University Press, 2005); and Michael Swaine and Ashley Tellis, *Interpreting China's*

Grand Strategy: Past, Present and Future (Santa Monica, CA: Rand, 2000). For an alarmist view, see Michael Pillsbury, *The Hundred Year Marathon: China's Secret Strategy to Replace America as the Global Superpower* (New York: Henry Holt and Co., 2015). The list of excellent studies of Chinese foreign relations continues to grow. The reader may refer to Odd Arne Westad, *Restless Empire* (New York: Basic Books, 2012); Chen Jian, *Mao's China and the Cold War* (Chapel Hill: University of North Carolina Press, 2001); and David Lampton, *Following the Leader: Ruling China from Deng Xiaoping to Xi Jinping* (Berkeley: University of California Press, 2014), among others. For a participant's view, see the intriguing Henry Kissinger, *On China* (New York: Penguin, 2011). The present volume is the first to attempt a comparative history of the grand strategies of China's leaders, exploring their similarities as well as their differences. Many of the sources it draws on were only recently declassified.

2. The ideas of a "structured, focused comparison" and "operational code" are drawn from Alexander George, "Case Studies and Theory Development: The Method of Structured, Focused Comparison," in *Diplomacy: New Approaches in History, Theory, and Policy*, ed. Paul Gordon Lauren (New York: Free Press, 1979), 43–68, and Alexander George, "The 'Operational Code': A Neglected Approach to the Study of Political Leaders and Decisionmaking," *International Studies Quarterly* 13, no. 2 (June 1969): 190–222, whose work I came to by way of the remarkable John Lewis Gaddis, *Strategies of Containment* (Oxford: Oxford University Press, 1982). The goal of this book—it falls to others to assess how far short I fell—is to do for China what Gaddis's work did for the United States. George, in turn, got the idea of an operational code from Nathan Leites, *A Study of Bolshevism* (Glencoe, IL: Free Press, 1953). Subsequent political scientists tried to quantify aspects of the operational code, but the results were not illuminating (see for example, He Kai and Feng Huiyun, "Xi Jinping's Operational Code Beliefs and Chinese Foreign Policy," *Chinese Journal of International Politics* 6, no. 3 (October 2013): 209–231. This was in part because, as George realized, people resist quantification and boxes.

3. Definitions of grand strategy abound. The most useful remains Paul Kennedy, ed., *Grand Strategies in War and Peace* (New Haven, CT: Yale University Press, 1991). See also Williamson Murray, Richard Hart Sinreich, and James Lacey, eds., *The Shaping of Grand Strategy* (Cambridge: Cambridge University Press, 2011); Lawrence Freedman, *Strategy* (Oxford: Oxford University Press, 2013); and Hal Brands, *What Good Is Grand Strategy?* (Ithaca, NY: Cornell University Press,

2015). Most of these works suggest that grand strategy is about careful planning; the Chinese case studies explored here suggest that instinct can produce much the same results in terms of the balancing of ends and means—a significant addition to the study of grand strategy.

4. For explanations focused on ideology and the nature of the communist state, see Chen Jian, *Mao's China and the Cold War;* Andrew Walder, *China under Mao: A Revolution Derailed* (Cambridge, MA: Harvard University Press, 2015); and John Garver, *China's Quest* (Oxford: Oxford University Press, 2015). For an explanation focused on security and geography, see Swaine and Tellis, *Interpreting China's Grand Strategy,* and the excellent Andrew Nathan and Andrew Scobell, *China's Search for Security* (New York: Columbia University Press, 2012). With the benefit of richer sources, this work builds on the works mentioned above by exploring how deeply being broken—and being broken in specific ways—defined China's understanding of security. It also differs significantly in its understanding of the means China used to pursue its objectives.

5. This comes close to, although it does not entirely meet, the idea of strategic culture. The idea of strategic culture has been the subject of much debate among political scientists, but if its limitations are properly grasped, it has its uses. Like other cultures, it can be multifaceted, often contradictory, and although one needs to be wary of reducing all a country does to ineluctable, overly determined "culture," there is value to recognizing that there are certain ways of understanding the world and one's position in it that come naturally. For a "strategic culture" approach to China, see Alastair Iain Johnston, *Cultural Realism: Strategic Culture and Grand Strategy in Chinese History* (Princeton, NJ: Princeton University Press, 1995). The approach and conclusions here differ from Johnston's, principally in arguing that there is a high degree of defensiveness to Chinese grand strategy.

6. The notion that there was such a consistency to Mao's policies is in itself controversial. For more on Mao, see, in addition to the works already mentioned, the biographies by Jung Chang and Jon Halliday, *Mao: The Unknown Story* (New York: Knopf, 2005); and Alexander Pantsov, with Steven Levine, *Mao: The Real Story* (New York: Simon and Schuster, 2012).

7. A word is in order here about the nature of Chinese power and offices. The presidency was created in the constitution of 1954 and went to Mao Zedong, who was chairman and general secretary of the party. The post of the president

was typically held by the general secretary. The title of chairman would fade from English language usage over time but would remain in Mandarin (*zhuxi*); Jiang Zemin, Hu Jintao, and Xi Jinping have all been called *zhuxi* (of the country) in Mandarin, president in English, and general secretary. As Deng's case shows, the actual title can be largely irrelevant: what matters is the influence wielded, through coalition building or control of the military portfolio or both. That position of "paramount leader"—not an official title—is the one a prospective Chinese leader should aspire to.

8. The literature on Deng is immense. For a starting point, see Ezra Vogel, *Deng Xiaoping and the Transformation of China* (Cambridge, MA: Harvard University Press, 2011). Surprisingly enough, previous studies have not really sought to piece together Deng's grand strategy—surprising because if anyone ever practiced that craft, it was he. Deng's views on power and its uses were much more nuanced and difficult to pin down than hitherto recognized.

1. Forging Great China

1. MZDNI, 1:64. All translations from foreign language sources in this book are my own, unless otherwise indicated.

2. For a comprehensive study of warfare in China at the time, see S. C. M. Paine, *The Wars for Asia, 1911–1949* (New York: Cambridge University Press, 2012). World War II is covered in Rana Mitter, *Forgotten Ally: China's World War II, 1937–1945* (Boston: Houghton Mifflin Harcourt, 2013); and Mark Peattie, Edward Drea, and Hans Van De Ven, eds., *The Battle for China: Essays on the Military History of the Sino-Japanese War of 1937–1945* (Stanford, CA: Stanford University Press, 2011). For a superb overview of the Chinese Civil War, see Odd Arne Westad, *Decisive Encounters: The Chinese Civil War, 1946–50* (Stanford, CA: Stanford University Press, 2003); as well as the pertinent chapter in Chen Jian, *Mao's China and the Cold War* (Chapel Hill: University of North Carolina Press, 2001), which emphasizes the importance of ideology. Mao himself has been well covered in the literature: two valuable studies are Jung Chang and Jon Halliday, *Mao: The Unknown Story* (New York: Knopf, 2005); and Alexander Pantsov, with Steven I. Levine, *Mao: The Real Story* (New York: Simon and Schuster, 2012). Missing in these works is the idea of Mao having a grand strategy during the times covered,

which is what this chapter seeks to add; it also gives due importance to that last crucial phase of the civil war, which is so often left unexplored. The idea of grand strategic goals shifting with circumstances deserves fuller exploration in the literature on strategic studies, but Robert Kagan, *Paradise and Power: America and Europe in the New World Order* (London: Atlantic, 2003) points in the right direction. I remain unconvinced that we need all shoot the bear just because we can, but the notion that states can feel more threatened the bigger they get is borne out by the historical record.

3. These developments are well covered in Joanna Waley-Cohen, *The Sextants of Beijing: Global Currents in Chinese History* (New York: W. W. Norton, 1999); and Odd Arne Westad, *Restless Empire: China and the World Since 1750* (New York: Basic Books, 2012). Arthur Waldron, *From War to Nationalism: China's Turning Point* (Cambridge: Cambridge University Press, 1995), is a superb account of the warlord era.

4. On Chiang, see Jay Taylor, *The Generalissimo: Chiang Kai-shek and the Struggle for Modern China* (Cambridge, MA: Harvard University Press, 2009).

5. MZDNI, 1:168.

6. Ibid., 271.

7. Ibid., 359.

8. Ibid., 361.

9. Ibid., 178.

10. Ibid., 281.

11. Ibid., 292.

12. Ibid., 316.

13. Ibid., 443.

14. Ibid. 529.

15. These events are well covered by most of the literature; see Mitter, *Forgotten Ally*, and Taylor, *The Generalissimo*, for starting points.

16. MZDNI, 2:15.

17. Ibid., 64, 107. Armies independent of both Mao and Chiang were springing up across China at the time. Much about them remains unknown; they merit far more scholarly attention than they have received. The opening of Japanese archives on the war offers a promising avenue of research.

18. The best account is the magisterial Xiaoyuan Liu, *Frontier Passages: Ethnopolitics and the Rise of Chinese Communism, 1921–1945* (Washington, DC:

Woodrow Wilson Center Press; Stanford, CA: Stanford University Press; 2004), which covers the outreach to Mongols, Hui, and Tibetans in detail. This book builds on Liu's work by arguing that minority policy was part and parcel of a larger diplomatic policy, aimed at preserving the communist state.

19. MZDNI, 1:438.

20. Zhonggong zhongyang tongzhan bu, ed., *Minzu wenti wenxian huibian: yi jiu er yi, qi, yi jiu si jiu, jiu* (Beijing: Zhonggong zhongyang dangxiao chubanshe, 1991), 210–211.

21. MZDNI, 1:491.

22. Ibid., 493.

23. Ibid., 496. See also Liu, *Frontier Passages.*

24. MZDNI, 1:543. See also Liu, *Frontier Passages.*

25. MZDNI, 2:150, 160–161, 169, 173.

26. Ibid., 1:490.

27. Ibid., 574–575.

28. Ibid., 2:325.

29. Ibid.

30. Ibid., 393, 421–422.

31. Ibid., 261.

32. On Pan Hannian, the memoir of the man he reached out to is intriguing: Iwai Eichii, *Kaiso No Shanhai* (Nagoya-shi: Kaisho no Shanhai shuppan linkai, 1983). The subject of Communist-Japanese relations is hard to dig into. Endo Homare, *Mo Takuto: Nihongun to kyoboshita otoko* (Tokyo: Shinchosha, 2015); and Xie Youtian, *Zhong gong zhuang da zhi mi: bei yan gai de Zhongguo Kang Ri zhan zheng zhen xiang* (Carle Place, NY: Mingjing chubanshe, 2002) are fascinating, but much more remains to be done on this subject.

33. MZDNI, 2:137.

34. Ibid., 312. On the hoped-for breakthrough to the Soviet border, see Liu, *Frontier Passages.*

35. MZDNI, 2:221.

36. Ibid., 280.

37. Ibid., 400.

38. Ibid., 343.

39. Ibid., 396.

40. Ibid., 522, 534, 537–538.

41. Ibid., 555–557.

42. Ibid., 560–561.

43. Ibid., 589.

44. Ibid., 602.

45. Ibid., 1:422.

46. Ibid., 2:29, 239.

47. Ibid., 487–88, 400–401.

48. Ibid., 491.

49. Ibid., 243.

50. Ibid., 444–445.

51. Ibid., 475.

52. Ibid., 591.

53. Ibid., 3:13.

54. Ibid., 15.

55. Ibid., 30. This is best covered by Steven I. Levine, *Anvil of Victory: The Communist Revolution in Manchuria, 1945–1948* (New York: Columbia University Press, 1987).

56. MZDNI, 3:31.

57. Ibid., 71, 74.

58. Ibid., 51.

59. Ibid., 70.

60. Ibid., 84.

61. Ibid., 107–108.

62. Ibid., 135, 173.

63. Ibid., 175, 180–181.

64. Ibid., 198.

65. Ibid., 191–192.

66. Ibid., 192.

67. Ibid., 264.

68. Ibid., 340.

69. Ibid., 356.

70. Ibid., 529.

71. Ibid., 2:572, 601.

72. Ibid., 3:248–249, 119.

73. Ibid., 208, 265, 268.

74. Ibid., 343–344.

75. Ibid., 264.

76. Ibid., 323.

77. Ibid., 401–402, 419–420, 430–431.

78. Ibid., 442. See also Westad, *Decisive Encounters*.

79. MZDNI, 3:448.

80. Ibid., 460–461.

81. Ibid., 476.

82. Ibid., 545.

83. Ibid., 491.

84. Ibid., 490.

85. Ibid., 499.

86. Chen Jian, *Mao's China*, and Yafeng Xia, *Negotiating with the Enemy: US-China Talks during the Cold War, 1949–1972* (Bloomington: Indiana University Press, 2006), provide first-rate accounts of the Huang-Stuart discussions. Chen Jian argues that America's "lost chance" in China was a myth but then, in very convincing detail, goes on to outline the conditions that America would have had to meet for a relationship to work. Those conditions seem to me to have been eminently achievable; they are no different, really, from what Richard Nixon and Henry Kissinger would do decades later (when the domestic political constraints on Washington were arguably even tougher).

87. FMPRC 102-00182-05.

88. Zhonghua renmin gongheguo waijiao bu, zhonggong zhongyang wenxian yanjiu shi, eds., *Mao Zedong Waijiao Wenxuan* (Beijing: Zhongyang wenxian chubanshe, 1994), 81.

89. Ibid., 82.

90. See here Odd Arne Westad, *Cold War and Revolution: Soviet-American Rivalry and the Origins of the Chinese Civil War, 1944–1946* (New York: Columbia University Press, 1993).

91. "Memorandum of Conversation between Anastas Mikoyan and Mao Zedong," January 31, 1949, Wilson Center, History and Public Policy Program Digital Archive, trans. Sergey Radchenko, http://digitalarchive.wilsoncenter.org

/document/112436. Reprinted in Andrei Ledovskii, Raisa Mirovitskaia, and Vladimir Miasnikov, *Sovetsko-Kitaiskie Otnosheniia*, vol. 5, bk. 2, 1946–February 1950 (Moscow: Pamiatniki Istoricheskoi Mysli, 2005), 37–43.

92. The tactic is well discussed in John Lewis Gaddis, *The Long Peace: Inquiries into the History of the Cold War* (New York: Oxford University Press, 1987); and Odd Arne Westad, *The Global Cold War: Third World Interventions and the Making of Our Times* (Cambridge: Cambridge University Press, 2005).

93. MZDNI, 3:538.

94. For an excellent account of the "lean to one side" idea, see Chen Jian, *Mao's China*, 50–53.

95. Zhonggong zhongyang wenxian yanjiu shi, ed., *Mao Zedong Wenji*, 6 volumes (Beijing: Renmin chubanshe, 1993–1999), 5:347. The line is often remembered as "We the Chinese people have stood up."

96. What is China? is one of the main motifs of Odd Arne Westad, *Restless Empire*.

97. Zhong gong zhong yang wen xian yan jiu shi, Zhong gong Xinjiang Weiwu'er Zizhiqu wei yuan hui, eds., *Xinjiang gongzuo wenxian xuanbian: yi jiu si jiu, er ling yi ling nian* (Beijing: Zhongyang wenxian chubanshe, 2010), hereafter cited as *Xinjiang gongzuo wenxian xuanbian*, 4–5.

98. For the imperial dimension, see Westad, *Restless Empire*. For an exploration of the forces behind expansion in the case of Tibet, see Sulmaan Wasif Khan, *Muslim, Trader, Nomad, Spy: China's Cold War and the People of the Tibetan Borderlands* (Chapel Hill: University of North Carolina Press, 2015).

99. Dangdai Zhongguo congshu bianji bu, ed., *Dangdai Zhongguo Jundui de Junshi Gongzuo*, 2 volumes (Beijing: Zhongguo shehui kexue chubanshe, 1989), hereafter cited as *Dangdai Zhongguo Jundui de Junshi Gongzuo*, 1:134.

100. Zhonggong zhongyang wenxian yanjiu shi, Zhongguo Renmin Jiefangjun junshi kexueyuan, eds., *Jianguo Yilai Mao Zedong Junshi Wengao*, 3 volumes (Beijing: Junshi kexueyuan chubanshe, 2010), hereafter cited as *Jianguo Yilai Mao Zedong Junshi Wengao*, 1:21.

101. *Dangdai Zhongguo Jundui de Junshi Gongzuo*, 1:113, 120.

102. Ibid., 121.

103. United States Consulate, *External Survey Detachment 44*, Department of State Telegram, September 4, 1949 (Digital National Security archive, *ProQuest*; Website accessed December 20, 2017); United States Central Intelligence Agency

Office of Research and Estimates, *Survival Potential of Residual Non-Communist Regimes in China*, October 19, 1949 (Digital National Security Archive, *ProQuest;* Website accessed December 20, 2017).

104. *Dangdai Zhongguo Jundui de Junshi Gongzuo*, 1:125.

105. Ibid., 133.

106. *Jiangyuo Yilai Mao Zedong Junshi Wengao*, 1:35.

107. *Dangdai Zhongguo Jundui de Junshi Gongzuo*, 1:188–193.

108. Ibid., 200–203. For more on this, see the remarkable Hsiao-ting Lin, *Accidental State: Chiang Kai-shek, the United States, and the Making of Taiwan* (Cambridge, MA: Harvard University Press, 2016).

109. *Dangdai Zhongguo Jundui de Junshi Gongzuo*, 1:234–237.

110. *Jianguo Yilai Mao Zedong Junshi Wengao*, 1:57.

111. Ibid., 1:119.

112. *Dangdai Zhongguo Jundui de Junshi Gongzuo*, 1:135.

113. *Jianguo Yilai Mao Zedong Junshi Wengao*, 1:104.

114. *Dangdai Zhongguo Jundui de Junshi Gongzuo*, 1:150, 238.

115. Ibid., 163.

116. Ibid., 168.

117. Ibid., 211.

118. *Jianguo Yilai Mao Zedong Junshi Wengao*, 1:64, 84–85.

119. "Record of Conversation between I. V. Stalin and Chairman of the Central People's Government of the People's Republic of China Mao Zedong in 16 December 1949," December 16, 1949, Wilson Center, History and Public Policy Program Digital Archive, trans. Danny Rozas, http://digitalarchive.wilsoncenter.org/document/111240.

120. "Record of Talks between I. V. Stalin and Chairman of the Central People's Government of the People's Republic of China Mao Zedong," January 22, 1950, Wilson Center, History and Public Policy Program Digital Archive, trans. Danny Rozas, http://digitalarchive.wilsoncenter.org/document/111245.

121. Ibid.

122. FMPRC 118-00294-01, June 14, 1950.

123. Zhonggong zhongyang wenxian yanjiu shi, Zhonggong Xinjiang Weiwu'er Zizhiqu weiyuanhui, eds., *Xinjiang Gongzuo Wenxian Xuanbian* (Beijing:

Zhongyang wenxian chubanshe, 2010), hereafter cited as *Xinjiang Gongzuo Wenxian Xuanbian*, 39–40.

124. "Record of Conversation between I. V. Stalin and Chairman of the Central People's Government of the People's Republic of China Mao Zedong in 16 December 1949," December 16, 1949, Wilson Center, History and Public Policy Program Digital Archive, trans. Danny Rozas, http://digitalarchive.wilsoncenter.org/document/111240.

125. *Jianguo Yilai Mao Zedong Junshi Wengao*, 1:117.

126. MZDN2, 1:62.

127. Westad, *Decisive Encounters*, 289.

128. *Xinjiang Gongzuo Wenxian Xuanbian*, 10–11.

129. *Jianguo Yilai Mao Zedong Junshi Wengao*, 1:43.

130. Ibid., 27.

131. The point is well covered in the literature on the Tibet; see Khan, *Muslim, Trader, Nomad, Spy*, for a starting point and suggestions for further reading.

132. *Xinjiang Gongzuo Wenxian Xuanbian*, 34–35.

133. Ibid., 50.

134. Ibid., 27.

135. MZDN2, 1:110–111.

136. *Jianguo Yilai Mao Zedong Junshi Wengao*, 1:96–97.

137. Ibid., 98.

138. Ibid., 121, 132.

2. Mao Zedong and the Balance of Power

1. "Telegram from the Leader of the Group of Soviet Specialists in Northeast China to the Chairman of the USSR Council of Ministers about the Results of the Chinese-Korean Talks on Military Cooperation," May 18, 1949, Wilson Center, History and Public Policy Program Digital Archive, trans. Gary Goldberg, http://digitalarchive.wilsoncenter.org/document/114898.

2. Ibid.

3. *Jianguo Yilai Mao Zedong Junshi Wengao*, 1:154–155. The best starting point for China's involvement in the Korean War is Chen Jian, *China's Road to the Korean*

War (New York: Columbia University Press, 1994), as well as the pertinent chapter in his *Mao's China and the Cold War* (Chapel Hill: University of North Carolina Press, 2001). See also the magisterial Shen Zhihua, *Mao, Sidalin, yu Chaoxian Zhanzheng* (Guangzhou: Guangdong Renmin chubanshe, 2003). For an overview of the international dimensions of the war, see William Stueck, *The Korean War: An International History* (Princeton, NJ: Princeton University Press, 1995); the shifting calculus in Washington is well served in John Lewis Gaddis, *Strategies of Containment* (Oxford: Oxford University Press, 1982).

4. MZDN2, 1:161–162, 165–166.

5. FMPRC 118-00080-01; see also Chen, *China's Road to the Korean War.*

6. *Jianguo Yilai Mao Zedong Junshi Wengao,* 1:198.

7. MZDN2, 1:168.

8. FMPRC 105-00009-01, September 9, 1950.

9. Ibid., October 3, 1950.

10. MZDN2, 1:201–203. See also Chen, *Mao's China*, 56; and Shu Guang Zhang, *Mao's Military Romanticism: China and the Korean War, 1950–53* (Lawrence: University Press of Kansas, 1995).

11. MZDN2, 1:201–203.

12. Ibid., 1:204. On the decision-making at the extended politburo meeting, see also Chen Jian, *China's Road to the Korean War.*

13. MZDN2, 1:204–205.

14. Ibid., 206–207.

15. "Telegram from Soviet Ambassador to China N. V. Roshchin to Stalin," October 7, 1950, Wilson Center, History and Public Policy Program Digital Archive, trans. Vladislav Zubok, http://digitalarchive.wilsoncenter.org/document/117314.

16. MZDN2, 1:208.

17. Ibid., 211.

18. Ibid., 211–212. It would take a few days and some discussion yet before the troops actually went through; see Chen Jian, *Mao's China*, for more on this point.

19. The best exponent of this line of thought is Shen Zhihua, *Mao, Sidalin, yu chaoxian zhanzheng* (Guangzhou: Guangdong renmin chubanshe, 2007).

20. MZDN2, 1:261.

21. Ibid., 265.

22. FMPRC 105-00009-01, "Memorandum of Conversation between Panikkar and Zhang Hanfu," December 25, 1950. See also Shen Zhihua and Xia Yafeng, "Mao Zedong's Erroneous Decision during the Korean War: China's Rejection of the Ceasefire Resolution in Early 1951," *Asian Perspective* 35, no. 2 (2011): 187–209.

23. MZDN2, 1:367–368.

24. Chen Jian, *Mao's China*, 104.

25. Even the best accounts tend to discuss the Korean War without connecting it to other theaters of war; viewed from Beijing, Korea was just one—albeit the most fierce—of a number of simultaneous, overlapping wars.

26. MZDN2, 1:240.

27. *Jianguo Yilai Mao Zedong Junshi Wengao*, 1:445.

28. Ibid., 452.

29. MZDN2, 1:578.

30. Ibid., 644.

31. Ibid., 493.

32. MZDN2, 2:33.

33. Ibid.

34. *Jianguo Yilai Mao Zedong Junshi Wengao*, 1:354.

35. On GMD activities in Tibet, see the remarkable Lin Hsiao-ting, *Tibet and Nationalist China's Frontier: Intrigue and Ethnopolitics* (Vancouver: University of British Columbia Press, 2006).

36. MZDN2, 1:280.

37. *Dangdai Zhongguo Jundui de Junshi Gongzuo*, 1:214–215.

38. For a discussion of Tibet's statelessness and the similarities of the agreement to that in Hong Kong, see Khan, *Muslim, Trader, Nomad, Spy*.

39. MZDN2, 1:397.

40. Ibid., 630–631.

41. On the Soviets as an economic model, see the nuanced Hua-yu Li, *Mao and the Economic Stalinization of China, 1948–1953* (Lanham, MD: Rowman and Littlefield, 2006).

42. On the Korean War's effects on the alliance, see Chen Jian, *Mao's China*, especially 60–61.

43. Information on aircraft is from MZDN2, I:263–264. On the factories, see Austin Jersild, *The Sino-Soviet Alliance: An International History* (Chapel Hill: University of North Carolina Press, 2014).

44. MZDN2, I:517–518, 438.

45. "Record of a Conversation between Stalin, Kim Il Sung, Pak Heon-yeong, Zhou Enlai, and Peng Dehuai," September 4, 1952, Wilson Center, History and Public Policy Program Digital Archive, trans. Gary Goldberg, http:// digitalarchive.wilsoncenter.org/document/114936. On the factories, see Austin Jersild, *The Sino-Soviet Alliance: An International History* (Chapel Hill: University of North Carolina Press, 2014).

46. MZDN2, 2:296.

47. Ibid., 349.

48. For more on the Sino-Soviet alliance and Moscow's conciliatory moves, see Odd Arne Westad, ed., *Brothers in Arms: The Rise and Fall of the Sino-Soviet Alliance, 1945–1963* (Washington, DC: Woodrow Wilson Center Press, 2009), 17.

49. Molotov's views are in "Cable from Zhang Wentian, 'Reporting the Preliminary Opinions of Our Side on the Geneva Conference to the Soviet Side,'" March 6, 1954, Wilson Center, History and Public Policy Program Digital Archive, PRC FMA 206-Y0054, trans. Chen Zhihong, http://digitalarchive .wilsoncenter.org/document/110039.

50. "Telegram, Zhou Enlai to Mao Zedong, Liu Shaoqi, and the CCP Central Committee, (excerpt)," May 30, 1954, Wilson Center, History and Public Policy Program Digital Archive, Zhou Enlai zhuan, 1949–1976, 168–169; Xiong Huayuan, Zhou Enlai chudeng shij wutai, p. 89; Zhou, vol. I, p. 372. Translated for the Cold War International History Project (CWIHP) by Chen Jian. http://digitalarchive.wilsoncenter.org/document/121150. See also Chen Jian, *Mao's China*, 62.

51. MZDN2, 2:549.

52. Chen Jian, *Mao's China*, 160.

53. MZDN2, 3:18; see also Chen Jian, *Mao's China*, 160.

54. MZDN2, 3:19–20.

55. Ibid., 246. Acheson's infamous quip about Tito is cited in, among others, John Lewis Gaddis, *The Cold War: A New History* (New York: Penguin Press, 2005), 33.

56. Geneva and the Chinese role in Indochina have been the subject of extensive scholarship. For starting points, see Zhai Qiang, *China and the Vietnam Wars, 1950–1975* (Chapel Hill: University of North Carolina Press, 2000); and Gregg Brazinsky, *Winning the Third World: Sino-American Rivalry during the Cold War* (Chapel Hill: University of North Carolina Press, 2017).

57. Zhai Qiang, *China and the Vietnam Wars*, 10–11.

58. MZDN2, 2:194–195.

59. "Telegram, Zhou Enlai to Mao Zedong," 168–169; Xiong Huayuan, Zhou Enlai chudeng shij wutai, p. 89; Zhou nianpu, vol. 1, p. 372. Translated for CWIHP by Chen Jian. http://digitalarchive.wilsoncenter.org/document /121150.

60. For the full text of the withdrawal agreement, see "Agreement on the Cessation of Hostilities in Viet-Nam," July 20, 1954, https://peacemaker.un.org /sites/peacemaker.un.org/files/KH-LA-VN_540720_GenevaAgreements.pdf.

61. On China's involvement in the Vietnam wars, see Zhai Qiang, *China and the Vietnam Wars, 1950–1975* (Chapel Hill: University of North Carolina Press, 2000).

62. FMPRC 106-00444-01.

63. FMPRC 106-00456-01, February 20, 1959.

64. FMPRC 203-00006-01, "Memorandum of Conversation between Zhou Enlai and Jawaharlal Nehru," June 25, 1954.

65. The Bandung principles can be found easily; see, for example, "The Ten Principles of Bandung," http://www.chinadaily.com.cn/english/doc/2005-04 /23/content_436882.htm.

66. FMPRC 105-00062-02, "Memorandum of Conversation between Zhou Enlai and Indian Ambassador to China, RK Nehru," November 5, 1955.

67. FMPRC 204-00037-04, September 23, 1957.

68. FMPRC 203-00006-01, June 25, 1954.

69. Author's interview with Sultan Khan, Karachi, June 20, 2009.

70. FMPRC 204-00004-03, October 7, 1954.

71. Ibid.

72. Ibid.

73. FMPRC 105-00464-04, October 1, 1956. The Sino-Thai relationship is a subject that cries out for further research, which is somewhat surprising given the

overall focus on China's relationship with Southeast Asia. Weaving the Thai relationship into the story of China's Asia policy is part of the historiographical contribution in this chapter.

74. FMPRC 105-00317-04, January 15, 1956.

75. Ibid., February 9, 1956.

76. Japan Foreign Ministry Archives, 2014–0065, January, 1961 report by Takasaki. Original in English. There remains a dearth of serious scholarship on the Sino-Japanese relationship during the Cold War, which was, as the brief discussion here shows, much more active than has hitherto been recognized. For a discussion of the economic dimensions, see Amy King, *China-Japan Relations after World War II: Empire, Industry and War, 1949–1971* (Cambridge: Cambridge University Press, 2016). For an account of China's conduct toward Japanese war prisoners, see Barak Kushner, *Men to Devils, Devils to Men: Japanese War Crimes and Chinese Justice* (Cambridge, MA: Harvard University Press, 2015).

77. FMPRC 111-00268-04, Memcon, Zhou and Indian Ambassador to China, January 12, 1958.

78. The Taiwan Strait crises are ably covered by Chen Jian, *Mao's China*. For an explanation that suggests this was an emotional response, see Yang Kuisong and Mao Sheng, "Unafraid of the Ghost: The Victim Mentality of Mao Zedong and the Two Taiwan Strait Crises in the 1950s," *China Review* 16, no. 1 (Spring 2016): 1–34. The explanation presented here emphasizes defensive and signaling considerations rather than ideological or emotional ones—although no doubt all of these had a role to play.

79. MZDN2, 2:244, 260.

80. Ibid., 263–264.

81. Ibid., 268.

82. See the superb Nancy Tucker, *Strait Talk: United States-Taiwan Relations and the Crisis With China* (Cambridge, MA: Harvard University Press, 2009).

83. MZDN2, 2:320, 338, 342.

84. Ibid., 370–371.

85. FMPRC 105-00351-01, January 4, 1956.

86. MZDN2, 5:29. The dislike came through at their first meeting: MZDN2, 5:22.

87. FMPRC 111-00146-01, September 10, 1958. The best account of the Warsaw talks is Yafeng Xia, *Negotiating with the Enemy: US-China Talks during the Cold War, 1949–1972* (Bloomington: Indiana University Press, 2006).

88. FMPRC 111-00146-03, September 18, 1958. On the origins of the defense pact, see Tucker, *Strait Talk.*

89. FMPRC 111-00146-03, September 18, 1958.

90. FMPRC 111-00147-02, September 25, 1958.

91. MZDN2, 2:337–338. The Chinese nuclear adventure is described in John Lewis and Xue Litai, *China Builds the Bomb* (Stanford, CA: Stanford University Press, 1988).

92. Three excellent books explore the Sino-Soviet relationship: Westad, ed., *Brothers in Arms*; Lorenz Luthi, *The Sino-Soviet Split* (Princeton, NJ: Princeton University Press, 2008); and Sergey Radchenko, *Two Suns in the Heavens: The Sino-Soviet Struggle for Supremacy, 1962–1967* (Washington, DC: Woodrow Wilson Center Press, 2009). See also the magisterial Shen Zhihua, ed., *Zhong Su Guanxi Shi Gang: 1917–1991 nian Zhong Su Guangxi Ruogan Wenti Zai Tan Tao* (Beijing: Shehui kexue wenxian chubanshe, 2016). For a view of how the Sino-Soviet conflict played out in the third world, see Jeremy Scott Friedman, *Shadow Cold War: The Sino-Soviet Competition for the Third World* (Chapel Hill: University of North Carolina Press, 2015). The view presented in this book differs from the preceding treatments in emphasizing how, even as conflict unfolded, the Chinese took conciliatory measures to maintain the productivity of the relationship. It also makes the argument that, contrary to the prevailing view, such damage as was done to the relationship did not harm the overall national security interests of the PRC too much—a point that was not lost on Beijing.

93. MZDN2, 3:367.

94. Ibid., 390.

95. Ibid., 391–393.

96. Ibid., 396–397.

97. Ibid., 397.

98. Ibid., 400–401.

99. Ibid., 413.

100. Ibid., 416.

101. Ibid., 420.

102. Ibid., 430.

103. Shelling promoting internal unity is well covered in Chen Jian, *Mao's China*, and Christensen, *Useful Adversaries.*

104. MZDN2, 3:438.

105. Ibid., 439.

106. Ibid., 456–457.

107. Ibid., 457. Shelling would continue on alternate days for a long while.

108. Ibid., 464.

109. Ibid., 436.

110. MZDN2, 4:194–196.

111. Ibid., 196–198.

112. Ibid., 198. On the role of Tibet and the Sino-Indian dispute in Sino-Soviet relations, see Luthi, *The Sino-Soviet Split.*

113. MZDN2, 4:231.

114. Ibid., 237.

115. Ibid., 436.

116. FMPRC 118-01764-04, April 24, 1962.

117. Ibid., Memorandum of Conversation between Zhang Hanfu and Soviet ambassador, April 24, 1962.

118. Ibid., Memorandum given by Soviet Ambassador to Zhang Hanfu, April 25, 1962.

119. FMPRC 118-01764-05, April 29, 1962.

120. FMPRC 118-01765-04, June 26, 1962.

121. FMPRC 118-01767-01, August 9, 1962.

122. FMPRC 118-01767-02, August 30, 1962. The document trail shows the Foreign Ministry drafting the memorandum that communicated these decisions as of August 23, 1962.

123. FMPRC 118-01097-05, October 12, 1963.

124. FMPRC 109-03861-03, February 23, 1963, and MZDN2, 5:194–196.

125. MZDN2, 5:381. See also Luthi, *The Sino-Soviet Split,* and Radchenko, *Two Suns in the Heavens.*

126. MZDN2, 5:417.

127. Ibid., 422.

128. Ibid., 431.

129. Ibid., 431–432.

130. The way the Sino-Soviet relationship played out in the rest of the world has garnered quite a bit of interest recently. The Korean case remains unexplored, largely because sources were, even at the best of times, almost impossible to come by. On the Vietnamese case, see the outstanding Lien-Hang T. Nguyen, *Hanoi's War: An International History of the War for Peace in Vietnam* (Chapel Hill: University of North Carolina Press, 2012); and Nicholas Khoo, *Collateral Damage: Sino-Soviet Rivalry and the Termination of the Sino-Vietnamese Alliance* (New York: Columbia University Press, 2011). The discussion here takes advantage of newly declassified sources to show, for the first time, how hard Ho tried to maintain the peace and how the Chinese worked to find a new balance of power in Southeast Asia, notably in cultivating Sihanouk. The early phases of the Sino-Cambodian relationship are ripe for further exploration; later years are covered by Andrew Mertha, *Brothers in Arms: Chinese Aid to the Khmer Rouge, 1975–1979* (Ithaca: Cornell University Press, 2014). For a look at Sino-Soviet rivalry in the third world, see Friedman, *Shadow Cold War.*

131. FMPRC 204-01454-01, July 11, 1961. The border dispute and its resolution remain difficult to study; the best account is Shen Zhihua and Xia Yafeng, "Contested Border: A Historical Investigation into the Sino-Korean Border Issue, 1950–1964," *Asian Perspective*, 37, no. 1 (January–March 2013): 1–30.

132. FMPRC 106-00717-01, December 13, 1963.

133. FMPRC 109-03640-02, April 21, 1965.

134. Ibid., April 30, 1965.

135. MZDN2, 4:438–439.

136. Ibid., 443–445.

137. Ibid.

138. FMPRC 204-01445-04, June 15, 1961.

139. FMPRC 106-01009-09, November 7, 1962.

140. FMPRC 204-01509-02, February 15, 1963.

141. FMPRC 204-01509-03, February 15, 1963.

142. FMPRC 204-01548-01, September 28, 1964.

143. FMPRC 204-01548-04, September 28, 1964.

144. FMPRC 106-01521-01, September 29, 1965.

145. For a full account, see Khan, *Muslim, Trader, Nomad, Spy.*

146. FMPRC 105-01774-03, July 16, 1961. The proffered swap is well-served by the literature; see John Garver, *Protracted Contest: Sino-Indian Rivalry in the Twentieth Century* (Seattle: University of Washington Press, 2001) for a starting point.

147. On China's willingness to settle territorial disputes (and the conditions under which it escalates them), the best account is M. Taylor Fravel, *Strong Borders, Secure Nation: Cooperation and Conflict in China's Territorial Disputes* (Princeton, NJ: Princeton University Press, 2008).

148. MZDN2, 5:138. On ROC activities with Tibetans and in India, see Khan, *Muslim, Trader, Nomad, Spy.* The fears on both fronts are omitted in most accounts of the Sino-Indian war; the best guide is still the classic Allen S. Whiting, *The Chinese Calculus of Deterrence: India and Indochina* (Ann Arbor: University of Michigan Press, 1975). See also Neville Maxwell, *India's China War* (New York: Pantheon Books, 1970); and John Garver, "China's Decision for War with India in 1962," in *New Directions in the Study of China's Foreign Policy,* ed. Alastair Iain Johnston and Robert Ross (Stanford, CA: Stanford University Press, 2006).

149. MZDN2, 5:164.

150. Ibid., 165.

151. For an account by one of the Pakistani boundary negotiators, see M. Yunus, *Awakened China Shakes the World and Is Now Pakistan's Mainstay: Memories of a Diplomat* (Islamabad: IPS Press, 2015).

152. FMPRC 105-01842-04, May 17, 1963. See also Khan, *Muslim, Trader, Nomad, Spy.*

153. FMPRC 105-01927-02, March 5, 1965.

154. FMPRC 105-01846-05, July 20, 1963.

155. FMPRC 204-01526-04, October 1964.

156. FMPRC 107-00240-08, September 30, 1960. The Algerian war is well covered by Matthew Connelly, *A Diplomatic Revolution: Algeria's Fight for Independence and the Origins of the Post–Cold War Era* (Oxford: Oxford University Press, 2002); and Jeffrey James Byrne, *Mecca of Revolution: Algeria, Decolonization, and the Third World Order* (New York: Oxford University Press, 2016). On Chinese aid to Algeria and its limitations, see Kyle Haddad-Fonda, "An Illusory Alliance: Revolutionary Legitimacy and Sino-Algerian Relations, 1958–1962," *Journal of North African Studies* 19, no. 3 (May 2014): 338–357.

157. FMPRC 106-01448-02, August 6, 1964.

158. On Tanzania, the Foreign Ministry still remembers its efforts: "China's Assistance in the Construction of the Tanzania-Zambia Railway," http://www.fmprc.gov.cn/mfa_eng/ziliao_665539/3602_665543/3604_665547/t18009.shtml, accessed December 20, 2017. See also Friedman, *Shadow Cold War.*

159. Zhonggong zhongyang wenxian yanjiu shi, ed., *Zhou Enlai Nianpu*, 3 volumes (Beijing: Zhonggong zhongyang wenxian chubanshe, 1997), hereafter cited as *Zhou Enlai Nianpu*, 2:610–611.

160. FMPRC 109-03748-03, August, 29, 1961.

161. On the costs, see Shu Guang Zhang, *Beijing's Economic Statecraft during the Cold War, 1949–1991* (Washington, DC: Woodrow Wilson Center Press, 2014).

162. MZDN2, 5:418.

163. Ibid., 355. The third-line is also discussed in Lorenz Luthi, "The Vietnam War and China's Third Line Defense Planning Before the Cultural Revolution, 1964–1966," *Journal of Cold War Studies* 10, no. 1 (Winter 2008): 26–51.

164. MZDN2, 5:490–491. On the signaling, see Chen Jian and James Hershberg, "Reading and Warning the Likely Enemy: China's Signals to the US about Vietnam in 1965," *International History Review* 27, no. 1 (March 2005): 47–84.

165. MZDN2, 5:492.

166. Information on missiles is from MZDN2, 5:312; information on Yongxing is from MZDN2, 4:437.

167. MZDN2, 2:172–173.

168. Ibid., 349, 350, 366.

169. Ibid., 399.

170. The Great Leap Forward has inspired some first-rate literature. See Andrew Walder, *China under Mao: A Revolution Derailed* (Cambridge, MA: Harvard University Press, 2015); Frank Dikotter, *Mao's Great Famine* (New York: Walker, 2012); and Yang Jisheng, trans. Stacey Mosher and Guo Jian, *Tombstone: The Great Chinese Famine, 1958–1962* (New York: Farrar, Straus, and Giroux, 2012). My small contribution made here is to emphasize the role of national security concerns in economic planning and the stuttering, contradictory course of

policy implementation, which I attribute largely to confusion. Mao simply did not understand economics. For violence before the Leap, see Frank Dikotter, *The Tragedy of Liberation* (London: Bloomsbury, 2013).

171. MZDN2, 3:370.

172. Ibid., 373.

173. The clearest account is Walder, *China under Mao;* what follows draws heavily on Walder, as well as Dikotter, *Mao's Great Famine.*

174. MZDN2, 3:384.

175. Ibid., 418.

176. Ibid., 456.

177. Ibid., 519.

178. Ibid., 549.

179. Ibid., 581; FMPRC 204-01241-04, June 17, 1962.

180. MZDN2, 3:592.

181. MZDN2, 5:74–75.

182. Estimates of the number of dead vary; Dikotter, *Mao's Great Famine* provides a good discussion.

183. MZDN2, 4:500, 502. The self-tilled plots are surprisingly unexplored in the literature.

184. Two excellent accounts of the Cultural Revolution are Frank Dikotter, *The Cultural Revolution: A People's History, 1962–1976* (London: Bloomsbury, 2016); and Roderick MacFarquhar and Michael Schoenhals, *Mao's Last Revolution* (Cambridge, MA: Belknap Press of Harvard University Press, 2006). See also the magisterial Roderick MacFarquhar, *The Origins of the Cultural Revolution,* 3 vols. (New York: Oxford University Press, 1974–1997). For a moving account from the ground up, see Yang Su, *Collective Killings in Rural China during the Cultural Revolution* (Cambridge: Cambridge University Press, 2011). For an intriguing account of the role of the Cultural Revolution in political activism, see Guobin Yang, *The Red Guard Generation and Political Activism in China* (New York: Columbia University Press, 2016). This chapter highlights, to a greater extent than previous works, how different the early part of the Cultural Revolution was from the rest and how Mao, taken aback by what he had unleashed, sought to mitigate the damage.

185. MZDN2, 3:309.

186. Ibid., 5:568–570.

187. On Burma, see Fan Hongwei, "The 1967 Anti-Chinese Riots in Burma and Sino-Burmese Relations," *Journal of Southeast Asian Studies* 43, no. 2 (June 2016): 234–256. The Pakistan case is crying out for further exploration, but sources are hard to come by; information on this and other Maoist activities is collated in a Central Intelligence Agency report, "Mao's Red Guard Diplomacy, 1967," POLO 31, June 21, 1968, https://www.cia.gov/library/readingroom/docs/polo-21.pdf.

188. MZDN2, 6:1.

189. Ibid., 31.

190. Ibid., 33.

191. Ibid., 34.

192. Ibid., 115.

193. Ibid., 170.

194. Ibid., 150.

195. Ibid., 66, 129.

196. Ibid., 184–185. The concern for energy security is not one typically noted in accounts of the conflict.

197. Ibid., 231. The best account of the Sino-Soviet border conflict is the remarkable Yang Kuisong, "The Sino-Soviet Border Clash of 1969: From Zhenbao Island to Sino-American Rapprochement," *Cold War History* 1, no. 1 (August 2000): 21–52, from which the information of 1968 clashes is drawn. The negotiations that followed have not hitherto been given much attention in the literature, but they are of immense importance in illustrating PRC conduct.

198. MZDN2, 6:232.

199. Ibid., 234.

200. Ibid.

201. Ibid., 231. See also *Zhou Enlai Nianpu, 1949–1976*, 3:283.

202. MZDN2, 6:240.

203. Ibid., 266. On Mao's doubts about how far the Soviets would uphold the agreement, see Yang, "The Sino-Soviet Border Clash."

204. MZDN2, 6:268.

205. Ibid., 269.

206. Ibid., 272.

207. Ibid., 274

208. Ibid., 282.

209. G. V. Kireev, *Rossiya-Kitai* (Moscow: ROSSPEN, 2006), 137.

210. MZDN2, 6:283.

211. In addition to the pertinent chapter in Chen Jian, *Mao's China*, see Margaret MacMillan, *Nixon and Mao: The Week That Changed the World* (New York: Random House, 2007). Li Danhui, in a remarkably perceptive essay, notes that Zhou deflected all Kissinger's praise for him toward Mao; see Li Danhui, "Da kai zhong mei guanxi jincheng zhong de Zhou Enlai," *Lengzhan Guoji Shi Yanjiu* 6 (Summer 2008): 141–173. See also the invaluable Richard H. Solomon, *Chinese Political Negotiating Behavior* (Santa Monica: Rand, 1995), which is impressively accurate in its overall portrait.

212. Chen Jian, *Mao's China*, makes the powerful argument that Mao could achieve the opening because he redefined the terms of the revolution, casting the Soviets as the prime enemy. The point is well taken, but Mao could have done this, had he so chosen, at just about any point in his reign. An opening to the Americans could have been explained as the relationships with the British and French were; if anything, doing it sooner would have been easier, requiring fewer explanations about why the reversal was wise. For the account by Mao's physician, see the titillating but telling Li Zhisui, trans. Tai Hung-chao, *The Private Life of Chairman Mao* (New York: Random House, 1994).

213. MZDN2, 6:278–279.

214. Steven E. Phillips, ed., *Foreign Relations of the United States, 1969–1976*, vol. 17, *China, 1969–1972* (Washington, DC: Government Printing Office, 2006), 815; "Joint Statement following Discussions with Leaders of the People's Republic of China" [the Shanghai communiqué], February 27, 1972, U.S. Department of State, Office of the Historian, https://history.state.gov/historicaldocuments /frus1969-76v17/d203.

215. "Memorandum of Conversation between Henry Kissinger and Zhou Enlai," July 10, 1971 from *MEMCONS of the Final Sessions with the Chinese Includes Memoranda of Conversations Dated July 10 and 11, 1971 and Draft Announcements*, 1971 (Digital National Security Archive, *ProQuest*; Website accessed December 20, 2017). See Tucker, *Strait Talk*, for a discussion of the implications for Taiwan.

216. MZDN2, 6:217–218. See also Nguyen, *Hanoi's War*.

217. MZDN2, 6:434, 460–461. I suspect that similar difficulties dogged the relationship with North Korea, but sources remain hard to come by.

218. "Memorandum of Conversation between Henry Kissinger and Zhou Enlai," July 11, 1971, from *MEMCONS of the Final Sessions with the Chinese Includes Memoranda of Conversations Dated July 10 and 11, 1971 and Draft Announcements,* 1971 (Digital National Security Archive, *ProQuest;* Website accessed December 20, 2017).

219. "Memorandum of Conversation Kissinger and Zhou Enlai," November 12, 1973, from United States Department of State. *Meeting between Henry Kissinger and Zhou Enlai, Guest House Villa #3, Peking,* 1973 (Digital National Security Archive, *ProQuest;* Website accessed December 20, 2017).

220. National Security Decision Memorandum 204, February 6, 1973, from United States Office of the Assistant to the President for National Security Affairs, *Sale of Inertial Navigation Systems to the People's Republic of China,* 1973 (Digital National Security Archive, *ProQuest;* Website accessed December 20, 2017).

221. MZDN2, 6:503–504.

222. Ibid., 505–506.

223. Ibid., 507.

224. Ibid., 615–616.

225. "Memorandum of Conversation," November 27, 1974 from United States Department, of State, *President's Visit; Nuclear War; SALT; Yugoslavia Meeting with Deng Xiaoping,* 1974 (Digital National Security Archive, *ProQuest;* Website accessed December 20, 2017). Sino-Soviet negotiations of the early seventies remain almost entirely unstudied and deserve much more attention.

226. Kireev, *Rossiya-Kitai* 153. These negotiations are crying out for further research, but Chinese sources are impossible to come by. Kireev's account provides a reasonable synopsis of the discussions.

227. MZDN2, 6:560–561.

228. Ibid., 575.

229. Odd Arne Westad has gone the furthest in making this argument: see Westad, "The Great Transformation: China in the Long 1970s," in *The Shock of the Global,* ed. Niall Ferguson, Charles Maier, Erez Manela, and Daniel Sargent (Cambridge, MA: Harvard University Press, 2010), 65–79; see also the intriguing Kazushi Minami, "Re-examining the End of Mao's Revolution: China's Changing Statecraft and Sino-American Relations, 1973–1978," *Cold War History* 16, no. 4 (2016): 359–375. The discussion here differs in stating,

starkly, that reform and opening were already underway in Mao's time—with Mao's blessing.

230. United States International Trade Commission Publication 1645, "China's Economic Development Strategies and Their Effects on US Trade," (Washington DC: February 1985), 115.

231. MZDN2, 6:552.

232. Ibid., 580–581.

233. The most judicious exploration of this political struggle to date is Xia Yafeng, "Myth or Reality? Factional Politics, US-China Relations, and Mao Zedong's Mentality in His Sunset Years," *Journal of American-East Asian Relations* 15 (2008): 107–130. Xia argues that Mao was the mastermind behind the Gang's denunciation of the Deng-Zhou course. I agree with this interpretation but add that Mao acted out of fear for his own position. This is all speculative: there is no smoking gun, but Mao's conduct would certainly suggest as much.

234. MZDN2, 6:523, 554–555.

235. Ibid., 570.

236. Ibid., 582–583.

237. Ibid., 593.

238. Ibid., 614–615.

239. Ibid., 621.

240. Ibid., 646–647.

3. Deng Xiaoping and Seeking Truth from Facts

1. DXN1, 1:8–9. Travel is typically noted when sketching the difference between Mao and Deng; left unmentioned is the nature of that travel. The best new treatment of Deng is Ezra Vogel, *Deng Xiaoping and the Transformation of China* (Cambridge, MA: Belknap Press of Harvard University Press, 2011). See also the biography by Alexander Pantsov, with Steven Levine, *Deng Xiaoping: A Revolutionary Life* (Oxford: Oxford University Press, 2015); and the invaluable David Shambaugh, ed., *Deng Xiaoping: Portrait of a Chinese Statesman* (Oxford: Oxford University Press, 1995). Useful too is Joseph Fewsmith, *Dilemmas of Reform in China: Political Conflict and Economic Debate* (Armonk, NY: M. E. Sharpe, 1994).

2. DXN1, 1:10.

3. Ibid., 35. This was a second name change: he had initially been named Deng Xianxi.

4. Ibid., 326.

5. Ibid., 2:850.

6. See Yang Gongsu, *Cang sang jiushi nian: yi ge waijiao teshi de huiyi* (Haikou: Hainan chubanshe, 1999); and Sulmaan Wasif Khan, *Muslim, Trader, Nomad, Spy: China's Cold War and the People of the Tibetan Borderlands* (Chapel Hill: University of North Carolina Press, 2015).

7. DXNI, 3:1953.

8. Ibid., 1952.

9. DXNI, 3:1960. The Lin Biao affair, as it came to be called, is covered in most accounts of the time, including Chen Jian, *Mao's China and the Cold War* (Chapel Hill: University of North Carolina Press, 2001).

10. DXNI, 3:1973.

11. DXN2, 1:25.

12. Ibid., 33.

13. Ibid., 75–76.

14. DXNI, 3:2016. The discussions with Kissinger are well served by American sources; see for example, United States Office of the Deputy Assistant to the President for National Security Affairs. *Report from Henry Kissinger regarding November 26 Discussions with Deng Xiaoping and Qiao Guanhua*, November 27, 1974 (Digital National Security Archive, *ProQuest;* Website accessed December 22, 2017).

15. DXNI, 3:2028.

16. Ibid., 2053.

17. Ibid., 1992.

18. DXN2, 1:147. See also Vogel, *Deng Xiaoping*.

19. The importance of Deng's intellectual wrestling with Maoism has been underestimated by scholars. Perhaps because his insights are taken for granted, we tend to ignore the near-Talmudic reinterpretations and explanations required to make them palatable to other party members. For Deng and for China, the intellectual struggle was crucial.

20. Hua's role is still crying out for a proper appraisal, but sources are hard to come by. The deepest exploration of the politics of this period is Frederick C.

Teiwes and Warren Sun, *The End of the Maoist Era: Chinese Politics during the Twilight of the Cultural Revolution* (Armonk, NY: M. E. Sharpe, 2007). See also the insightful treatment in Vogel, *Deng Xiaoping.*

21. DXN2, 1:152.

22. Ibid., 261; see also Vogel, *Deng Xiaoping.*

23. DXN2, 1:170–171.

24. Ibid., 319–320.

25. Ibid., 162–163.

26. DXN2, 2:1267.

27. Ibid., 730.

28. Teiwes and Sun, *The End of the Maoist Era,* makes this point.

29. DXN2, 1:264. On Nepal's requests for aid in the Mao years, see Khan, *Muslim, Trader, Nomad, Spy.* The general changes in China's aid policy are well chronicled in S. G. Zhang, *Beijing's Economic Statecraft during the Cold War, 1949–1991* (Washington, DC: Woodrow Wilson Center Press, 2014).

30. DXN2, 2:712.

31. DXN2, 1:494.

32. DXN2, 2:738.

33. This being the main point of Paul Kennedy, *The Rise and Fall of the Great Powers* (New York: Random House, 1987).

34. Zhonggong zhongyang wenxian yanjiu shi; Zhongguo renmin jiefangjun junshi kexueyuan, eds., *Deng Xiaoping Junshi Wenji*, 3 volumes (Beijing: Junshi kexueyuan chubanshe, 2004), hereafter cited as *Deng Xiaoping Junshi Wenji*, 3:264.

35. DXN2, 1:672. For a starting point on demographics, see Mei Fong, *One Child: The Story of China's Most Radical Experiment* (Boston: Houghton Mifflin Harcourt).

36. DXN2, 2:729–730.

37. Ibid., 889.

38. The role of Japan, discussed later in the chapter, still awaits a full reckoning; see Vogel, *Deng Xiaoping*, for a starting point. Lee Kuan Yew, *One Man's View of the World* (Singapore: Straits Times Press, 2013) recalls conversations with Deng. The Western role is discussed in David Lampton, *Following the Leader: Ruling China, from Deng Xiaoping to Xi Jinping* (Berkeley: University of California Press,

2014), with Robert McNamara's role getting particular attention; and Julian Gewirtz, *Unlikely Partners: Chinese Reformers, Western Economists, and the Making of Global China* (Cambridge, MA: Harvard University Press, 2017). See Vogel, *Deng Xiaoping,* for Deng's travel in Guangdong; Deng's observations on Chinese getting material from Hong Kong are mentioned in Odd Arne Westad, *Restless Empire: China and the World since 1750* (New York: Basic Books, 2012). My hunch is that Deng's own observations of what had and had not worked in China were of far greater importance than anything foreigners had to tell him (accounts of Western influence rely very heavily on Western accounts) but that he was too savvy to say so. It is always useful to let people feel that they have taught you something.

39. On Wan Li's role, see Vogel, *Deng Xiaoping,* 437.

40. Zhao Ziyang Wenji bianji zu, eds., *Zhao Ziyang Wenji,* 4 volumes (Hong Kong: Xianggang zhongwen daxue chubanshe, 2016), hereafter cited as *Zhao Ziyang Wenji,* I:44–45.

41. See Barry Naughton, "Deng Xiaoping: The Economist," in Shambaugh, *Deng Xiaoping,* 83–106.

42. DXN2, I:334.

43. Ibid., 366.

44. Ibid., 323–324.

45. Ibid., 407–413.

46. Ibid., 241.

47. Ibid., 637.

48. Ibid., 268.

49. Ibid., 519.

50. DXN2, 2:885.

51. Ibid., 1153–1154.

52. United States Congress Office of Technology Assessment. *Technology Transfer to China Includes Photographs and Tables,* 1987 (*ProQuest;* Website accessed December 20, 2017).

53. *Zhao Ziyang Wenji,* I:43. On Chen's objections, see Vogel, *Deng Xiaoping,* 427–429.

54. For a discussion of such cycles, see Richard Baum, *Burying Mao: Chinese Politics in the Age of Deng Xiaoping* (Princeton: Princeton University Press, 1994). On the broken contracts, see Vogel, *Deng Xiaoping.*

55. DXN2, 1:447–448, 578.

56. DXN2, 2:1099.

57. Ibid., 1:423–424.

58. Ibid., 501.

59. Ibid., 506, 510. The discussion of special zones (which the bureaucrats refined to special economic zones) does not mention Taiwan, but there was no other reason to look to Xiamen.

60. Ibid., 509.

61. Author's interview with locals in Jinmen, who preferred to remain anonymous, January 4, 2015.

62. DXN2, 2:892.

63. Ibid., 958, 960, 963.

64. *Zhao Ziyang Wenji*, 4:171.

65. DXN2, 2:854. See also Vogel, *Deng Xiaoping*.

66. SMA B 1-798-1, January 6, 1982.

67. DXN2, 1:500–501.

68. Ibid., 2:982–984.

69. Ibid., 997.

70. Ibid., 999.

71. Ibid., 991.

72. Ibid., 971.

73. Ibid., 1019–1020.

74. Ibid., 990.

75. Hoover Institution Archives, Wei Yung Papers.

76. Information compiled from the several folders in Hoover Institution Archives, Wang Sheng Papers, Box 5.

77. Ibid.

78. DXN2, 2:1010–1011.

79. Ibid., 1007.

80. Ibid., 1122.

81. Ibid., 1227.

82. Ibid., 993–994.

83. SMA B 1-9-798-1, October 11, 1981.

84. SMA B 1-9-798-12, April 19, 1982.

85. SMA B 1-9-798-49, September 8, 1982.

86. *Zhao Ziyang Wenji*, 2:27–36.

87. DXN2, 2:841–842.

88. Ibid., 1186–1187.

89. SMA B 1-9-798-30, August 21, 1982.

90. See Garver, *Protracted Contest: Sino-Indian Rivalry in the Twentieth Century* (Seattle: University of Washington Press, 2001).

91. DXN2, 2:1265.

92. DXN2, 1:188–189.

93. Ibid., 268.

94. Ibid., 507–508.

95. SMA B 1-9-798-22, June 1, 1982.

96. SMA B 1-9-798-37, September 8, 1982.

97. SMA B 1-9-798-37, September 8, 1982.

98. DXN2, 1:505–506.

99. SMA B 1-9-798-37, September 8, 1982.

100. DXN2, 1:465.

101. Ibid., 476.

102. Ibid., 667.

103. Ibid., 2:778.

104. SMA B 1-9-798-22, June 1, 1982.

105. SMA B 1-9-798-37, September 28, 1982.

106. SMA B 1-9-798-37, September 28, 1982.

107. SMA B 1-9-798-37, September 26, 1982.

108. SMA B 1-9-798-61, October 24, 1982.

109. SMA B 1-9-798-37, September 8, 1982. The concerns about Afghanistan, Indochina, and Soviet troops on the border were issues Chinese diplomats and policymakers raised consistently at this time. The best account of Sino-Soviet relations at this time is the outstanding Sergey Radchenko, *Unwanted Visionaries: The Soviet Failure in Asia at the End of the Cold War* (Oxford: Oxford University Press, 2014).

110. SMA B 1-9-798-37, October 13, 1982.

111. SMA B 1-9-798-61, October 24, 1982.

112. Li Peng, *Heping, Fazhan, Hezuo: Li Peng Waishi Riji* (Beijing: Xinhua Chubanshe, 2008), 14–16.

113. "Transcript of Conversation between Todor Zhivokov and Zhao Ziyang in Beijing," May 6, 1987, Wilson Center, History and Public Policy Program Digital Archive, trans. Kalina Bratanova, http://digitalarchive.wilsoncenter.org /document/110018.

114. "Memorandum of Conversation between George H. W. Bush and Chairman Deng Xiaoping in Beijing," February 26, 1989, Wilson Center, History and Public Policy Program Digital Archive, http://digitalarchive .wilsoncenter.org/document/116507.

115. Li Peng, *Heping, Fazhan, Hezuo,* 33. See also Radchenko, *Unwanted Visionaries.*

116. "Note by Vladimir Lukin regarding Soviet-Chinese Relations," August 22, 1989, Wilson Center, History and Public Policy Program Digital Archive, trans. Sergey Radchenko, http://digitalarchive.wilsoncenter.org/document /119292.

117. The war is discussed in Zhang Xiaoming, *Deng Xiaoping's Long War: The Military Conflict Between China and Vietnam, 1979–1991* (Chapel Hill: University of North Carolina Press, 2015). Although Zhang's evidence is compelling, my judgment of how the Chinese came off in the contest is harsher—I simply have a harder time swallowing the PRC's rationalization of the outcome given the military defeat. Zhang's case is plausible, however, and superbly documented. See also Odd Arne Westad and Sophie Quinn-Judge, eds., *The Third Indochina War: Conflict between China, Vietnam, and Cambodia, 1972–79* (New York: Routledge, 2006); Edward O'Dowd, *Chinese Military Strategy in the Third Indochina War: The Last Maoist War* (New York: Routledge, 2007); and Nayan Chanda, *Brother Enemy: The War after the War* (San Diego: Harcourt Brace Jovanovich, 1986). Merle Pribbenow has been a true fount of wisdom on the subject.

118. Zhongwen chuban wufu zhongxin, eds., *Zhonggong zhongyao lishi wenxian cailiao huibian,* vol. 24, hereafter cited as *Zhonggong zhongyao lishi wenxian cailiao huibian* (Los Angeles: Zhongwen chaban wufu wu zhongxin, 1995), 1–6.

119. SMA B 1-9-798-30, August 21, 1982.

120. *Zhonggong zhongyao lishi wenxian cailiao huibian,* 24:8–12.

121. Tran Quang Co, "Tran Quang Co: A Memoir," trans. Merle Pribbenow. Until recently this document was available only on the Internet. Merle Pribbenow generously shared his translation with me, which is what I have used here. The Vietnamese Ministry of Foreign Affairs, however, recently adopted it

as an internal document: "Hoi Uc va Suy Nghi" [Tran Quang Co, Memories and Thoughts], Diplomatic History Research Committee, Hanoi, 2008.

122. SMA B 1-9-798-57, November 11, 1982.

123. "Information of I. A. Rogachev about the Visit of the Minister of Foreign Affairs of the USSR in the PRC," February 11, 1989, Wilson Center, History and Public Policy Program Digital Archive, trans. Sergey Radchenko, http://digitalarchive.wilsoncenter.org/document/121765.

124. "Tran Quang Co: A Memoir." See also Zhang, *Deng Xiaoping's Long War.*

125. *Deng Xiaoping Junshi Wenji*, 3:177–178.

126. Ibid., 111–123.

127. Ibid., 153.

128. Ibid., 160–161.

129. SMA B 1-9-798-22, June 8, 1982.

130. Ibid, April 21, 1982.

131. Anyone writing about the Tiananmen Square massacre has to decide what use to make of the compilations of documents by Zhang Liang (a pseudonym), edited by Andrew Nathan and Perry Link, available in English as *The Tiananmen Papers* (New York: Public Affairs, 2001) and in Chinese as *Zhongguo Liusi Zhenxiang* (Hong Kong: Mingjing chubanshe, 2001). The authenticity of the compilations has been the subject of much debate; to my mind, the gist material does have the ring of truth when set against the other sources available, even though the tone at certain points seems artificial. These compilations do not, however, materially alter the picture presented here, which was garnered from the sources cited, so I have opted not to use them in depth. The best account of what happened at the square remains the classic Jan Wong, *Red China Blues* (Toronto: Anchor Books, 1996). See also Louisa Lim, *The People's Republic of Amnesia: Tiananmen Revisited* (Oxford: Oxford University Press, 2014); and M.E. Sarotte, "China's Fear of Contagion: Tiananmen Square and the Power of the European Example," *International Security* 37 (2): 156–182.

132. *Zhao Ziyang Wenji*, 4:650–653. On the group interested in democracy, see Merle Goldman, *Sowing the Seeds of Democracy in China: Political Reform in the Deng Xiaoping Era* (Cambridge, MA: Harvard University Press, 1994).

133. DXN2, 1:499.

134. Ibid., 2:1160–1162.

135. Ibid., 1171.

136. Ibid., 2:1272–1273.

137. Ibid., 1282, 1284. On Deng after Tiananmen, see also Vogel, *Deng Xiaoping.*

138. DXN2, 2:1285.

139. Ibid., 1279–1280.

140. For an account of the southern march, see Baum, *Burying Mao.*

4. Jiang Zemin, Hu Jintao, and the Virtue of Dullness

1. Jiang and Hu remain less studied than their predecessors or Xi Jinping. The best starting point is the insightful David Lampton, *Following the Leader: Ruling China from Deng Xiaoping to Xi Jinping* (Berkeley: University of California Press, 2014). For a starting point on Jiang that is useful and is, unusually, a little more positive than most coverage on him, see Bruce Gilley, *Tiger on the Brink: Jiang Zemin and China's New Elite* (Berkeley: University of California Press, 1998); see also Willy Wo-Lap Lam, *The Era of Jiang Zemin* (New York: Prentice Hall, 1999). Robert Kuhn, *The Man Who Changed China* (New York: Crown, 2004), verges a little too closely on the hagiographic, although the insights on Jiang's political skills are sound. On Hu, see Willy Wo-Lap Lam, *Chinese Politics in the Hu Jintao Era: New Leaders, New Challenges* (Armonk, NY: M. E. Sharpe, 2006). Part of the problem is the availability of sources; we do not have the detailed chronologies we do for the Mao and Deng eras. The argument that Jiang and Hu had grand strategies is unusual; their dullness has been such as to obscure their grand strategy. But clinging to a tried and tested course and keeping the state afloat— especially when that state was China—required grand strategy as much as luck.

2. On the search for something to believe in, see the fascinating Arthur Kleinman, ed., *Deep China* (Berkeley: University of California Press, 2011). For a different, equally fascinating exploration, see Ian Johnson, *The Souls of China: The Return of Religion After Mao* (Pantheon: New York, 2017).

3. Jiang Zemin, *Jiang Zemin Wenxuan*, 3 volumes (Beijing: Renmin chubanshe, 2006), hereafter cited as *Jiang Zemin Wenxuan*, 1:94–96.

4. Ibid., 318–322.

5. Ibid., 57–61.

6. See Ezra Vogel, *Deng Xiaoping and the Transformation of China* (Cambridge, MA: Belknap Press of Harvard University Press, 2011).

7. *Jiang Zemin Wenxuan*, 3:374–396.

8. Ibid., 2:157–162.

9. Ibid., 1:20–33.

10. Ibid., 346–348.

11. Author's telephone interview with Joseph Prueher, May 5, 2017.

12. Hu Jintao (principal author), Zhonggong zhongyang wenxian bianji weiyuanhui, eds., *Hu Jintao Wenxuan*, 3 volumes (Beijing: Renmin chubanshe, 2016), hereafter cited as *Hu Jintao Wenxuan*, 2:261. The three represents are listed in many places; the English text here is taken from "What is 'Three Represents' CPC Theory?," http://www.china.org.cn/english/zhuanti/3represents/68735.htm, accessed December 14, 2017.

13. *Jiang Zemin Wenxuan*, 1:217.

14. Ibid., 224.

15. Ibid., 187.

16. *Hu Jintao Wenxuan*, 3:227–230.

17. Ibid., 374.

18. Ibid., 316–319.

19. The classic account is the phenomenal Huang Yasheng, *Capitalism with Chinese Characteristics* (Cambridge: Cambridge University Press, 2008), a meticulous and groundbreaking account of the changes in the PRC's economy. On corruption and crony capitalism, see Minxin Pei, *China's Crony Capitalism: The Dynamics of Regime Decay* (Cambridge, MA: Harvard University Press, 2016).

20. *Jiang Zemin Wenxuan*, 1:98.

21. Ibid., 511–513.

22. *Hu Jintao Wenxuan*, 2:411–422. See also Huang, *Capitalism with Chinese Characteristics*.

23. Li Peng, *Shichang yu Tiaokong: Li Peng Jingji riji* (Beijing: Xinhua Chubanshe, 2007), 1428–1429.

24. The Chinese Foreign Ministry's summary of its actions during the crisis is at "Proactive Policies by China in Response to Asian Financial Crisis," http://www.fmprc.gov.cn/mfa_eng/ziliao_665539/3602_665543/3604_665547/t18037.shtml.

25. *Hu Jintao Wenxuan*, 3:117–118.

26. Ibid., 458.

27. Ibid., 216–220. The BRICS countries are Brazil, Russia, India, China, and South Africa.

28. Ibid., 137–140.

29. For an intriguing look at the American influence on Poland, see Gregory F. Domber, *Empowering Revolution: America, Poland, and the End of the Cold War* (Chapel Hill: University of North Carolina Press, 2014).

30. *Jiang Zemin Wenxuan*, 1:134–136.

31. The allusion to the end of history is, of course, to Francis Fukuyama, "The End of History?" *The National Interest*, Summer 1989, 3–18, which lays the idea out most clearly.

32. Charles Krauthammer used the term "unipolar"; see Krauthammer, "The Unipolar Moment," *Foreign Affairs*, January 1990, 23–33. For academic explorations of the idea, see Hal Brands, *Making the Unipolar Moment: U.S. Foreign Policy and the Rise of the Post-Cold War Order* (Ithaca, NY: Cornell University Press, 2016); Christopher Layne, "The Unipolar Illusion Revisited: The Coming End of the United States' Unipolar Moment," *International Security*, 31 (Fall 2006): 7–41; and G. John Ikenberry, ed., *America Unrivaled: The Future of the Balance of Power* (Ithaca, NY: Cornell University Press, 2002).

33. *Jiang Zemin Wenxuan*, 1:241–242.

34. Ibid., 2:195–196.

35. Li Peng, *Heping, Fazhan, Hezuo: Li Peng Waishi Riji* (Beijing: Xinhua Chubanshe, 2008), 15.

36. *Jiang Zemin Wenxuan*, 1:84–85.

37. Ibid., 312.

38. Ibid., 330–334.

39. Details drawn from author's interview with Prueher, May 5, 2017. My gratitude to Prueher, who was head of PACOM during the crisis, for pointing out that at no point during the actual crisis was a carrier put in the Taiwan Strait

and for highlighting the lack of a U.S. response in 1995. For further coverage of the crisis, see Robert Ross, "The 1995–6 Taiwan Strait Confrontation: Coercion, Credibility, and the Use of Force," *International Security* 25, no. 2 (Fall 2000): 87–123; and Michael Swaine and Zhang Tuosheng, eds., with Danielle F. S. Cohen, *Managing Sino-American Crises: Case Studies and Analysis* (Washington, DC: Carnegie Endowment for International Peace, 2006). For a Chinese diplomat's account, see Qian Qichen, *Ten Episodes in China's Diplomacy* (New York: Harper-Collins, 2005).

40. Memorandum of Conversation, "Meeting with Former Secretary of State Henry Kissinger and Three Others re China," July 13, 1995, National Security Council and Records Management Office, "Declassified documents on Henry Kissinger," *Clinton Digital Library*, https://clinton.presidentiallibraries.us/items /show/47988, accessed December 8, 2017.

41. *Jiang Zemin Wenxuan*, 2:151–155.

42. Ibid., 3:442–450.

43. Ibid., 2:324.

44. Author's interview with an American official who preferred to remain anonymous, May 20, 2017.

45. *Jiang Zemin Wenxuan*, 3:447–448.

46. Author's interview with Prueher, May 5, 2017.

47. Ibid.

48. Ibid.

49. See Odd Arne Westad, *Restless Empire: China and the World since 1750* (New York: Basic Books, 2012).

50. *Jiang Zemin Wenxuan*, 3:367–368.

51. Ibid., 353.

52. Ibid., 304–312.

53. Ibid., 354.

54. Ibid., 257–260.

55. Ibid., 355. The original five countries in the club were China, Russia, Kazakhstan, Kyrgyzstan, and Tajikistan. References to the three evil forces abound in media outlets such as the *China Daily.*

56. *Hu Jintao Wenxuan*, 3:592–595.

57. Normalization with Vietnam is covered in Li Peng, *Heping, Fazhan, Hezuo.*

58. *Jiang Zemin Wenxuan*, 3:315–318.

59. A video of the performance can be found at Lian Zhan hui mian muxiao Zaihoumen xiaoxue de xiao pengyou, https://www.youtube.com/watch?v=z929wkSANGc, accessed December 21, 2017.

60. *Hu Jintao Wenxuan*, 2:306–313.

61. Ibid.

62. *Jiang Zemin Wenxuan*, 2:371–374.

63. Ibid., 3:238–242.

64. *Hu Jintao Wenxuan*, 3:143. On China's relations with Latin America, see Kevin Gallagher, *The China Triangle: Latin America's China Boom and the Fate of the Washington Consensus* (Oxford: Oxford University Press, 2016).

65. *Jiang Zemin Wenxuan*, 1:524–529. On China's relations with Africa, see Deborah Brautigam, *The Dragon's Gift: The Real Story of China in Africa* (Oxford: Oxford University Press, 2009); and Howard French, *China's Second Continent: How a Million Migrants Are Building a New Empire in Africa* (New York: Knopf, 2014).

66. *Hu Jintao Wenxuan*, 2:532.

67. *Jiang Zemin Wenxuan*, 1:142–150.

68. Ibid. The literature on China's military modernization after the Cold War and on shifts in doctrine abounds, although given the nature of the sources, firm conclusions are hard to come by. An excellent guide is Robert Haddick, *Fire on the Water: China, America, and the Future of the Pacific* (Annapolis, MD: Naval Institute Press, 2014). On naval power, see Toshi Yoshihara and James R. Holmes, *Red Star Over the Pacific* (Annapolis, MD: Naval Institute Press, 2010). The work of M. Taylor Fravel is invariably meticulous and thought-provoking; see, for example, M. Taylor Fravel, "China's Search for Military Power," *Washington Quarterly* 31 (3): 125–141, which argues that China's goals are "largely conservative, not expansionist."

69. *Jiang Zemin Wenxuan*, 1:473.

70. Ibid., 2:82–85.

71. Ibid., 1:286.

72. Ibid., 490–493.

73. Author's interview with Prueher.

74. *Jiang Zemin Wenxuan*, 1:487–494.

75. James Kynge, "Military to Quit Business," *Financial Times* (London), November 16, 1998, 8. The extent and nature of the PLA's involvement in the Chinese economy is almost impossible to gauge accurately, but Kynge's article goes remarkably far.

76. *Hu Jintao Wenxuan*, 2:259. The aversion to militarizing space is well covered; see for example, James Mulvenon, "Rogue Warriors? A Puzzled Look at the Chinese ASAT Test," *China Leadership Monitor*, no. 20 (Winter 2007), available at http://media.hoover.org/sites/default/files/documents/clm20jm.pdf.

5. Xi Jinping and the Insecurity of Power

1. Details drawn from Xi Jinping, *Xi Jinping tan zhi guo li zheng* (Beijing: Waiwen chubanshe, 2014), hereafter cited as Xi, *Tan zhi guo li zheng*, 432–433. An English version is available, titled *Xi Jinping, The Governance of China* (Beijing: Foreign Languages Press, 2014); I consulted the original Chinese version for this chapter. The details of Xi's life in the Cultural Revolution have been well covered; see the very useful Evan Osnos, "Born Red," *New Yorker*, April 6, 2015, for a summary that includes Chinese accounts. Xi in general has been very well covered; see for a starting point, Kerry Brown, *CEO China: The Rise of Xi Jinping* (London: I. B. Tauris, 2016).

2. Xi, *Tan zhi guo li zheng*, 434.

3. This is, of course, the problem that vexes Sinologists and leads them to such radically different conclusions on the country's future. See Martin Jacques, *When China Rules the World* (London: Penguin, 2012); Gideon Rachman, *Easternisation: War and Peace in the Asian Century* (London: Bodley Head, 2016); and David Shambaugh, "The Coming Chinese Crack-Up," *Wall Street Journal*, March 6, 2015. For a sense of how this haunts Chinese leaders, see the aptly titled Susan Shirk, *China: Fragile Superpower* (Oxford: Oxford University Press, 2008).

4. The writing of Xi Jinping thought into the constitution and the declaration that China could be a model were covered by the international press; see, for example, Chris Buckley, "China enshrines 'Xi Jinping Thought,' Elevating Leader to Mao-like Status," *New York Times*, October 24, 2017; and Tom Phillips, "'A Huge Deal' for China as the Era of Xi Jinping Thought Begins," *Guardian*, October 18, 2017. On the reassurance that China would not export its model, see

Reuters Staff, "President Xi says China will not export its political system," *Reuters*, December 1, 2017.

5. Xi, *Tan zhi guo li zheng*, 85.

6. Most coverage on the 2013 plenum instantly harkens back to the American National Security Council; see, for example, Reuters, "China Appoints Xi to Head National Security Commission," January 24, 2014, http://www.reuters.com /article/us-china-politics-xi-idUSBREA0N0LM20140124.

7. Xi, *Tan zhi guo li zheng*, 200–201.

8. Ibid., 369, 388, 389.

9. Ibid., 90, 144–145, 153–154.

10. The names of Xu Caihou, Gao Xiaoyan, and Guo Zhenggang made most news accounts at the time of indictment. Perhaps the most useful tracking device for the anticorruption campaign was set up in *ChinaFile*, "Visualizing China's Anti-corruption Campaign," January 21, 2016, http://www.chinafile.com /infographics/visualizing-chinas-anti-corruption-campaign.

11. Sulmaan Khan, "The Coming Coup in China?," *American Interest*, 10 (4): 1–10.

12. Khan, "The Coming Coup in China?" A *ChinaFile* discussion of Xi's cult of personality covers the main ground. *ChinaFile*, "Xi Jinping: A Cult of Personality?" March 4, 2016, http://www.chinafile.com/conversation/xi-jinping-cult -personality.

13. Xi, *Tan zhi guo li zheng*, 116.

14. China as a rising power and reviving long-lost glory are the core arguments of Graham Allison, *Destined for War: Can America and China Escape Thucydides's Trap?* (Boston: Houghton Mifflin Harcourt, 2017), and Howard French, *Everything under the Heavens: How the Past Helps Shape China's Push for Global Power* (New York: Knopf, 2017), respectively.

15. Xi, *Tan zhi guo li zheng*, 247–249.

16. Ibid., 279–280.

17. Ibid., 130–131.

18. See Kelly Sims Gallagher, *The Global Diffusion of Clean Energy Technologies: Lessons from China* (Cambridge, MA: MIT Press, 2014).

19. Xi Jinping, "New Asian Security Concept for New Progress in Security Cooperation" (Fourth Summit of the Conference on Interaction and Confidence

Building Measures in Asia, Shanghai, May 21, 2014), http://www.fmprc.gov.cn /mfa_eng/zxxx_662805/t1159951.shtml.

20. For an account of how the relationship developed, see Qian Qichen, *Ten Episodes in China's Diplomacy* (New York: Harper Collins, 2005).

21. Bryan Harris, Charles Clover, and Sherry Fei Ju, "Beijing and Seoul Reset Frayed Relations," *Financial Times,* October 31, 2017. On the resumption of the tour group ban, see Bryan Harris, Kang Buseong, and Charles Clover, "Tensions Rise Again between China and South Korea," *Financial Times,* December 21, 2017.

22. See Sulmaan Khan, "Unbalanced Alliances," *Foreign Affairs,* February 28, 2016. On discussions between Beijing and Washington regarding a North Korean collapse, see Charles Clover, "US and China Broach Sensitive Topic of North Korea Regime Collapse," *Financial Times,* December 19, 2017.

23. Xinhua, "Xi Jinping hui jian riben shouxiang Anbei Jinsan," September 5, 2016, http://news.xinhuanet.com/world/2016-09/05/c_1119515029.htm. The Voldemort barbs were traded in the pages of the *Daily Telegraph* and well-covered by the press.

24. Xi, *Tan zhi guo li zheng,* 230–231, 233, 237.

25. See Andreo Calonzo and Cecilia Yap, "China Visit Helps Duterte Reap Funding Deals Worth $24 Billion," *Bloomberg Markets,* October 21, 2016, https://www.bloomberg.com/news/articles/2016-10-21/china-visit-helps -duterte-reap-funding-deals-worth-24-billion; and Alexis Romero and Richmond Mercurio, "Philippines, China Sign $24-B Deals," *Philippine Star,* October 22, 2016, http://www.philstar.com/headlines/2016/10/22/1636102 /philippines-china-sign-24-b-deals.

26. The best account of antiaccess and area denial is Robert Haddick, *Fire on the Water: China, America, and the Future of the Pacific* (Annapolis, MD: Naval Institute Press, 2014). The base in Djibouti was announced after his book was published.

27. Zhongguo Junwang, "Telangpu jing gongkai yu Cai Yingwen tong dianhua, dapo 'jinji' he yiwei," December 3, 2016, http://www.81.cn/jwgz/2016-12/03 /content_7390426_2.htm.

28. Associated Press, "China Provisionally Grants Trump 38 Trademarks— Including for Escort Service," *Guardian,* March 8, 2017, https://www.theguardian .com/us-news/2017/mar/08/china-approves-trump-trademarks-businesses.

29. Xinhua, "Xi Jinping tong Telangpu juxing ZhongMei yuanshou di er chang zhengshi huiwu," http://news.xinhuanet.com/world/2017-04/08/c_129527507.htm.

30. On Xi as a "good man," see Chris Buckley, "A Spring Thaw? Trump Now Has 'Very Good' Words for China's Leader," *New York Times*, April 29, 2017, https://www.nytimes.com/2017/04/29/world/asia/trump-xi-jinping-china.html. Trade information is in Shawn Donnan and Tom Mitchell, "Trump Administration Hails US-China Trade Deal," *Financial Times*, May 12, 2017, https://www.ft.com/content/9a5ee6b8-36c0-11e7-bce4-9023f8c0fd2e.

31. See "Donald Trump Notes Xi Jinping's 'Extraordinary' Rise," *BBC*, October 26, 2017, http://www.bbc.com/news/world-asia-china-41756769; and Demetri Sevastopulo, Tom Mitchell, and Charles Clover, "Trump Rolls Back the China Rhetoric on China visit," *Financial Times*, November 9, 2017.

32. National Security Strategy of the United States of America, December 2017, https://www.whitehouse.gov/wp-content/uploads/2017/12/NSS-Final-12-18-2017-0905.pdf, accessed December 21, 2017.

33. Xinhua, "Telangpu ru zhu baigong yu shidai bianqian," http://news.xinhuanet.com/world/2017-03/14/c_129508934.htm.

34. Xi Jinping, "Jointly Shoulder Responsibility of Our Times, Promote Global Growth" (World Economic Forum, Davos, Switzerland, January 17, 2017), https://america.cgtn.com/2017/01/17/full-text-of-xi-jinping-keynote-at-the-world-economic-forum. The English text is from the site.

35. Xi, *Tan Zhi Guo Li Zheng*, 292–294.

36. Ibid., 271–275.

37. Ibid. On Arctic gas exploration, see Jack Farchy, "Chinese Lend $12bn for Gas Plant in Russian Arctic," *Financial Times*, April 29, 2016, https://www.ft.com/content/4ca8886e-0e14-11e6-ad80-67655613c2d6. On hydrocarbon pipelines, see Reuters, "China to Complete Russia Oil, Gas Pipeline Sections by End-2018: Vice Governor," May 12, 2017, http://www.reuters.com/article/us-china-silkroad-russia-pipelines-idUSKBN18819I. On water transfer, see Zhang Yu, "Lanzhou Govt Resurrects Plans to Divert Water from Siberia to China's Arid Northwest," *Global Times*, March 6, 2017, http://www.globaltimes.cn/content/1036247.shtml.

38. See the fascinating article by Jeffrey Mankoff, "Russia's Asia Pivot: Confrontation or Cooperation," *Asia Policy*, January 2015, 65–87.

39. Xi, *Tan zhi guo li zheng*, 341–342.

40. J. P., "What Is China's Belt and Road Initiative?," *Economist*, May 15, 2017, http://www.economist.com/blogs/economist-explains/2017/05/economist -explains-11.

41. Xi, *Tan zhi guo li zheng*, 303–304, 312, 314, 325.

42. This phenomenon is far from exclusively Chinese. Robert Kagan documents it wonderfully in the case of the United States: see Robert Kagan, *Of Paradise and Power: America and Europe in the New World Order* (London: Atlantic, 2004), and *Dangerous Nation: America's Place in the World, from Its Earliest Days to the Dawn of the 20th Century* (New York: Knopf, 2006).

43. For an intriguing perspective on this, see Edward Luttwak, *The Rise of China versus the Logic of Strategy* (Cambridge, MA: Harvard University Press, 2012).

44. For the workings of imperial overstretch across the centuries, see Paul Kennedy, *The Rise and Fall of the Great Powers* (New York: Random House, 1987).

45. See Tracy Rucinski, "China's Sinopec Sues Venezuela in Sign of Fraying Relations," *Reuters*, December 6, 2017.

46. Stories abound on China's pollution woes; see, for example, Reuters, "China's Environment Ministry Finds Patchy Progress on Water and Soil Pollution," April 24, 2017, http://www.reuters.com/article/us-china-pollution -idUSKBN17R02V. On pikas, see Richard Harris, *Wildlife Conservation in China: Preserving the habitat of China's Wild West* (Armonk: M.E. Sharpe, 2008); and M. C. Wilson and A. T. Smith, "The Pika and the Watershed: The Impact of Small Mammal Poisoning on the Ecohydrology of the Qinghai-Tibetan Plateau," *Ambio* 44, no. 1 (February 2015): 16–22.

Conclusion

1. On ideology as a driving force in the Soviet-American competition, see the magnificent Odd Arne Westad, *The Global Cold War: Third World Interventions and the Making of Our Times* (Cambridge: Cambridge University Press, 2005). Jeremy Friedman, *Shadow Cold War: The Sino-Soviet Competition for the Third World* (Chapel Hill: University of North Carolina Press, 2015), suggests that there was an ideological

competition between Moscow and Beijing; Gregg Brazinsky, *Winning the Third World: Sino-American Rivalry during the Cold War* (Chapel Hill: University of North Carolina Press, 2017), highlights the contest between America and China. My own view, as made clear here, is that the overriding precept in China's approach to the world is the simple belief that, to stay safe, you make friends wherever you can. Competition, when it existed, has been incidental.

FURTHER READING

This book relies chiefly on primary sources, but my thinking has been shaped by much of the excellent work that other scholars have produced on China and grand strategy. What follows is a selection of the books in English that I found most useful and that could provide the basis for hours of fruitful reading. The list is by no means exhaustive; those interested in delving deeper are encouraged to peruse the notes.

On grand strategy, the best starting point is Paul Kennedy, ed., *Grand Strategies in War and Peace* (New Haven, CT: Yale University Press, 1991). Chinese grand strategy is explored in Michael Swaine and Ashley Tellis, *Interpreting China's Grand Strategy: Past, Present and Future* (Santa Monica, CA: Rand, 2000). See also the insightful Andrew Nathan and Andrew Scobell, *China's Search for Security* (New York: Columbia University Press, 2012).

China's foreign relations in general are served by the remarkable Odd Arne Westad, *Restless Empire: China and the World since 1750* (New York: Basic Books, 2012). For a participant's view, see Henry Kissinger, *On China* (New York: Penguin, 2011). The best general history remains Jonathan Spence, *The Search for Modern China* (New York: W. W. Norton, 2012).

The pre-1949 communist experience is treated in a number of books. Xiaoyuan Liu, *Frontier Passages: Ethnopolitics and the Rise of Chinese Communism, 1921–1945* (Washington, DC: Woodrow Wilson Center Press; Stanford, CA: Stanford University Press; 2004), is remarkable in scope and execution. The war is well served by Rana Mitter, *Forgotten Ally: China's World War II, 1937–1945* (Boston: Houghton Mifflin Harcourt, 2013), which offers a wealth of suggestions for further reading. On the Chinese Civil War, see Odd Arne Westad, *Decisive Encounters: The Chinese Civil War, 1946–50* (Stanford, CA: Stanford University Press, 2003).

The classic on the Mao era is still Chen Jian, *Mao's China and the Cold War* (Chapel Hill: University of North Carolina Press, 2001). The groundbreaking work done by Chinese scholars is now thankfully available in English: see Zhihua Shen and Yafeng Xia, *Mao and the Sino-Soviet Partnership, 1945–1959: A New History* (Lanham, MD: Lexington Books, 2014). On the split, see Lorenz Luthi, *The Sino-Soviet Split* (Princeton, NJ: Princeton University Press, 2008), and Sergey Radchenko, *Two Suns in the Heavens: The Sino-Soviet Struggle for Supremacy, 1962–1967* (Washington, DC: Woodrow Wilson Center Press, 2009). For domestic issues, Andrew Walder, *China under Mao: A Revolution Derailed* (Cambridge, MA: Harvard University Press, 2015), is superb.

The monumental Ezra Vogel, *Deng Xiaoping and the Transformation of China* (Cambridge, MA: Belknap Press of Harvard University Press, 2011), is indispensable and an excellent starting point for further research. Sergey Radchenko, *Unwanted Visionaries: The Soviet Failure in Asia at the End of the Cold War* (Oxford: Oxford University Press, 2014), is a remarkable guide to Asia in Deng's time. Any student of China must read Jan Wong, *Red China Blues* (Toronto: Anchor Books, 1996), which in its insight and detail is likely to remain unsurpassed.

Approaching the post–Cold War era, material becomes thinner. Jiang Zemin and Hu Jintao remain understudied; Xi Jinping, of course, is something of a moving target. For starting points, see Bruce Gilley, *Tiger on the Brink: Jiang Zemin and China's New Elite* (Berkeley: University of California Press, 1998), Willy Wo-lap Lam, *Chinese Politics in the Hu Jintao Era: New Leaders, New*

Challenges (Armonk, NY: M. E. Sharpe, 2006), and Kerry Brown, *CEO China: The Rise of Xi Jinping* (London: I. B. Tauris, 2016). For books about China's role in contemporary security issues, see Graham Allison, *Destined for War: Can America and China Escape Thucydides's Trap?* (Boston: Houghton Mifflin Harcourt, 2017), Howard French, *Everything under the Heavens: How the Past Helps Shape China's Push for Global Power* (New York: Knopf, 2017), and Gideon Rachman, *Easternisation: War and Peace in the Asian Century* (London: Bodley Head, 2016). Richard H. Solomon, *Chinese Political Negotiating Behavior* (Santa Monica: Rand, 1995), remains invaluable to practitioners.

ACKNOWLEDGMENTS

Odd Arne Westad's decision to move to Cambridge, Massachusetts, brought the perfect reader and a delightful dinner companion to my neighborhood. Arne believed in this book when it was still just the faintest of glimmers and read chapters of it while on transoceanic flights and train rides across the China plains. He and Ingunn Bjornson also provided the ideal respite from research at their Norfolk haven; I will forever treasure the memories of dinner at The Lifeboat and our walk across the marshes.

Christopher Kavanagh, Jackie Page, Sarah Golkar, and Rachel Vandenbrink offered valuable feedback on parts of this manuscript. So did Mary Sarotte, whose advice and friendship have added much to my life. Joseph Prueher generously took the time to chat with me about his dealings with China and then provided a thoughtful review of Chapter 4. Merle Pribbenow shared Vietnamese memoirs that he had translated. For points of superior wisdom, I turned to Chen Jian, Liu Xiaoyuan, Lin Hsiao-ting, Sergey Radchenko, Lien-Hang Nguyen, Wang Wenlung, and Zhao Xiaoxue. As I wrote, I found myself drawing often on insights forged in conversation with Jonathan Spence, Peter Perdue, Simon Long, Bill Emmott, and Timothy Snyder. My thoughts on civil-military relations, water security, and North Korea were first worked out in essays for *The American Interest* and *Foreign Affairs;* my thanks to Adam Garfinkle, Cameron Abadi, and Kathryn Allawala for giving me space to work those thoughts out.

At David Higham Associates, Andrew Gordon's integrity and wisdom were clear from our earliest dealings; I am fortunate to have him as a literary agent. My thanks too to Andrew's predecessor at David Higham, Bruce Hunter, who believed I had a book in me when I was just an aimless young backpacker, and to David Evans. At Harvard University Press, Kathleen McDermott was a thoughtful and caring editor. The two expert reviews she commissioned were both helpful and encouraging. The Smith Richardson Foundation funded much of the research here; my thanks to Marin Strmecki, both for the funding and for helping me think through the book at an early stage. Kelly Sandefer of Beehive Mapping was as superb as ever in producing the book's maps.

In China, Shen Zhihua and Li Danhui continue to exemplify all that scholars should be; they have taught me lessons in courage and resourcefulness, as well as in Cold War history. Dai Chaowu's comradeship over the years has enriched both my research and my time in China. Xu Laoshi's Mandarin lessons stood me in good stead. Mehvesh Mumtaz Ahmed, friend and big sister of my youth, welcomed me into her family and home in Hong Kong; I am grateful to her for a crash course on Hong Kong's political economy, and to Naeem, Faiz, and Amal for a marvelous stay. In Japan, Ami Nomura, Taka Okada, Yasuko Kimura, and Shin Mikami were wonderful company. My thanks to my hosts at the Japan Institute of International Affairs, particularly Iijima-san, who arranged my time at the archives, Nami-san for the occasional Japanese lesson, Kadozaki-san for lunch, and Nishimura-san for bearing with me in the library. Swapping stories with Akio Takahara was a privilege and education. I was able to spend time in Tokyo thanks to the Council on Foreign Relations International Affairs Fellowship in Japan, sponsored by Hitachi; my thanks to the fellowship committee, especially Carl Green, and to Miho Ochai, who taught me much about Japan. My Japanese got to the point where it could be useful thanks to two wonderful Fletcher students: Ayako Kubodera and Mio Yamada. Mio's company on a jaunt across Japan was eye opening. Thanks to Tara Dominic and Brian

O'Keefe for making those trips possible by cat-and-house-sitting. In Britain, Usman Manzoor waited for me for four hours at the Heathrow airport. Riyaz-ul-Haque spent a day taking me to chat with Pakistani diplomats in Islamabad. Marina Ivanova and Inga Zemlenuhina taught me Russian; Inga also discussed some of my translations of Russian sources (not to mention the meaning of life), to my immeasurable benefit. Archivists and librarians in various places helped in more ways than I can tally.

Christian Ostermann rallied his marvelous team at the Cold War International History Project to help with my research. My friendship with Christian has been the best part of being a member of the CWIHP family; I am glad that we got to add Lahore and Berlin to the list of places where our paths have crossed. Laura Deal and Chuck Kraus helped immensely. Chuck, in particular, answered e-mails day and night, and tolerated my requests with good humor and grace. At home, Emery Ku and Elyssa Weber have been dream neighbors. For all they have done, I am grateful to Chia-Chun Chang, Chen Yun-Ru, Zaka Shafiq, Rushdia Yusuf, Susan Cohen, Paul Roberts, and Allie Sacharuk. I drew comfort and support along the way from old friends: Toni Dorfman, Cynthia Farrar, Tracy, Lee, Alyssa, and Chloe Jackson, Susie Jakes, Zhang Taisu, Ryan Irwin, and Ranger Dan Barvir.

This book bears the unmistakable marks of the Fletcher School, Tufts University, where I am fortunate to work. Deans are not generally expected to tutor their faculty, but Jim Stavridis agreed to educate me in matters military, thereby improving this book immensely. Toni Chayes, tempestuous force of nature and partner in crime, has never been anything less than inspiring. My thoughts on civil-military relations originated in a class she allowed me to teach. Eileen Babbitt's reminders to breathe came in handy long after she first gave them. Dan Drezner told me not to be an idiot; Michael Klein made the same point by hurling a napkin at me. An annual walk with Michael Glennon around Mount Auburn Cemetery was a welcome break. Kelly Sims Gallagher tossed me the keys to the Water and Oceans Program at the Center for International Environment and Resource Policy, and, in a moment of crisis, rode to my aid with a broken shoulder. At the Center, my thanks to Jenny Aker (who shared her coffee machine and her inexhaustible fund of jokes), Mieke van der Wansem, and Jillian DeMair for all their help. Elayne Stecher printed reams of documents and put up with my loss of countless receipts. Special thanks to the incomparable Penny Storey, trusted colleague and dear friend, who conjured up funds and kept me sane. I have yet to reconcile myself to the fact that she, Neil, and Nora are moving back to Ireland. Lupita Ervin has always had my back; one could ask for no better security. Karen Jacobsen forbore to call in my debts to her while I was at work. Kim Wilson let me talk to her class on financial inclusion and encouraged me along the way. Dyan Mazurana threw open her Newburyport home. Dick Shultz, Bobbi Kates-Garnick, Alan Henrikson, Shin Tanaka, Bhaskar Chakravorti, Alex de Waal, Katie Mulroy, Jerry Sheehan, Leila Fawaz, Steven Block, Mary Dulatre, Katrina Burgess, Jonathan Brookfield, Kate Ryan, Michele Malvesti, Yoon Lee, Chris Miller, and Ian Johnstone put up with a colleague who became increasingly eccentric as the writing wore on. Cyndi Rubino provided everything from tech support to driving practice to cake. Lee LaFleur, Brad Macomber, and Anulfo Baez were always welcoming when I entered the Ginn Library sanctum. The Peanut Gallery—Liz Ludan (who threw in last-minute research assistance and her lucky pencil), Liz Mori Tornheim, and Phil Ehrig—dragged me back to fiction and hawks when I needed them most. I miss them.

Ellen McDonald, the original Wonder Woman and the smartest person at Fletcher, has come to my rescue more times than I can remember. Whether rooting out semicolons, hunting down facts that seemed impossible to find, or baking seven-layer bars for a fractious friend, she has been simply wonderful.

My sister Maryam kept all safe on the home front. My mother, for the first (and, I suspect, last) time in my life, told me that it was all right to blow past a deadline. She did a better job with me than she realizes. My father was understanding beyond belief when I left him stranded in British Columbia; I had the best of times with him when I eventually joined him there. Koshka the cat kept long and impish vigil with me in the hours before dawn. I cannot do justice to all that Anna Beth Keim has brought to this book and to my life. The days we have spent together, mulling translations, debating word choices, gallivanting across Asia, or just working side by side quietly, have been days of deep joy. One could ask for no more.

This book is, in many ways, an extended assignment for a class I took with the Gang of Three at Yale about a decade and a half ago. I could go on forever about them: about how John Gaddis would turn his students loose, to use his phrase, on newly declassified documents, and of how his twinkling wisdom moved his charges to do more than they had ever dreamed they could; of how Charlie Hill dragged an axe to his class on *The Odyssey* and remains the only person I know who would suggest going back to the Arthurian legend when confronted with a draft of this manuscript; of how Paul Kennedy, when not plotting to seize the president's lawn for a game of croquet, could evoke the entire world in a few choice phrases and show you the ships that sailed between the continents. Magic happened when they came together and clashed in a classroom. They will not agree with everything I have written here; they would be disappointed if they did, for they encouraged irreverence in their students, and in doing so inspired respect. With thanks, affection, and a contrarian grin, this book is hereby dedicated to them.

INDEX

Index

People's Republic of China, 48; and
Sino-Soviet relations, 94. *See also*
Sino-Indian relations
Indochina: and Mao Zedong's balance of
power politics, 65, 70–71, 73; and
Sino-American relations, 120; and
Sino-Soviet relations, 67, 96, 97, 158;
and United States, 162
Indonesia, 72, 75, 199, 229
Internet, 198
Iraq War of 2003, 196

Japan: China's war with, 10, 14; Deng
Xiaoping's diplomacy toward, 131,
140–141, 142, 154; and Diaoyu/
Senkaku Islands dispute, 131, 157, 217,
239; and economic policy of Deng
Xiaoping, 140–141, 142; and economic
policy of Mao Zedong, 48; and Jiang
Zemin's balance of power politics, 183;
and Korean peninsula, 157; Mao
Zedong's diplomacy toward, 65, 86;
shipping industry of, 140; treaties with
Qing dynasty, 11; U.S.-Japan alliance,
76, 217. *See also* Sino-Japanese relations;
Sino-Japanese war
Jiang Jingguo, 151
Jiang Qing, 121, 124, 125, 126, 133
Jiangshan Island, 79
Jiangxi soviet: fall of, 15, 40; Mao
Zedong's founding of, 13–14; and
Zhu De, 112
Jiang Zemin: and anti-imperialism,
201–203; and balance of power
politics, 171, 181–184, 191–199,
202–203; blandness of, 171, 208;
and continuation of Mao-Deng era

concerns, 7; and Deng Xiaoping's
retirement, 168–169; economic
policy of, 7, 178–179, 184, 191–192,
194, 197, 198, 202, 204–205, 242;
grand strategy of, 171, 183–184,
188–189, 208, 246; and ideology of
Chinese Communist Party, 172–175,
213; and Kim Il Sung, 181; and
multipolarization, 198, 202; national
security planning of, 192, 196, 203,
204; and one-China principle, 189;
operational codes of, 2, 4; and
reform and opening, 171, 172,
176–177, 189–190, 208; and Taiwan
Strait crisis of 1996, 7, 184–188;
"three represents," 176, 214; and
Western development policy, 177;
Xi Jinping compared to, 208, 210,
211, 212, 215–216. *See also* military
power
Jinmen: Mao Zedong's battles with
Nationalist Party over, 43, 52, 63, 67,
78, 86–87, 88; and Mao Zedong's
talks with U.S., 80, 89
Johnson, Lyndon, 118

Karakoram Highway, 231
Kasimi, Ahmed Jan, 48
Kenya, 203
Khan, Sultan, 73
Khrushchev, Nikita: and Albania, 104;
and Mao Zedong's diplomacy, 83,
84–85, 88–90, 95, 98; and peaceful
coexistence, 48; secret speech
criticizing Stalin, 67–68; Josef Stalin
compared to, 67; and U.S. relations,
96–97, 105–106

311

Index

Party members, 34–35, 48, 51; diplomacy towards Soviet Union, 37–38, 45–48, 52, 54, 60; economic policy of, 25–26, 31, 32, 33–34, 37, 46–47, 48, 49–51, 54, 58, 65, 73, 75, 107–111, 121, 123–124, 126, 128, 131, 135, 136–137, 144–145, 150, 237, 242; and Gang of Four, 124–125, 132; grand strategy of reunification, 5–6, 9–11, 17, 18, 19, 29, 40–41, 43, 45, 51–52, 53, 79, 82, 107, 111, 117, 121, 126, 238, 243, 246; instinctive understanding of grand strategy, 10; and Nikita Khrushchev's secret speech criticizing Stalin, 67–68; and Korean War, 6, 52, 54–55, 57–65, 78, 85, 119; national goals defined by, 1, 14; national security planning of, 45, 60, 62, 67, 82–83, 94, 100, 101, 103, 106, 114, 119, 120, 144; and nuclear weapons, 82; operational codes of, 2, 3; and peasant mobilization, 13, 14, 25–26, 29, 31, 50; pragmatism of, 10–11, 32, 33, 77; ruling by force of personality, 8, 211, 215; and self-created chaos, 87; state founded in Jiangxi soviet, 13–14; and strategic environment, 54–65; survival of his China as core interest of, 22, 23; and Taiwan, 52, 63, 77–82, 88–89, 105; vision of great China, 9–10, 12–13, 15, 213; water management of, 235; Xi Jinping compared to, 214; Xi Jinping's homage to, 214. *See also* military power

Marco Polo Bridge incident of 1937, 15

Marshall, George, and Zhou Enlai, 28–29

Marx, Karl, 98, 135, 147, 173, 175, 216

Marxism, 40, 168, 174, 175

Marxism-Leninism, 135, 214

May Fourth Movement, 12

Ma Ying-jeou, 224

Ma Zhanshan, 19

Mazu: Mao Zedong's battles with Nationalist Party over, 67, 78, 86–87, 88; and Mao Zedong's talks with U.S., 80, 89

McMahon Line, 102

Mexico, 232

Miao, and Long March, 17–18

Middle East, 239

Mikoyan, Anastas, 37

military power: and active defense, 163–164, 203–204, 206–207, 218, 241; anti-access, area-denial capabilities, 7; and Chinese Communist Party, 205–207, 240; and Cultural Revolution's protection of troops, 112–113; and Deng Xiaoping's economic policy, 131, 137–138, 204–205; Deng Xiaoping's military retirement system, 138; and Deng Xiaoping's modern warfare, 130–131, 132, 163–164, 204–205; and Deng Xiaoping's naval warfare, 163–164; and Deng Xiaoping's nuclear policy, 131; and establishment of People's Republic of China, 40–41; and Hu Jintao's modern warfare, 171, 206–207; Hu Jintao's use of, 212; and Jiang Zemin's economic policy, 204–205; and Jiang Zemin's modern warfare, 171, 192, 203–206,

South Korea: and Soviet Union, 96; and
trade, 134; and United States, 217,
220, 222; and Xi Jinping's balance of
power politics, 220–222
South Vietnam, 99, 100, 120
Soviet Union: and Chinese civil war, 27,
44–47; and Chinese Communist Party,
16, 22, 37–38, 44–45; dissolution of,
196; Mao Zedong's diplomacy toward,
37–38, 45–48, 54; and revisionism,
91, 92, 94, 95, 98, 99, 100, 113; threats
of war with, 7; and United States,
90–91, 154, 181, 212; and Zhou Enlai,
66, 88–89, 95, 102, 115, 116. *See also*
Russia; Sino-Soviet relations
splittism, 198
Stalin, Josef: on Afghan king, 100; and
Chinese Communist Party, 22,
37–38; Nikita Khrushchev's secret
speech criticizing, 67–68; Mao
Zedong's diplomacy toward, 45–48,
52, 55, 57, 58, 59, 60, 66–67, 83, 84,
85, 98; on military power of People's
Republic of China, 241; and North
Korea, 54, 55, 57, 59, 60; relationship
with satellite countries, 69
state: Mao Zedong's changing definition
of, 10, 13, 14, 15, 17, 38–39, 42, 81;
Zhou Enlai's defining of, 39–40
state-run enterprise: and Hu Jintao's
economic policy, 178; and Mao
Zedong's economic policy, 25, 26; and
Xi Jinping's economic policy, 216, 234
Strategic Arms Limitation Talks
(SALT), 158
Strategic Economic Dialogue, 219
Stuart, John Leighton, 36

Sukarno, 201–202
Sun Yat-sen, 12

Taiwan: Chiang Kai-shek in, 42; Deng
Xiaoping's policy toward, 129, 131,
141, 143, 147, 148–151, 155, 157; Hu
Jintao's policy toward, 200–201;
Japanese position on, 76–77, 158;
Japanese seizure of, 11; Jiang Zemin's
policy toward, 184–189, 200, 205;
and Korean War, 58–59, 61; and Mao
Zedong, 52, 63, 77–82, 88–89, 105;
and Nationalist Party, 39, 63, 149; and
People's Republic of China's
sovereignty claims, 87–88, 119, 238,
239, 241; and renewal of Chinese civil
war, 32; separatist forces of independence, 201, 205, 207, 224; and trade,
134, 200, 201; and United States, 40,
55, 56, 58, 61, 72, 78–82, 87, 88–89,
119, 148, 149, 153, 155–156, 157,
184–189, 200, 217, 227; Xi Jinping's
policy toward, 223–224, 233
Taiwan Relations Act, 148, 155, 156,
157, 184
Taiwan Strait crisis of 1954, 78
Taiwan Strait crisis of 1958, 83,
86–88
Taiwan Strait crisis of 1996, 7, 184–188,
194
Takasaki, Tatsunosuke, 76–77
Tanzania, 104, 231
technology transfer: and Jiang Zemin,
177, 184; and Sino-American
relations, 121, 141–142, 184
Terminal High Altitude Area Defense
system (THAAD), 220–221, 222